The Individual Investor's Guide to Winning on Wall Street

The Individual Investor's Guide to Winning on Wall Street

■

PETER J. DeANGELIS, CFA

CB
CONTEMPORARY
BOOKS

CHICAGO

DeAngelis, Peter J.
    The individual investor's guide to winning on Wall Street / Peter
J. DeAngelis.
        p.   cm.
    ISBN 0-8092-4202-8 (cloth)
        0-8092-3934-5 (paper)
    1. Investments.   2. Stocks.   3. Investment analysis
4. Portfolio management.   I. Title.
HG4521.D43   1991
332.6'78—dc20   91-3403
                                                                             CIP

    Quotations in Chapter 9, "Thinking of Using a Professional?,"
from One Up on Wall Street: How to Use What You Already Know
to Make Money in the Market, copyright © 1989 by Peter Lynch and
John Rothchild (New York: Simon & Schuster), reprinted by
permission of Simon & Schuster
    Quotations in Chapter 9, "Thinking of Using a Professional?,"
from Secrets for Profiting in Bull and Bear Markets, copyright ©
1988 by Stan Weinstein (New York: Dow Jones–Irwin), reprinted by
permission of Dow Jones–Irwin Publishers
    "Introduction," "Just the Facts," "Beauty and the Beast," "When to
Sell and Pin Down Your Profits," and "Wall Street Folklore"
copyright © 1991 by Peter J. DeAngelis
    "Footprints in the Sand" copyright © 1991 by David Krell
    "The Last Hurrah?" copyright © 1991 by Arthur K. Carlson
    "An Introduction to Exchange-Traded Options," copyright © 1991
by Cheryl Curley-Dukoff
    "All That Glitters" copyright © 1991 by Ira U. Cobleigh
    "All Debts, Public and Private," ". . . And All That Jazz," and
"Thinking of Using a Professional?" copyright © 1991 by Van W.
Knox III
    "Fads" copyright © 1991 by Richard L. Evans

Published by Contemporary Books, Inc.
180 North Michigan Avenue, Chicago, Illinois 60601
Manufactured in the United States of America
International Standard Book Number: 0-8092-4202-8 (cloth)
                                            0-8092-3934-5 (paper)

CONTENTS

ABOUT THE AUTHOR AND THE CONTRIBUTING AUTHORS

Foreword by Monte Gordon: Gordon is the retired Research Director, Dreyfus Corporation (a world-renowned multibillion-dollar money manager/mutual fund organization), and a regular panelist on the award-winning television series "Wall Street Week with Louis Rukeyser." With over forty year's of hands-on experience as a security analyst, research director, economist, and money manager, Gordon is an acclaimed investment authority.

Author: Peter J. DeAngelis, CFA, is coauthor of *The $2 Window on Wall Street*, president of PDA Associates, Inc., a comprehensive financial consulting firm, and chairman of Dowbeaters®, an investment advisory research service. Over the past 30 years, he has been involved in the investment industry as an investment research director, security analyst, economist and portfolio manager, and investment strategist. He is a Chartered Financial Analyst and past president of the New York Society of Security Analysts, Inc. He is also is a member of the board of directors of Worldwide Computer Services Inc. Before forming PDA Associates and Dowbeaters®, he was an officer and senior portfolio manager of a major New York investment advisory firm.

Contributing Author: David Krell, CMT, is a vice president of
the New York Stock Exchange, past president of the Market Technicians Association, and an instructor with the New York Institute
of Finance. His expertise is market timing and the use of technical
analysis for stock selection. He is a world-renowned expert in
trading options and derivative products, and he is a past director
of the Options Clearing Corporation.

Contributing Author: Richard L. Evans is a Registered Investment Advisor and Principal of Richard L. Evans Investments,
personally managing investment portfolios and retirement plans
for accounts over $250,000. He is an established investment author-
ity, appearing on numerous radio and television programs and
quoted in the nation's leading financial publications, including
Money Magazine, Barron's, Business Week, Forbes, the *Wall
Street Journal*, the *Chicago Tribune*, and the *New York Times*.

Contributing Author: Ira U. Cobleigh, Sc.D., is a nationally
known author, economist, investment professional, and financial
consultant to corporations. He has been the feature and financial
editor of the *Commercial and Financial Chronicle* and a senior
executive with a leading financial communications firm, as well as
director of several corporations. He is the author of many books,
including the bestselling *Happiness Is a Stock That Doubles in a
Year*. He coauthored the bestselling *The Dowbeaters*.

Contributing Author: Cheryl Curley-Dukoff is a vice president
for Bearbull Investment Products (U.S.A.) Inc., a newly formed
subsidiary of the Bearbull Group of companies, continental Europe's largest portfolio management firm. Before her current position, she was Manager of Options Marketing with the New York
Mercantile Exchange, where she presented option seminars across
the country, as well as in Europe, the Far East, and the Soviet
Union. She has authored articles in numerous publications, including *Barron's, Financial World*, and *Futures* magazine. Before
joining the New York Mercantile Exchange, she was with Merrill
Lynch as a National Marketing Specialist for futures and options
investments.

Contributing Author: Arthur K. Carlson is a retired senior vice president and manager of the $14 billion Valley National Bank, Trust Division. He is also past president of The New York Society of Security Analysts, Inc., and a known authority on tax-exempt investments. He is trustee and director of the Tax-Free Trust of Arizona, Tax-Free Fund of Colorado, Hawaii's Tax-Free Fund, The Cash Assets Trust, Tax-Free Cash Assets Trust, U.S. Treasuries Cash Assets Trust, and various other financial boards.

Contributing Author: Van W. Knox III is founder and president of Van William Knox, Inc., a registered investment advisory firm located in Chatham, New Jersey. Originally founded to meet the specific needs of an international clientele, his firm works with a number of individuals and pension and retirement accounts in the United States, Europe, and Latin America.

CAVEAT

THIS BOOK IN NO WAY, AND UNDER NO CONCEIVABLE CIRCUM-
stances, should be construed as offering, recommending, or endors-
ing any securities, for consideration, purchase, or sale, at any time.
The information given about any securities mentioned is incomplete and outdated, and provides absolutely no basis for an intelligent decision as to the securities' worth, merit, potential, or possible future market action.

Moreover, each security mentioned or partially described appears only as an illustration or example or part of a general list.
Under no circumstances is it suggested as suitable for possible
purchase or sale. If any security mentioned interests or attracts
the reader, he or she is urged to obtain the most recent and official
information about it from (1) the issuing company, (2) a responsible
financial publication or investment service, and (3) an underwriting, investment, or brokerage firm with adequate statistical facilities. In fact, no investment or speculative decision should ever be
made without assembling and reviewing the latest financial data
with respect to the subject company. Such data are not presented
in this book.

The authors and persons associated with them may from time to time acquire, hold, or sell a position in securities, including the securities of companies mentioned in this book.

The views expressed in this book are solely those of the authors.

FOREWORD

———————————————— Monte Gordon

When Peter J. DeAngelis asked me to write the foreword to this book, I was still active as Vice President–Director of Research of the Dreyfus Corporation. The information in this guide, and my foreword to it, are an extension of what I had been doing for more than forty-three years. To my perspective, I now add about three months in retirement, for I retired as of December 31, 1990.

I offer this brief personal history to emphasize the point that Peter and the various contributing authors seek to establish: certain verities have always been evident to investors since they first sought to codify their knowledge and perceptions. Those verities are that investing is really a relatively uncomplicated activity and that one should strip away the perception of mystery and get down to those principles that remain constant. Thus, for all the so-called new techniques, the application of computer capabilities, the extraordinary increase in the flow of information, and the speed with which it is disseminated, the basic principles upon which the value of an investment is determined remain unchanged. Many integral elements of the investment scene today are not substantially different from the basic principles enunciated back in the 1920s, when the first perceptions of the value of common stocks as a long-term investment were set forth, or in the early 1930s, when the concept of intrinsic value was published in a book that became the bible of security analysis.

Peter has gathered into one volume the work of seven people who write from experience. The variety of contributions here serves to emphasize that, while there are many ways to skin a cat in the pursuit of successful investments, it still is necessary to adhere to certain basic points that make up the value of a security and that cause that value to be influenced and realized. Peter and his group of professionals present here the keys that will enable the individual to open the door to investment success.

In the decades since I first entered the investment business, there have been many changes in structure and approach, but, as I look back, I see that the basics have not changed. And, *The Individual Investor's Guide to Winning on Wall Street* points the way to those factors that have been proved valid by many years of experience. Indeed, this effort will be an invaluable aid to those who are willing to apply its perceptive advice with care and diligence.

Wishing you good reading and successful investing!

Monte Gordon
retired Vice President
Director of Research
Dreyfus Corporation
April 1991

INTRODUCTION

SUCCESS AND THE INDIVIDUAL INVESTOR

———————————————— Peter J. DeAngelis, CFA

IT IS STILL POSSIBLE TO MAKE A KILLING ON WALL STREET!

Judging from my 30-plus years in the financial markets, there are a good number of individual investors who consistently outperform the stock market indexes and the market gurus. They are ordinary people who prudently take a bit of time before investing hard-earned and saved dollars. They don't rush in and invest on hunches, fads, and scant knowledge. Instead, armed with mastery of a relatively few key investment principles and tools of investment analysis, they investigate and understand financial markets and companies, as well as the forms of investment available— stocks, options, bonds, or one of the more exotic investment vehicles. These investors not only beat the market but bring home the bacon in the form of consistent capital gains.

Remarkably, these successful investors don't have the badges or credentials of the career professional. Nor do they work full-time at the art of investing, since they are gainfully employed in unrelated professions. Instead they are serious individuals with a keen desire to profit and build capital. They are willing to make the effort to gain the winning edge. That effort, incidentally, provides enjoyment and satisfaction in short order.

Although it may seem incredible, the individual investor enjoys some major advantages over the professional. In terms of size, flexibility, liquidity, and even investment analysis, the individual investor can be way ahead of the pros. Tie these advantages to some work, and the individual is a favorite on the money track.

Conversely, professional investment analysts, who spend their entire working day at the task, may actually be laboring under a handicap. After all, they get paid for—and are hard-pressed to produce—product (the synonym for investment ideas) for their firm. It is product that the pros probably aren't investing in themselves but that will generate the commissions to directly or indirectly support their livelihood. The pressure to perform and to provide a constant stream of new investment ideas rarely produces consistently winning results.

Similarly, the institutional investor is hamstrung. Institutional investors are typically managers of billion-dollar pools of capital. They aren't necessarily smarter, just bigger. They rarely discover value and are rarely innovative or, for that matter, terribly selective. But by virtue of their very domination of the stock market, blind faith in computer program trading, herd investment techniques, and narrow focus, they set the stage for the serious individual investor to succeed. In all those market highs, who do you think was investing and making the new highs happen? Not the smart individual investor. No. It was the institutional element; the institutions created those peaks. And it is the very same institutions that are caught in the subsequent market collapses.

Believe it or not, the cards are stacked in your favor. All you have to do is spend a little time to learn the basic principles in this book—and I mean just a *little* time! Your performance cannot help but improve when you do this.

I never fail to be amazed when I see people put no appreciable time and effort into a decision that involves a large sum of money. I witness more effort in the purchase of a vacuum cleaner than I do in a $1,000, $5,000, or even a $10,000 stock market purchase. People from the entire social and economic spectrum are guilty of this. Such behavior is the basis of the general belief that the majority of individual investors lose in the market. But it doesn't have to be that way. This book is for the person who takes his or her investments seriously. That person is destined to get involved and be a winner. This book is not for the person who isolates himself from the process or has positioned herself to lose.

The beauty is that there just isn't that much to it! Forget the overzealous and ponderous textbook approaches with their contrived complexities that impair the understanding and use of successful investment techniques. One book—this one—covers the tools you need to measure the investment mettle of specific industries and companies.

This book was conceived as a concise, down-to-earth guide for the individual investor. It is designed to show you how to apply investment principles in the key areas of investment decisions and techniques. In each of its 12 chapters, a seasoned investment authority discusses a specific topic. My colleagues and friends David Krell, Van William Knox III, Arthur Carlson, Cheryl Curley-Dukoff, Ira Cobleigh, and Richard Evans have collaborated to bring this book to fruition. The diversity of talents, viewpoints, and writing styles combine to provide a readable investment bible.

The book focuses on identifying and evaluating opportunities. Your winning edge is in recognizing these values by applying proven analytical methodology. The topics covered by this group of financial authorities and investment veterans are a unique collection. The authors strip away the mystery of Wall Street and consider those few key elements that make up a winning investment. This wealth of easy-to-read wisdom will enhance your ability to understand and use the investment techniques vital to a consistent, successful program.

Also in this book, the seasoned professionals discuss the variety of investment vehicles available to choose from. Among those covered are common stocks, options, debt, and tax-free issues. You must have an understanding of all these so that you may adapt them to your personal goals and aspirations. If you seek long-term capital gains and growth, you will be drawn to the opportunities offering growth potential. If you seek income, then the fixed-income and high-yielding equities will be your port of call. The more aggressive investors will seek out special situations, such as asset plays and turnarounds. All these and more are covered in the book, together with prudent methods for analyzing them.

Those topics may sound like a lot, but, believe me, it isn't complicated at all. You can refer to specific chapters specializing in an
appropriate area and gain a firm understanding of each . . . but
the most interesting and beneficial way is to start at the beginning
and read right through to the end.

I hope that this book opens new doors to rewarding investment.

1

JUST THE FACTS

APPLYING FUNDAMENTAL RESEARCH

———————————— Peter J. DeAngelis, CFA

AT THE ROOT OF MOST, IF NOT ALL, INVESTMENT DECISIONS IN the financial marketplace is the process of stock picking. Whether you choose to invest in common stocks, options, futures, or even corporate debt instruments (bonds), the foundation upon which you select a particular investment is ultimately the attractiveness of the company and its common stock. So while investors prefer different kinds of investments, we are all stock pickers under the skin.

Stock picking is one part fundamental and one part art. The fundamental aspect lies in knowing the key facts about a company and how to analyze them properly. It is always desirable to begin by determining whether you are on a firm footing to invest in a particular company. Plod through the basic numbers. You'll be amazed at what they can tell you. After a while you'll feel downright clairvoyant. The numbers will talk to you. They will praise, shout warnings, and wave banners. Heed their conversation.

The art portion of stock picking is being sensitive to the patterns of stock prices and market behavior in concert with the fundamentals of a particular situation. Here, very much like the art critic, you will develop a talent for recognizing true value in an invest-

1

ment's presentation and position in the financial arena. Also, an important aspect of the art of stock selection is recognizing an important trend or development. Much like the inventor who perceives a better mousetrap, the investor may recognize the merit of a new process, product, or service where others don't. History is full of examples. The entry and growth of fast-food restaurants is a good illustration. A serious investor recognizing fast food's potential to become an American institution would have investigated the industry and companies. Fundamentals notwithstanding, this investor would have enjoyed many years of reward long before the megabuck pros hopped on the bandwagon.

Getting into the process of successful stock picking is a bit like first learning to drive an automobile or use a personal computer. At first glance the process appears overwhelming. But upon close inspection it's really quite simple, relatively effortless, and, most important, fun! As with the auto and the computer, once you overcome the psychological barriers, it's just a question of knowing what pedal to push (clutch, brake, gas) or what buttons to push (keyboard strokes). With some experience behind the wheel or keyboard, you're a seasoned driver or computer jockey.

We have to begin somewhere. As a stock picker, I'm inclined to start with the fundamental approach. Therefore, this chapter discusses fundamental research—one of the two basic methods of universal securities and market study employed to determine future values in the stock market.

APPROACHES TO SECURITIES ANALYSIS

Though the methods have many variations, there are basically only two approaches to predicting future values: fundamental and technical. Fundamental research, the topic of this chapter, focuses upon the basic financials and economics of the individual company. Technical analysis considers how the price of the individual stock has performed historically, as well as the past behavior of stocks in the industry group and the stock market overall. Technical analysis is the subject of Chapter 2.

By using the terms *research* and *analysis*, both methods imply a scientific approach. These implications are misleading. Any effort to assign future value to a common stock, even in the most mathematical form, is not a precise science, no matter how well packaged the reasoning is with formulas and charts. Scores of professionals worldwide ply their art and deploy their judgments to brokerage customers while the professional institutional investors allocate the assets they control according to their own efforts at in-house security analysis.

Apostles of these two methods dispute as to which is more effective. The fundamentalist proclaims that understanding the financials, the economics of the industry, and dynamics of management is the key to future values. Conversely, the technician (chartist) argues that the stock price and volume of shares traded already reflect all the vital information and expectations, and hence point the way to future price levels.

Both views are correct and vital to the process of seeking value and making investment judgments. The most prudent strategy is a blend of the two approaches. A winning parlay would be strong fundamentals combined with a favorable technical (chart) position. When technical and fundamental approaches are sending different signals, it is a red flag. When it happens, as a fundamentalist, I revisit the fundamentals and delve further to reaffirm the judgment before moving ahead against a negative or poor technical position.

Interestingly, the opposite is often true of the technician. Of the two types of stock analysts, the fundamentalists I have known are more prone to consider the stock chart as well as their analysis of the fundamentals. In contrast, the chartists have been more likely to ignore negative fundamentals and go full speed ahead—a sort of "damn the torpedoes" mentality.

When reading this chapter, you may want to keep in mind that I am a fundamentalist with a healthy respect for the technical approach (if for no other reason than the fact that the followers of charts are legion and can create self-fulfilling prophecies). There is always the possibility that a chart is telling me that someone out there may indeed know more than I. Reaffirming a fundamental analysis in the face of a weak price chart makes good sense.

DOING FUNDAMENTAL RESEARCH

Professional security analysts spend their entire workday analyzing companies and industries. They have the advantage of frequent industry and management contact as well as interaction with their peers. Often analysts will specialize by covering a particular industry or industries. They may or may not have industry background, but all are financial in approach.

How can an individual investor compete with these professionals? Easy. First, recognize that, as in other professions, overkill rules the day. Most fundamental analysts go far beyond the key data. They become mired in more detail than is necessary—or desirable, for that matter. Further, industry and management contact is overrated. It misleads at least as often as not.

To enhance their understanding and performance, individual investors need only stick to basics. Deal in facts, and keep it simple. The primordial matter is already available because publicly owned companies must comply with disclosure requirements. The problem is that individual investors rarely take advantage of the data available. Instead many of them make investments on the basis of tips, brokerage reports, and personal hunches. As a result, as has been documented, the individual investor is too often a loser in the stock market.

It is OK to listen to your broker or to be guided by intuition. But before investing, you must make the effort to investigate and understand the security and its fundamentals. Otherwise you're doing little more than rolling the dice, in which case the odds are against you.

The first step is to get data from the primary source—that is, the company itself. The company is normally referred to as the "issuer." The information available from the issuer is in the shareholder reports, press releases, financial results, and filings with federal, state, and stock exchange regulatory bodies, primarily the Securities and Exchange Commission. Getting this material is as easy as writing a quick note or making a phone call to the person in charge of shareholder/investor communications at corporate headquarters. Phone numbers and addresses are available in the phone directory or from your broker. The issuer or its representative (public relations firm) will in most cases be only too happy to supply the data.

For several reasons, it is best for the individual investor to request and receive this material direct from the issuer. First, the data sent will be complete and current. Also, you will be placed on the issuer's shareholder mailing list and will receive future data in

a timely manner. Finally, you will have a direct contact with the
shareholder communications representative, which may be helpful
for future inquiry.

WHAT TO ANALYZE

When you ask to be placed on the company's mailing list for future
shareholder communications, you will receive the documents
needed to do fundamental analysis. These are the annual report
and proxy; most recent quarterly shareholder reports; interim
reports and press releases for the past six months; and the 10K,
latest 10Q, 8Ks, and 13Ds. These items are described on the following pages.

ANNUAL REPORT

The most popular and best-known shareholder communication is
the annual report, even though the 10K in some ways is a much
more informative financial document. (The 10K is covered later on
in this chapter.) Despite its limits, the annual report does provide
a wealth of information. The company publishes this report card to
shareholders after the close of its fiscal year but well before the
shareholders' annual meeting. Depending on the company, the
annual report may be extensive or modest in size and scope. In any
event it must, by law, carry certain vital data.

The annual report contains the following information:

- Company description
- Letter from management to shareholders
- Financial highlights
- Statement of income (profit and loss)
- Balance sheet
- Statement of cash flow
- Statement of changes in shareholders' equity
- Management's discussion and analysis of financial condition and
  results of operations
- Notes to financial statements
- Independent auditor's report

The following discussion will cover these typical items succes-
sively. My purpose is to explain what each item is and what its
significance is in the general picture. When appropriate, I shall

suggest a few key standards, tests, and ratios that you may use to determine whether a company's position is favorable or unfavorable. Some of this may appear elementary. However, it is the elementary aspects of a subject that reveal the important values and pitfalls.

The financial community would have you believe that to succeed in the stock market, you must have command over a multitude of sophisticated and complicated financial tools. Not true. There are relatively few basic tools. All are easy to calculate, understand, and use.

As much as half of the annual report can be hype. But even the hype is worthy of attention. Management's letter to shareholders; description of the company's businesses, products, and services; and rhetoric about the past year's performance and future prospects and direction all provide insight into how management sees and conducts itself. In some instances the text can be as helpful as the financial statements.

A winning stock and a company mentioned later in the book is Mylan Laboratories, Inc. (As a financial consultant to Mylan, I am very familiar with their stockholder communications.) The text of Mylan's annual report contains a wealth of factual information on its industry, the company, and its products. It has always carried a candid management evaluation of problems as well as achievements. An investor who used this information would have had at least as good, if not a better, understanding of the company and industry as a career security analyst. As of this writing, even after advancing over 6,500 percent, the stock still traded near its high. Many professional investors who sold early and wrong have been dramatically outperformed by informed individual Mylan shareholders, many of whom have held their stock for the long pull.

So read the text of the annual report. If management is defensive and vague, that's the first red flag. If you are looking at more pictures than hard facts, that's the second red flag. If management appears to be preoccupied with the stock market and the company's stock price, that's another warning signal. On the other hand, if the report to shareholders discusses the business and the company while addressing the year's progress and difficulties intelligently, you can gain important insight into the company's management culture.

It is also sound policy to read management's prior-year letter to shareholders and compare it to the most recent. This will enable you to measure how management followed through on its expectations of a year earlier. That information can boost or diminish your confidence in management's current postulating.

The Proxy

Read the proxy in tandem with the annual report. The proxy is the document that accompanies the shareholder's vote. The proxy is surprisingly easy to read and relatively brief. It is required reading before making an investment. It spells out the issues to be voted upon by the shareholders at the annual meeting, as well as providing, under securities law, disclosures concerning the directors, management, and related transactions between the company and interested parties. The proxy discloses the compensation of officers and board members in dollars and option awards.

The salary levels and incentives of the top executives are important to consider in evaluating a company. Abuses will be evident. For example, compensation of more than $250,000 for the chief executive officer (CEO) of a modest-sized (under $50 million revenue) company is excessive. Similarly if a CEO's salary is too large a portion of the company's total income (10 percent or more), it indicates management abuse and a disregard for the interests of shareholders.

Pay particular attention to any business before the shareholders that goes beyond what is normally conducted at the annual meeting. To illustrate, the creation of a new class of security can telegraph a number of important future developments. It can signal a management entrenchment if the new securities will be used to stall or defeat a takeover move. The issuance of a new class of stock is usually triggered when an outside interest crosses an ownership threshold (typically 20 percent). Shareholders could benefit because those who buy stock in a takeover move pay a material premium over the prevailing market price. But even though an offer may be fair and attractive, the company's ability to issue a new class of stock will discourage a potential takeover—and the likely financial gain to shareholders. Therefore, this management strategy—commonly referred to as a "poison pill"—can be at odds with the shareholders' best interest.

   This and other devices can be and are used to entrench management and thwart takeover interest, regardless of whether such acquisitions are or aren't in the best interest of the shareholder. For example, the creation of employee stock ownership plans (ESOPs) with voting rights firmly positioned in favor of the status quo can roadblock a beneficial interloper. Golden parachutes (generous severance pay for executives let go following a takeover) discourage acquisitions by increasing the cost to an unacceptable level. Staggered terms for the board of directors are a means by which only a minority portion of the board is elected annually. Consequently, a raider with a majority stock position can at first gain only a minority position on the board of directors. This discourages buyers by extending the period of time necessary to take complete control.

   Fortunately, most of these tactics require shareholder approval. Consequently, they must be disclosed in the proxy as an item to be voted upon at the shareholders' meeting. Even golden parachutes are disclosed as executive and board compensation.

   Also look for these items in the proxy:

- *All shareholder items added to the agenda*—Such items raise issues where shareholders might be at odds with management and the board.
- *Stock ownership of the management, board, and large holders (5 percent and more)*—Large "insider" ownership is, up to a point, beneficial. When people in the firm invest their own money, rewarding the shareholders becomes a first priority. On the other hand, if incompetent management has a stranglehold on the company, control is complete, and salaries plus perks become the top priority. Obviously this is a situation to avoid. (Identifying incompetent management is dealt with in a later section of this chapter.)
- *Related business transactions and property ownership between the company and members of management or the board*—This raises the issue of conflicts of interest and their influence on conducting the company's business.
- *Increase in the number of authorized common shares*—This is a clear sign of change. It's good if the increase is for future stock splits and dividends or to create shares available for acquisitions.

It's bad for the near-term performance of stock prices if the move is to provide for another future public stock offering (called a secondary). Newly issued common stock may flood the market and depress the stock price.

Remember, disclosing a fact doesn't make it right or OK. But the company's disclosure is a tool that you, a potential shareholder, should use in reaching your investment judgment.

Financial Statements
The annual report's financial statements are intended to give an accurate snapshot of a company's condition and operating results. The report is prepared and presented so every investor, large and small, can understand it. The ability to analyze these statements and know what the figures mean is essential for good investment judgment. If you have a handle on the company's present financial position and its past operating record, you are better equipped to judge its future potential—and it is the future developments that ultimately determine whether an investment succeeds.

The standard financial statements are the statement of income, the balance sheet, and the statements of changes in financial position. Later on, this chapter discusses each of them in detail.

Financial Highlights
Normally the financial highlights appear as a table at the beginning of the annual report just after the description of the company's business but before the management's letter to shareholders. This table presents a two- to five-year history and comparison of selected financial data such as total revenues, net income before taxes and extraordinary items, net income, total assets, working capital, stockholders' equity, net income per share, book value per share, cash dividend per share, and average number of shares outstanding.

Like the overall annual report, the financial highlights presentation varies in style and content from one company to another. Some are extensive with graphics, while others are a simple table. While a bare bones approach may merely show that management is frugal, it also may reflect a less than rosy picture—one that management isn't too proud of. This is particularly true if the annual report is little more than a 10K (the required annual SEC filing) with a cover. This presentation is known as a "brown wrapper" and portends financial ills. Conversely, an eye-catching and comprehensive statistical report coupled with a sound performance record reflects management's pride of achievement.

Rule number one: The figures speak more eloquently than management's rhetoric. In studying the financial highlights, you will get your first factual insight into the company. This summary shows the trend of the key measurements of the company's health and momentum. Ask yourself one simple question: have the key financial items summarized improved during the years depicted? With the exceptions of turnarounds, which are risky ventures at best, most companies continue on track pretty much along their historic patterns. If there has been cyclical, uneven, or erratic behavior, it's likely to continue. Unless there is a compelling reason to believe otherwise, you will be swimming against the tide—and that rarely works.

Rule number two: Form without substance is a trap. Companies with a lot of promise but a poor record and no earnings are for a gambler, not an investor. These companies are generally loosely defined as concepts, development stage, or start-ups.

The "concept company" is one where the plan of business is little more than a twinkle in the founder's eye. It is literally an idea in search of a business.

A company in the development stage is one small step further along from the concept company. While the business is still largely on the drawing board, there is some early movement in business activity. There may even be preliminary customer interest and tentative orders.

Start-up companies have made the transition from the concept and early-development phases to the beginning of operations. However, these companies are nowhere near large enough to be considered seriously.

These situations all rank the highest on the risk scale; the investor's capital is at great risk. They almost always have two common characteristics. First, they all harbor the hope of becoming the next IBM and an enormous hit in the market. Second, these companies almost always have no revenues, no earnings, no cash, and no assets.

The biggest mistakes made by investors, myself included, are with stocks of companies "all on the come." There will be ample time to purchase later on when some substance and credibility is evident. You will pay up some for the stock at that time, but the odds for a successful investment will have increased geometrically in your favor. Besides, in the long run it matters little whether you pay $1 or $10 per share for a stock if it is going to move up to $200. So, at this point in your analysis, if the annual report's message promises much but delivers nothing historically, you're better off to pass on the stock and investigate sounder opportunities.

Management's Discussion and Analysis of Financial Condition and Results of Operations

Today public companies are required to provide a commentary in which management describes and analyzes the company's financial condition and the results of its operations. Do not confuse this report with the letter to shareholders presented early in the annual report. Here management compares four years of operating results, frequently referring to percentage and dollar changes and the reasons underlying them.

This a valuable part of the annual report. Modern investors are blessed to have this section. Armed with your understanding of the annual report, you may be able to find here answers to many of the questions raised by your study of the financials. When I began in the industry, this report wasn't required, and we had to meander through the annual report as best we could. So take advantage of it.

Notes to Financial Statements, and Independent Auditor's Report

The remaining items in the annual report are the notes to the financial statements and the report of the auditor, or independent accountants. While notes to the financial statements vary, they typically cover summaries of accounting policies, inventory valuation methods, depreciation schedules, income tax data, details of bank loans and long-term debt, retirement plans, employee stock option plans, accounting treatment of acquisitions, and financial contingencies such as litigation, as well as data on unusual items pertaining to the specific company. When you are confused by an item in the financial statements, seek clarification in the notes to the financial statements. The answer is usually there.

The auditor's report is almost always a letter only a few paragraphs long and using standard language as shown in Figure 1-1. But go through the exercise of reading it. On the rare occasions where there is a problem, you can bet that the independent accountants are not going to stick their necks out! They will instead give the dreaded "Qualified Opinion." That is, they will hedge like hell. Statements like one questioning the financial ability of the firm to continue in business without financing will leap out at you. If that isn't a red flag, I don't know what is. The few minutes it takes to read the letter are well worthwhile, if for no other reason than to determine the absence of a negative.

INTERIM REPORTS AND PRESS RELEASES

Beyond the annual report, companies will issue press releases on mundane and important interim events in the corporation. News to look for includes announcements of quarterly results for the fiscal year, dividend payments, stock splits, management changes, mergers, contract awards, and product introductions. These announcements are brief and easy to read. Be sure to read any press release issued after the annual report. Equally important are the interim financial reports to the shareholders, which companies sometimes issue with a message from management.

10Ks, 10Qs, AND SIMILAR REPORTS

When you buy a new car, you get a complimentary owner's manual. If you are into cars, you ask for the shop manual. The difference between the two is measured in light-years. One is 10 pages, and the other is an indexed 300 pages or more. I know I'll never use the whole shop manual, but I also know that if I ever have to go beyond the comic book simplicity of an owner's manual, I'll find an answer in the shop manual.

The 10K and the 10Q are the shop manuals of the annual and quarterly reports, respectively. They are very detailed and coincide with the issuance of the formal annual report and the quarterly reports. When requesting information from the company, always ask to be put on the mailing list to receive these documents as well as any 8Ks filed. (An 8K is a document a company is required to file if there is a material change in the company, such as new senior management, sale of an asset, or an acquisition.)

Finally, there is the 13D. This is a document that must be filed

FIGURE 1-1

Report of Independent Accountants

To the Board of Directors and
Shareholders of Worldwide Computer Services Inc.

In our opinion, the accompanying balance sheets and the
related statements of operations, of changes in shareholders'
equity, of cash flows and of changes in financial position
present fairly, in all material respects, the financial position
of Worldwide Computer Services Inc. at December 31,
1989 and 1988, and the results of its operations for each of
the three years in the period ended December 31, 1989, its
cash flows for each of the two years in the period ended
December 31, 1989, and changes in its financial position
for the period ended December 31, 1987, in conformity
with generally accepted accounting principles. These
financial statements are the responsibility of the Company's
management; our responsibility is to express an opinion on
these financial statements based on our audits. We conducted our audits of these statements in accordance with
generally accepted auditing standards which require that we
plan and perform the audit to obtain reasonable assurance
about whether the financial statements are free of material
misstatement. An audit includes examining, on a test basis,
evidence supporting the amounts and disclosures in the
financial statements, assessing the accounting principles
used and significant estimates made by management, and
evaluating the overall financial statement presentation. We
believe that our audits provide a reasonable basis for the
opinion expressed above.

As discussed in Note 2, in 1988 the Company adopted
prospectively the provisions of Statement of Financial
Accounting Standards No. 95, "Statement of Cash Flows."

Price Waterhouse

PRICE WATERHOUSE
Morristown, New Jersey
February 27, 1990

by any party, group, individual, or corporation that has purchased at least a 5 percent ownership position in a public company. It always helps to know who you are in bed with. A 13D filing could mean anything from a straightforward investment position to the beginning of a takeover attempt. The filer must by law state its intention in the filing.

STATEMENT OF INCOME (PROFIT AND LOSS)

If the company you're looking into seems OK based on the letter from management and the financial highlights, move on to the nuts and bolts of security analysis: the actual financial reports. Turn to the portion of the annual report that presents the financial statements; it's clearly labeled. Although most reports will lead off with the balance sheet (a statement of the assets and liabilities), I recommend you begin with the statement of income. It is commonly known as the profit and loss (P&L) statement. This is simply the report of the past two years' operations but in much greater detail than the financial highlights. Start here because you must determine whether the company is growing and operating at an acceptable level of profitability before you review the company's balance sheet to determine its financial strength.

REVENUES

In studying the P&L, begin at the top line. The essence of the company—the true measure of the company's purpose in corporate life—is its sales, or gross revenues. You first saw the size and trend of gross revenues while perusing the financial highlights. Now you may see a breakdown of total revenues by its components such as product sales, licensing fees, consultant fees, investment profits, interest income, and dividend income. By way of example, the December 31, 1989, annual report of Leisure Concepts, Inc., shown in Figure 1-2 (pages 16–17) does just that.

Look at where the revenues are coming from. Money-making money—interest, dividend, and investment income—is considered "passive" revenue and isn't valued as highly as revenues generated by selling a product or service. There's no future in corporate America from managing the return on a pool of capital. Wall Street tends to reward operations that exhibit growth and profitability from operations, while it discounts passive revenue. You do the same. Take note of each component. If gross revenues have grown but the increase is attributed to nonoperating revenues, then there is a problem. Back off and go fishing elsewhere. With so many fish in the sea, why look for trouble? Instead, look for revenues that are largely derived from operations and are *growing*.

COSTS AND EXPENSES

Working down the P&L takes you to the cost of operations. This item is also broken down. In the case of Leisure Concepts, it shows development costs and selling, general, and administrative (SG&A) expenses. (Sometimes officers' salaries are shown separately, as in the Leisure report. More often than not, however, they are lumped in with the SG&A. As described earlier, you can obtain this figure in the proxy.)

Gross Margin
With this information you can already compute your first financial ratio: gross margin. To try this, use the Statement of Income of Lechters, Inc., shown in Figure 1-3 (page 18).

To compute gross margin, you must first find the *gross profit*. That is the money remaining after deducting the cost of goods sold but not SG&A and other expenses from total operating revenues. Thus, gross profit is an intermediate figure between gross revenues and net income. On the Lechters P&L, the gross revenues (net sales), cost of goods sold, and gross profit are already labeled. A company's P&L often provides these calculations for its shareholders, as in the case of Lechters. Here the gross profit is $51,763,000. When calculating gross profit, be careful to use only revenues generated from operations. Exclude passive revenues.

The *gross margin* is the gross profit expressed as a percent of total revenues. For example, the gross margin of Lechters is the gross profit of $51,763,000 divided by net sales of $156,833,000, or 33 percent.

The higher (wider) the gross margin, the better. A company working with a very narrow gross margin (under 15 percent) may have a host of difficult problems, ranging from inept management to poor cost control, highly competitive business with severe price sensitivity, a weak market for the company's goods and services, and poor pricing. As a rule of thumb, the narrower the gross margin, the less is the margin for error. An economic downturn or

FIGURE 1-2

LEISURE CONCEPTS. INC.

CONSOLIDATED STATEMENTS OF INCOME

	Year Ended December 31,		
	1989	1988	1987
Revenues			
Licensing and consulting fees—net	**$5,398,235**	$4,001,302	$4,153,236
Dividend income	—	—	198,666
Interest income	**490,144**	352,846	128,785
	5,888,379	4,354,148	4,480,687
Costs and expenses			
Concept development costs	**470,636**	456,945	232,197
Selling, general and administrative	**2,000,634**	1,925,657	1,480,464
Officers' salaries	**1,216,587**	999,218	803,263
Interest	**50,678**	21,856	105,060
Loss on sale of marketable securities	—	—	307,881
	3,738,535	3,403,676	2,928,865
Income before taxes on income	**2,149,844**	950,472	1,551,822
Taxes on income	**929,000**	376,000	843,000

Income from continuing operations	1,220,844	574,472	708,822
Discontinued operations			
Share of partnership loss (net of income taxes of $25,000 in 1989 and $26,000 1988)	(33,323)	(33,855)	—
Loss on investment and advances to partnership (net of income taxes of $154,000)	(204,390)	—	—
Loss on discontinued operations	(237,713)	(33,855)	—
Income before cumulative effect of change in accounting for income taxes	983,131	540,617	708,822
Cumulative effect of change in accounting for income taxes	—	—	141,000
Net income	$ 983,131	$ 540,617	$ 849,822
Net income (loss) per common share			
Income from continuing operations	$ .39	$ .18	$ .23
Discontinued operations			
Loss from discontinued operations	(.01)	(.01)	—
Loss on investment and advances to partnership	(.07)	—	—
Loss on discontinued operations	(.08)	(.01)	—
Income before cumulative effect of change in accounting for income taxes	.31	.17	.23
Cumulative effect of accounting change	—	—	.04
Net income	$ .31	$ .17	$ .27
Weighted average number of common shares and common share equivalents outstanding	3,126,984	3,165,543	3,112,246

FIGURE 1-3

LECHTERS, INC. and Subsidiaries

CONSOLIDATED STATEMENTS OF INCOME
(Dollar amounts in thousands, except per share data)

	January 27, 1990	Fiscal year ended January 28, 1989	January 30, 1988
Net sales	$156,833	$120,754	$ 89,621
Cost of goods sold (including occupancy and indirect costs)	105,070	80,680	60,343
Gross profit	51,763	40,074	29,278
Selling, general and administrative expenses	35,094	26,539	18,783
Income from operations	16,669	13,535	10,495
Interest expense	2,081	2,205	1,339
Income before income tax provision	14,588	11,330	9,156
Income tax provision (Note 5)	5,567	4,334	3,985
NET INCOME	$ 9,021	$ 6,996	$ 5,171
Net income per share	$ 1.35	$ 1.15	$ .85
Number of shares used in computing net income per share	6,694,582	6,078,110	6,078,110

an increase in the cost of doing business could be devastating to net income.

Calculate the gross margin for the current year and the year earlier. You may wish to go back even another year by using the last year's annual report. Compare the current margin with those past. If there is a material change or trend, for the worse or the better, make a note of it. Later on, other sections of the annual report and attending documents will help you discover the reasons for these changes.

Now you have the first financial ratio. There are no complicated coefficients or formulas—just simple financial sense. Suffice it to say that, if you throw a "KISS" (Keep It Simple and Short) at all your analysis, you'll come out ahead. All that other stuff amounts to little more than mental gymnastics designed to cloak the entire process in mystery and provide job security for the analyst. As you continue through the P&L, you'll follow a similar process of comparing other items to total revenue.

Selling, General, and Administrative Expense (SG&A)
It is important to note the distinction between cost of goods sold and SG&A. The cost of goods sold measures what it costs to make a product or service—the cost of raw material, components, and occupying the facility where the product is made. SG&A includes officers' salaries, marketing, and all the cost related to operations.

To analyze SG&A, look for any material change from the prior year, and also compare it to changes in cost of goods sold. In the instance of Lechters, 1990 revenues rose 30 percent, cost of goods sold rose 30 percent, but SG&A increased a disproportionate 32 percent. The earlier year's SG&A rose 41 percent compared with a 35 percent revenue gain, while the cost of goods sold actually declined relative to sales, with a lesser increase of 34 percent. Therefore, by a few simple calculations and comparisons it is determined that the erosion in Lechter's pretax profit margins lies in SG&A. This is an important piece of intelligence.

INCOME FROM OPERATIONS
To find income from operations, or operating profit, start with total operating revenues, and deduct the cost of goods sold, SG&A, and other expenses except for interest expense and income tax provision. In the Lechters example, this would be $16,669,000:

$156,833,000 revenues less $105,070,000 cost of goods sold less $35,094,000 SG&A.

To find the operating income margin of profit, divide the income from operations by total revenues. For Lechters, the $16,669,000 operating profit divided by $156,833,000 in revenues gives an operating margin of 10.6 percent.

This ratio indicates operating efficiency. In the case of Lechters, for every dollar of sales, the company had 10.6 cents left after paying all costs of operations. From this amount (plus other income such as net realized gains from the sale of properties, equity interests or securities, and dividend and interest income), the company must pay its interest expense and income taxes. Operating margins under 10 percent are considered too narrow.

INCOME BEFORE TAXES (PRETAX INCOME)

The very last expense item is income taxes. The amount of taxes that companies pay varies. Some companies are tax-exempt or pay lesser rates due to offshore operations, tax shelters, or loss carry-forwards. Hence, to evaluate this important margin on a level playing field, you must find the pretax margin, that is, the income before taxes as a percentage of revenues. Ideally, pretax margins should run at least 15 percent. Lechters' pretax margin is 9.3 percent ($14,588,000 pretax income divided by $156,833,000 revenues).

EXTRAORDINARY ITEMS

As the name implies, extraordinary items are items outside the boundaries of the company's ordinary business. They can be large enough to materially affect the P&L. Examples would be gain from the sale of an asset, write-offs, discontinued operations, severance costs, and loss due to fire or similar catastrophe. Extraordinary expenses include settled lawsuits, inventory write-downs, discontinued operations and projects, and fire and storm damage.

Some, like inventory write-downs, are bookkeeping entries that lower the carrying value of the asset but have no impact on operations. Others, such as the sale of an asset or a division, can boost the company's cash position and eliminate hard-dollar expenses. In assessing the present impact on the financial reports and future business of the company, consider each item separately. And remember, they are extraordinary developments, so they should be factored out when analyzing the company's long-term outlook.

An extraordinary item on the P&L for Cascade International shown in Figure 1-4 (page 22) is the gain on sale of fixed assets under Other Income. If you were analyzing this company's long-term potential, you would factor out this item as a nonrecurring benefit.

In contrast, the Boonton Electronics P&L in Figure 1-5 (page 23) shows a material expense (nearly 40 percent of pretax income) under the label "Unusual Item." Note 11 to the financial statements identifies this item as costs associated with an unsolicited tender offer. This is a nonoperating expense and probably a nonrecurring one. In attempting to determine Boonton's true earning power, it would be prudent to adjust income as if the expense hadn't occurred.

NET INCOME, EARNINGS PER SHARE, AND PRICE-EARNINGS RATIO

The bottom line is, of course, net income. That is the amount remaining after paying all expenses, the cost of doing business, and taxes.

The attractiveness or the success of an investment depends upon its future earning power, or ability to generate net income. In formulating expectations, investors are compelled to use current and past earnings as a guide. Based on the financial highlights and the P&L, you can assess the trend and quality of the company's earnings, so that you can begin to reasonably estimate future earnings.

Earnings per Share

Since the value of a company's stock is quoted as a price per share, you must know the company's earnings on a per-share basis. You first encountered net income per share in the financial highlights. It is repeated throughout the report. In the unlikely event there is an annual report that doesn't report the figure, the arithmetic is simple: divide net income by the number of shares outstanding at year-end.

Price-Earnings Ratio

The relationship between the company's earnings and the market price of its stock is expressed as the *price-earnings ratio*. The P/E, as it is called, is the market price per share of stock divided by the company's net income per share. For example, a $32 stock of a

FIGURE 1-4

CASCADE INTERNATIONAL, INC. and Subsidiaries
Consolidated Statements of Income

	(In thousands, except per share data) Years Ended June 30		
	1989	**1988**	**1987**
REVENUES:			
Boutiques	$15,875	$14,138	$11,187
Cosmetics	9,833	7,759	4,651
TOTAL REVENUES	25,708	21,897	15,838
COST OF SALES (including occupancy costs)			
Boutiques	10,550	9,689	7,416
Cosmetics	4,418	4,098	2,430
TOTAL COSTS	14,968	13,787	9,846
GROSS PROFIT	10,740	8,110	5,992
SELLING AND ADMINISTRATIVE EXPENSES	3,743	2,700	1,874
OPERATING INCOME	6,997	5,410	4,118
OTHER INCOME:			
Gain on sale of fixed assets	92	355	—
Interest income	337	264	—
TOTAL OTHER INCOME	429	619	—
INCOME BEFORE TAXES	7,426	6,029	4,118
PROVISION FOR INCOME TAXES	2,710	2,208	1,649
NET INCOME	$ 4,716	$ 3,821	$ 2,469
Weighted Average Number of Shares Outstanding	13,479	12,216	12,401
Earnings per share	$ .35	$ .31	$ .20

FIGURE 1-5

Boonton Electronics Corporation

Consolidated Statement of Income and Retained Earnings

| | For the Year Ended September 30, | | |
	1988	1987	1986
Net Sales	$13,530,002	$12,609,802	$9,910,254
Cost of Goods Sold	6,842,285	6,747,099	4,651,233
Gross Profit	6,687,717	5,862,703	5,259,021
Commissions	1,454,684	1,298,967	1,332,829
Research and Development	1,519,358	1,502,651	1,577,962
Other Operating Expenses	1,917,412	1,866,239	1,867,309
Income from Operations	1,796,263	1,194,846	480,921
Unusual Item (Note 12)	317,969	0	0
Interest Expense (Net)	128,674	94,837	73,760
Other (Income)/Expense	67,582	98,186	52,554
Income Before Provision for Income Taxes	1,282,038	1,001,823	354,607
Provision for Income Taxes (Note 5)	450,373	382,930	72,857
Net Income	831,665	618,893	281,750
Retained Earnings—Beginning of Period	3,442,400	2,823,507	2,541,757
Retained Earnings—End of Period	$ 4,274,065	$ 3,442,400	$2,823,507
Weighted Average Number of Common Shares Outstanding	1,436,993	1,480,297	1,479,485
Earnings Per Share	$ 0.58	$ 0.42	$ 0.19

company earning $4 per share has a P/E of 8 or is said to be selling at eight times earnings. P/Es are calculated on latest annual earnings, 12-month running earnings (the total of the most recent 12 months' earnings), and estimated future earnings.

The P/E is a simple and valuable ratio for comparing stocks of companies in similar and different industries and of varying size. It serves as a common denominator. First, compare the stock's P/E to the general market. To do this, look up the P/Es of the popular market indexes: Dow Jones Industrial Average and S&P 500. These are easily located in the Market Lab section of *Barron's* each week under the heading "Indexes, P/Es and Yields." By comparing these numbers, you will be able to determine whether your stock pick is in line or out of line with the general market. Next, compare your stock's P/E with the average for its industry group. The easy way to do this is to use the *Value Line Investment Survey*, a premier investment service. Listed in the service, under composite statistics, are P/Es by industry grouping. The *Value Line Investment Survey* is available in the public library.

Entire texts have been written on analyzing P/Es, and this ratio has many variations. But by sticking to a few basic rules, you have all you need. A relatively low P/E indicates a less attractive stock, and a high P/E is associated with the more attractive or popular stocks. As a general rule, a low P/E is 8 or less, and a high P/E is at least 15. If the P/E exceeds 18, then you have hardly discovered the stock at the bottom price, and the stock may well be approaching a good selling rather than buying price.

Who determines the P/E? The majority of the buyers and sellers in the market do by the prices at which they buy and sell. Value, like beauty, is in the eyes of the beholder or, in this case, in the actions of the investors. If a stock is selling at a P/E of 5 based on last year's earnings, then the majority believes it to be a poor value. By acting as if a company is worth only five times what it earned last year, investors are showing more than a little skepticism as to the earnings they expect in the immediate future.

Based on this information, how do you approach the market? Keep in mind that the majority is wrong the majority of the time. If the stock holds up under analysis, you can make an investment even if the majority have placed a low P/E valuation. Just the reverse is true on stocks with high P/Es. Normally a P/E in excess of 18 based on next year's estimated earnings is a sell signal. There are exceptions, of course, such as companies that have made medical and technical breakthroughs. But most of the time, you would be wise to pass by the high P/Es. When the market ticks down, these are the stocks that get slammed the hardest. On the other hand, a stock with a low P/E has a worst-case scenario already built into the price. It is likely to fare better in a down market. If your pick is good and earnings move up, then you will be rewarded with a double bang—a higher P/E on higher earnings.

BALANCE SHEET

Once you have reviewed the P&L, it is appropriate to move to the balance sheet. The balance sheet is a statement of the company's financial condition as of a particular date. It is the equivalent of an annual checkup. Unlike the P&L, which presents a historical pattern of operations to the most recent year-end, the balance sheet is a still-life portrait or a snapshot of the company's financial status at a given time. The specific items in a balance sheet vary, but Figure 1-6 (pages 26–27), a balance sheet for Mylan Laboratories, illustrates the general format.

Begin with the balance sheet presented in the most current annual report. (And remember that more current data are available in the interim financial reports and regulatory filings.) Here you will find the financial makeup of the company at the close of the last year's business, which is also the beginning of the current year's business.

Analyzing the balance sheet need not be complicated. It has three basic sections: Assets, Liabilities, and Shareholders' Equity. Each is measured alone, then they are measured against each other and in combination with selected elements of the P&L. Again, use the KISS approach. Only a few key yardsticks and ratios need be applied to evaluate the balance sheet.

ASSETS

The lead section and the place to start analyzing the balance sheet is Assets. This category consists of current assets, fixed assets (sometimes called property, plant, and equipment), and some miscellaneous items.

FIGURE 1-6

CONSOLIDATED BALANCE SHEETS

March 31	1990	1989
ASSETS		
CURRENT ASSETS		
Cash, including cash equivalents	$ 21,919,000	$ 29,865,000
Accounts receivable	17,381,000	13,979,000
Inventories		
Raw materials	11,925,000	10,590,000
Work in process	5,925,000	4,467,000
Finished goods	5,317,000	7,892,000
	23,167,000	22,949,000
Prepaid expenses	421,000	996,000
Total Current Assets	62,888,000	67,789,000
PROPERTY, PLANT AND EQUIPMENT – AT COST		
Land and land improvements	3,862,000	3,362,000
Buildings and improvements	15,445,000	15,131,000
Machinery and equipment	22,766,000	19,591,000
Construction in progress	1,922,000	652,000
	43,995,000	38,736,000
Less accumulated depreciation and amortization	13,088,000	10,934,000
	30,907,000	27,802,000
OTHER ASSETS	19,653,000	15,609,000
INVESTMENT IN AND ADVANCES TO SOMERSET	24,072,000	1,500,000
TOTAL ASSETS	$ 137,520,000	$ 112,700,000

March 31	1990	1989
LIABILITIES AND SHAREHOLDERS' EQUITY		
CURRENT LIABILITIES		
Trade accounts payable	$ 3,388,000	$ 2,123,000
Income taxes payable	1,563,000	1,505,000
Other liabilities	2,219,000	2,926,000
Current maturities of long-term obligations	53,000	50,000
Total Current Liabilities	7,223,000	6,604,000
LONG-TERM OBLIGATIONS–LESS CURRENT MATURITIES	1,086,000	526,000
DEFERRED INCOME TAXES	1,978,000	1,292,000
SHAREHOLDERS' EQUITY		
Preferred stock, par value $.50 per share, authorized 5,000,000 shares, issued and outstanding–none	—	—
Common stock, par value $.50 per share, authorized 100,000,000 shares, issued 36,443,334 shares at March 31, 1990 and 36,385,959 shares at March 31, 1989	18,223,000	18,193,000
Additional paid-in capital	597,000	159,000
Retained earnings	108,793,000	86,306,000
	127,613,000	104,658,000
Less–Treasury stock 239,173 shares–at cost	380,000	380,000
Net Worth	127,233,000	104,278,000
TOTAL LIABILITIES AND SHAREHOLDERS' EQUITY	$137,520,000	$112,700,000

Current Assets
The major current assets are:

• Cash and cash equivalents.
• Accounts receivable.
• Inventories.
• Short-term notes receivable.
• Investments.
• Prepaid expenses.

Don't be overwhelmed by the titles or number of items. Take the items one by one, and you will find that you need only simple arithmetic and common sense.

Cash and Equivalents: Hard dollars and items that are as good as cash, such as short-term Treasury obligations, commercial paper, certificates of deposit, and the like, are called "cash and equivalents." All these have a specific cash value that the owner may realize in a very short period of time (30, 60, or 90 days). All may be sold in the financial markets at a price above, at, or near their dollar face value, or they can be used as collateral for short-term bridge borrowing. Because they share these common characteristics, there is no useful way to distinguish cash itself from cash equivalents. For all practical purposes, the various kinds of cash assets may be considered interchangeable.

A company must have enough cash to support its day-to-day operations, to say nothing of getting through any recessions, extraordinary events, or occasional disruptions. If too little of the company's current assets are in the form of cash, the company will be stuck trying to fend off creditors while it waits for its accounts receivable to be collected or its inventory to be sold for cash. In general, businesses sell inventories, then must collect the cash on the resulting accounts, which may take 30 to 60 days or more. Meanwhile the business needs cash to pay for mundane things like salaries, supplies, and rent.

Unfortunately, a common problem is for companies to have trouble collecting on accounts just when they need cash the most. If you think about it for a moment, it makes sense. When business is soft, the company needs extra cash. If the business slowdown is due to an industrywide condition, many of the company's customers are likely to be in financial difficulty as well. They will be slow in paying, due to their own cash needs.

Of course, there are other reasons for cash needs. For example, expansion, acquisitions, product development and marketing, and construction projects all legitimately eat cash. However, these are optional undertakings and lend themselves to planning and structured financing. They're less likely to drain dollars from the business's daily capital needs. Reasons to the contrary given by management are suspect and symptomatic of weak financial planning.

So play it safe. Seek and require liquid current assets with a healthy level of cash and equivalents.

What is a satisfactory level? Eyeball it. A company that has $100 million in revenues but only $1 million in cash is in a tight position. Cash at any level less than 4 percent of sales is courting a squeeze.

If the companies you are investigating are modest to small firms, your requirement for liquidity should be larger. The smaller the company, the more critical is its cash position and the higher its level of cash should be as a percentage of sales. For example, the immediate cash needs of a modest-sized or fledgling company of $10 to $25 million include such mundane items as payroll, rent, and payments to vendors. No matter how promising the future, failure to meet near-term cash obligations will sink a company faster than you can say "bankruptcy."

On the other hand, a large corporation has an edge in that it may have access to quick (even though expensive) cash from short-term bridge financing. Witness Donald Trump's last-minute bailout. Had Trump's operations been smaller, he wouldn't have had a chance. Rather than negotiate, the banks would have confiscated. Within a heartbeat, the company would have been in an unmarked grave on corporate Boot Hill with no one of any consequence to mourn its passing (except, of course, its employees, debtors, and shareholders). Don't take the chance. Insist on a minimum liquidity level.

On the other hand, if cash holdings are exceptionally large in relation to the market price of the stock, the company deserves favorable investment attention. The stock may be worth more than the earnings record and outlook indicate, because a material part of the stock price may be represented by cash holdings. Eventually, stockholders are likely to benefit from large cash assets, when the company distributes them or uses them more productively in the business.

Admittedly, an opposite school of thought considers large cash positions a weakness. Disciples of this view reason that excess cash is symptomatic of poor financial management and that the cash should be deployed gainfully to improve the company's return to shareholders. On the surface this approach has merit. However, there are considerations and drawbacks to ponder. For example, the level at which cash becomes excessive isn't clearly defined, but surely too much cash is better than not enough. Second, given the unstable domestic and world economies, with attending social and political unrest, it's best to have a substantial cushion. This protects the company against unforeseen developments and arms it to benefit from opportunities that may develop due to a stressful business climate. All things considered, I prefer a bit more cash than is prudent and, with little effort, will tolerate even more than that.

Accounts Receivable: After cash and equivalents, the most liquid current asset is accounts receivable. This is what purchasers of the company's products owe it over the near term. Collection time—the period of time it takes to collect the monies due—is called "aging." Aging varies by firm and industry. The shorter the aging (the quicker the company collects what is due it), the better. The reason is simple. If a company is to meet its payroll, rent, and current payables weekly, semimonthly, or monthly, then it must collect the money on time. Otherwise, it will get into a cash crunch before long. More than one corporation has died of prosperity. The more business it does, the greater its obligations become. While the company may seem to be doing well, the stretched out receivables actually have it on the ropes. This is not exactly a complicated economic theory; nevertheless, it is a vital measure of a company's survivability.

As a general rule, an average collection period of 30 to 45 days is acceptable; 45 to 60 days is slow; 60 to 90 is unacceptable. These are average collection periods, since each industry's practice varies. Nevertheless, anything longer than 120 days threatens to become a "bad" (uncollectible) receivable. The banks would call a bad receivable a nonperforming loan. Anybody else would call it worthless!

The people in management are human like everybody else. Their tendency is to carry an overdue account and resist undertaking a legal collection action, which could acknowledge it as a "bad" account. Management doesn't want to take a loss or look bad. The hope, often forlorn, is that the customer will restore itself to a good rating. Of course, most times it doesn't happen. Ultimately, the independent auditors will force a write-down of any accounts that are in arrears for 120 days and over.

Only unpleasant surprises await stretched-out receivables. The P&L takes a hit, and the balance sheet loses liquidity. A receivable account that is too large and too aged is symptomatic of a much deeper problem: poor financial management. The stock market has unmercifully punished stocks of companies with such problems.

So how do you spot this weakness? Normally an annual report does not provide an average collection period. But measuring receivables by aging is in effect studying them in relation to total sales. The very size of the accounts receivable in relation to the total operating revenues (from the P&L) is an indicator of how "good" (collectible) and well managed the accounts receivable are. If receivables are more than 25 percent of total sales, look out! Chances are they're on the edge of becoming problems.

It is also important to scrutinize receivables in relation to changes shown over a period of years. Any sudden increase as a percentage of sales could signal an unduly liberal credit policy— maybe indicative of an attempt to boost sagging sales volume.

Conservative management will make allowances for the prospect of uncollectible receivables by setting aside a reserve for bad debts. This provision usually appears in the financial footnotes following the financial statements. Sometimes the bad-debt reserve is identified right on the balance sheet as a notation in parentheses. A 2 percent allowance for doubtful accounts is standard. More than that could mean a receivables problem exists and is acknowledged by management.

Inventories: Considerably less liquid than cash and accounts receivable are inventories. This current asset consists of raw materials, work in process, and finished goods. For a manufacturing company, inventories include the material from which the company's product is manufactured, as well as the product itself. Sale of the product generates revenues, accounts receivable, and eventually cash. As certain receivables may go bad, so may inventories go bad due to obsolescence as a result of market forces and technology advances.

Rising inventory levels can be a warning. They are a precursor to a world of worry. Needed money is tied up in stockpiled material and product, the work force becomes idle, and poor management controls are in evidence. When studying inventory levels, be certain to consider the seasonality, if any, of the business being analyzed. For example, a retailer will increase inventories in anticipation of the December holiday season. To avoid receiving a false signal, compare inventory as a percentage of sales over this and preceding years.

The chief criterion of inventory soundness is turnover. As in the case of receivables, study inventory in relation to sales. Divide the gross sales by the year-end inventory figure to derive turnover. The more times inventory turns over in a year, the faster and healthier sales are and the less the danger of inventory becoming obsolete.

The standards on this point vary from industry to industry. Nevertheless, a turnover of 5 or more is indicative of a robust business. For example, a company with $100 million in sales and an inventory of $20 million turns its inventory five times a year ($100,000,000 \div $20,000,000 = 5$). Less than three turns annually is low and risky, whatever industry the company is operating in. A good example is the automobile industry. If the cars aren't selling, they pile up on the dealers' lots and in the manufacturers' stockyards. Inventory is high. Next year's model is coming. What follows are markdowns and losses. That's not a good scenario and certainly not one you want to invest in. So watch those inventory levels relative to sales.

Other Current Assets: Other current assets are short-term notes receivable (those with terms of less than a year), investments, annual prepaid expenses, and miscellaneous items. As you may have anticipated, these are less liquid than the other current assets. Investments, for example, can be anything from various classes of stock to long-term Treasury and commercial notes. Technically they qualify as current assets because they are traded in the financial markets and have a quoted value at any given time. But their value may fluctuate month to month, week to week, and day to day. For this reason, these investments are carried on the books at the lower of either their cost or their market value.

A footnote to the financial statement provides the details concerning the makeup of these investment items. If these items are minor (under 5 percent of total current assets), you may pass them by. If the investment amount is more, then check it out by inquiring of your broker or referring to the financial pages of the *Wall Street Journal*, *Barron's*, or other papers for their present values and volume of activity. This is easy to do by looking up the name of the investment and reading across to the price of the last transaction and the daily and weekly volume. Bear in mind that although these investment items have a market value, they may be difficult to convert into cash, depending upon the size of the investment and the activity of the market for them.

Personally, I look somewhat askance at public companies speculating in the market with their cash resources. Managing the most favorable return on the company's cash assets is one thing, and a desirable one. It involves using high-quality, short-term, liquid money instruments. However, in today's volatile markets, investing in the securities of other companies is another thing altogether. I am more comfortable with management that tends to its business and runs the operations of its own company than with a management that wheels and deals in the stock market. If you see too much size (more than 5 percent of current assets), poor quality (speculative equities), and limited marketability (thinly traded securities), it is probably best to pass on this one. Management's priorities are all wrong, and the future of the company (your stock) is not commanding the attention it deserves.

Usually, the remaining current assets are so small that they are not listed individually. They are grouped under a category called Prepaid Expenses and Miscellaneous. If this category is not large, don't give it more than passing notice. But if it is significant, you should understand what it includes and how to treat those assets.

Prepaid expenses represent amounts paid to others for services to be rendered during the year. Almost always this item is treated as a current asset. Presumably, if these services were terminated before being completed, they would have some residual or surrender value to the corporation. Don't you believe it. That money is already spent—so don't count on it. In fact, you would be wise to pull the prepaid expense item from your valuation altogether.

Another miscellaneous item is the deferred charge. In contrast with prepaid expenses, this represents amounts paid that will benefit future operations but for which no specific service or benefit will be received in the present. Such expenses are considered properly chargeable to future operations. Thus, they are "deferred." Examples are research and development (R&D), costs of introducing a product, or the expense of moving a plant. Such items might be logically expensed against future operations. If small, deferred charges may fall into current assets. If large, this item may appear at the bottom of the list of assets on the left-hand side of the balance sheet ledger, where the assets are recorded.

On rare occasions, a deferred charge is a large item. When it is, it can be an important checkpoint for the investor, because it can be a killer! When an expense applies to a fixed asset, it is a deferred charge. When it refers to an expense such as R&D, then it is a capitalized expense. The result is the same: a bomb waiting to go off. These are expenses already incurred and paid for but not accounted for. That's the fact. The fiction is the expectation that future sales and earnings will be there to apply these expenses against.

If the sales and earnings don't materialize, you can bet you're in that great American corporate tradition known as the write-off. Here the auditors and the regulating bodies such as the SEC will require the company to take the loss by expensing it into the P&L. Earnings can be unexpectedly hit hard. And that will spell disaster for your stock.

Capitalized expenses and deferred expenses are easy to spot. They stand out on the asset side of the balance sheet like a toad in a punch bowl. Steer clear.

Fixed Assets
"Hard," long-term assets are called fixed assets. They consist of buildings and improvements, fixtures, machines and equipment, tools, land and land improvements, and so on. Fixed assets are the roots, the bedrock, of a company. An auto company without its manufacturing facilities, a printer without its presses, or an air-

line without its planes isn't much to write home about. So unless you are investigating a pure service company, fixed assets play an important role in evaluating a company.

Valuation of Fixed Assets: Fixed assets have several kinds of value. First is the book value. This is the value reported in the annual report. It is the net of the cost of the assets less accumulated depreciation.

Fixed assets (other than land, which is carried at cost) are assumed to have a limited life for tax purposes, so a portion of the assets' value, usually calculated at cost, is depreciated. That is, this portion of asset value is expensed each year against income. Depreciation (described later) reduces the value of the assets each year for reporting purposes. However, in the real world, these assets may appreciate in value. For example, a well-maintained manufacturing facility increases, not declines, in value. So the dollar values assigned by the accountants to fixed assets on the balance sheet are often worthless. These values can cloak hidden assets—assets with values well in excess of those reported on the balance sheet. Thus, the manufacturing facility whose value increased is likely to have a greater value than stated.

Some fixed assets, such as computers, transportation equipment, and office furnishings, do have a definable life. For these assets, you can take the depreciated values at face value. Otherwise, understand that the company may have more than you first see.

To find the true worth of a fixed asset, use one of these measures:

• Its worth as an operating manufacturing facility.
• The cost to replace it.
• Its value in the industry if an outside party were to buy it.

Annual reports don't give this sort of data directly. However, by reading the footnotes and observing the amount of depreciation, you can estimate the approximate age of the fixed asset. If the depreciation is large compared with the value of the asset shown, then you know that the asset has been on the books for a while and that it is probably way undervalued.

Depreciation, Depletion, and Obsolescence: As mentioned earlier, fixed assets are subject to a gradual loss of value through age and use. The allowance made for this loss in value is expressed as depreciation, obsolescence, depletion, or amortization. Don't get lost in the terminology and feel like a novice. Again, the concepts are merely obscured by the technical jargon and formulas of the accountants. Simply stated:

- *Depreciation* is the ordinary wear and tear of buildings and equipment.
- *Obsolescence* refers to the loss of value due to technological and similar changes.
- *Depletion* is the gradual removal from the ground of mineral and timber resources by the company, which either sells them or turns them into products for sale.
- *Amortization* is the process of gradually extinguishing a liability over a period of time. Certain liabilities, deferred charges, and capital expenditures all may be expensed gradually with annual charges to the P&L. The term *amortization* refers to essentially the same procedure as depreciation, except that it involves charging off the cost of an intangible asset such as goodwill or a patent.

These items appear as charges against earnings in the profit and loss statement and as a deduction from the original value of the fixed asset in the balance sheet. The original cost of the property, before the allowance for these items, is called its gross value. The amount remaining after deducting accrued depreciation is called net value. As discussed, there is the real world, and then there is the accountant's world. The net values assigned to depreciated assets often grossly understate the assets' true value.

Land: The value of land is reported at cost. Since corporate land holdings tend to be long-lived, you can expect they have increased in value. For almost every company I have investigated over many years as an analyst, I have found the true value of fixed assets to be substantially above that given in the financial statements. These hidden assets are desirable.

Goodwill: If a company's assets include goodwill, it is usually carried separately toward the bottom of the asset side of the balance sheet ledger. Despite its position on the balance sheet, goodwill can be an important item and is worthy of your close attention.

A quick reference to the financial footnote will identify the good-will item and its history.

No matter what you find in the footnotes, remember that good-will is fluff. Don't let anyone tell you differently. It is a created paper value. That's why it's called an intangible asset. It has no substance, and worst of all, it will reduce the earnings of the corporation you own stock in for a very long time—40 years!

Where does this monster come from? Mostly acquisitions of other companies and/or assets. It is how the bean counters (accountants) balance the books when a company buys something at a price in excess of its stated or true value. Don't let it confuse you. Look at it this way: Often a company purchases a plant, a patent, equipment, a label, or a whole other company at a price higher than the entity or asset is valued on the seller's books. The amount paid in excess of that value is goodwill.

Is this a polite way of saying that a company has overpaid? Probably yes. But what about the fact that fixed assets can be substantially undervalued on the financial statements? Isn't it then reasonable to expect that a sale at fair market value would create an accounting profit for the seller and goodwill for the buyer? If so, the buyer wouldn't have necessarily overpaid. Rather, the accounting abnormality of establishing value for financial statements is off the mark, not the buyer.

That's all true for textbooks, but it doesn't work that way in real life, because a conservative and financially savvy buyer would immediately "write up" purchased assets as much as the law permits. That is, the asset will be valued higher than the purchase price based upon its true market worth. This is done for several reasons. It permits the buyer to increase the depreciation of the asset over its tax life. The noncash depreciation charge reduces the buyer's tax obligation and therefore increases cash flow. What remains is the amount in excess of the value at which the company can carry the asset. It is goodwill and is likely to be the true fluff. Under generally accepted accounting principles (GAAP), goodwill must be expensed against income annually in 40 equal amounts.

How can a company be so foolish as to pay up? I really don't know, but it is conventional wisdom that the majority of corporate buyers are losers when they acquire other companies or their assets. The seller seems almost always to be the winner, often being overpaid for the wares. Acquiring companies simply overpay for underperforming assets and/or businesses. It is a nondiscriminatory truism among macro and micro corporations. Size doesn't seem to be a factor for the corporate spendthrift. That's the reason to be wary of goodwill buildup. You may not wish to own stock in a free-spending company.

Miscellaneous Assets

Miscellaneous assets are grouped together under the heading Other Assets. They appear at the very bottom of the asset side of the balance sheet. They are usually insignificant.

LIABILITIES AND SHAREHOLDERS' EQUITY

If the balance sheet is a snapshot of a company's financial status, that snapshot contains two portraits. The left side of the balance sheet shows assets, just described. On the right-hand side of the balance sheet are liabilities and shareholders' equity. The total for the two sides are equal.

Liabilities consist of current liabilities, long-term obligations, and accrued income taxes.

Current Liabilities

Corresponding to the current assets are the current liabilities. For the most part, these are the company's debts and the obligations payable within a year and incurred in the ordinary course of business. Those most generally encountered are:

- Trade accounts payable (amounts owed by the corporation to its vendors).
- Accrued liabilities payable (accrued payroll bonus and other small debts, no one of which is substantial enough to warrant an individual label).
- Income taxes accrued (unpaid portion of income taxes due on various dates in the ensuing year).
- Current maturities (that portion of originally long-term obligations that must be paid within a year).
- Bank loans or notes payable (money borrowed from banks or others for the short term).

In addition, miscellaneous items tailored to the nature of the company's business will appear among the current liabilities. These include accrued restructuring costs, dividends payable, and customer advances and deposits.

Long-Term Obligations

As their name indicates, long-term obligations are simply debts with maturities of over one year. They are normally held over many years and include permanent bank loans and debt instruments such as bonds and notes.

The fact that a company borrows from the banks or issues public debt is not in itself a sign of weakness but more likely indicates that the company needs long-term capital to finance operations. This is true particularly if the company is expanding. The danger arises when the amount of long-term debt is too high relative to shareholders' equity. The acceptable level of long-term debt is measured by a debt-to-equity ratio. The calculation of this and other balance sheet ratios is covered later in this chapter.

Reserves

A company may have set aside sums to provide for a future obligation or recognize a potential liability. Such funds are called reserves. They can provide important insight into the company's real or probable liabilities. There are three basic categories of reserves:

1. *Liability reserves*—These represent an obligation due at some future point. Liability reserves are set up for taxes, pending litigation, customer refunds, and for certain future operating charges. These are twilight zone liabilities, neither current nor long-term liabilities. These reserves are separated from the current liabilities in the balance sheet and appear in an intermediate position.
2. *Valuation reserves*—These are offsets against the stated value of an asset. This type of reserve applies to depreciation and the like.
3. *Surplus or "voluntary" reserves*—With these, the company sets aside part of its reinvested earnings. This is a vague item that is essentially an offset reserve. It is rarely encountered now. But on the off chance it does appear, bear in mind that it is usually there to provide for a decline in inventory value. In dealing with such reserves, it is essential to discover whether the reserve reflects a real exposure in inventory or is merely a conservative

management's provision for an unlikely contingency. A history of, or lack of, inventory write-offs will tell the story.

Again, the footnotes to the financial statements will provide the detail necessary to determine the true nature and importance of reserve accounts. As a rule of thumb, reserves that keep growing year to year, are never used, and are of an indefinite nature should be returned to the earned surplus account (an item appearing under shareholders' equity). Conversely, reserves representing real potential liabilities should be classified as current liabilities when computing the key balance sheet ratios.

Shareholders' Equity
The interest or equity of the shareholders of the company is represented on the balance sheet under the heading Shareholders' Equity. It is the net worth. There are just two major ingredients to this account: capital and surplus.

In the typical case, the monies paid in by the stockholders are designated as *capital*. This in turn is broken out into subcategories by classes of equity, such as preferred stock and common stock. The equity category is more likely to show the equity at par value (the value stated on the face of the stock certificate). Par value is not in the slightest degree informative. It is frequently stated far below the actual amount paid in by shareholders. The balance of the original shareholders' investment is stated in some surplus account—usually under the label Additional Paid-In Capital or Capital Surplus. Combine the three, and you have the total injection of initial capital into the company.

The other major item is Retained Earnings or Earned Surplus. This is the total of the company's net income or losses to date.

There may be a few miscellaneous items such as treasury stock (stock repurchased and held by the company). In the case of treasury stock, it is deducted from the total shareholders' equity.

Combine all of these items, and you have shareholders' equity. Divide by the number of shares issued and outstanding (a number provided in the financial highlights section or on the balance sheet under common stock), and you have book value per share. The book value of company assets theoretically is the value available to each share of common stock. It is a measurement of value per share but has no practicable value unless the company is actually being liquidated.

BALANCE SHEET FINANCIAL RATIOS

In addition to the ratios and valuations discussed so far, there are a handful of other key financial ratios and yardsticks that are easy to calculate and necessary to master:

- Current ratio.
- Acid test ratio.
- Working capital.
- Debt-to-equity ratio.
- Return on invested capital.

All may be computed readily from the balance sheet and, in one case, the P&L. In some instances, the company has already calculated them for the shareholder and published them in the financial summary. Nevertheless, it is important to understand how they are derived.

Current Ratio

In analyzing balance sheets, the most frequently used figure is the current ratio. It is the ratio of current assets to current liabilities and is arrived at by dividing the total current assets by the total current liabilities. This ratio measures a company's ability to meet its near-term debts as they come due.

Remember, current liabilities represent all the obligations that must be paid within a year, whereas current assets include items such as inventory and accounts receivable that are considered current but are not necessarily liquid enough to pay current debts on short notice. Thus, for a company to be financially sound, its current assets should exceed its current liabilities by a wide margin. In that case, the company will have no difficulty in paying its bills.

What constitutes a satisfactory current ratio varies by lines of business. For example, if inventory turns over frequently and/or receivables are promptly collected (as previously discussed), the cash is generated quickly. Such a business would need less of a margin over current liabilities. It follows that the slower these items turn, the wider the margin needs to be.

In general, a standard minimum is a current ratio of 2 to 1. That is, current assets should be at least twice the size of current liabilities. Anything less is trouble. A ratio of 3 or more to 1 is preferable.

Acid Test or Quick Test Ratio

You should analyze the current ratio further and more stringently. To do this, consider only the current assets with high liquidity and weigh them against current liabilities. This is the so-called acid test or quick test. Specifically, divide the total of cash items and receivables by current liabilities.

It is customary to require that the cash items and receivables exceed all the current liabilities. To the extent that an acid test fails, it indicates that a company depends upon the less liquid inventory to turn over in order to meet its near-term obligations. (An informative reference would be glancing back at your earlier calculation of inventory turnover.) Whenever that is the case, look into the situation with some care. Failure to pay current liabilities will cut off the company's lifeblood. Always apply the acid test.

Working Capital

As you can see, when studying the current position of an enterprise, never consider the current assets only by themselves, but in relation to current liabilities. Besides the current and acid test ratios, you can do this by computing working capital. To do so, subtract current liabilities from current assets.

In this absolute figure is the measure of the company's ability to meet the demands of carrying on operations comfortably. All the fixed assets in the world are of little aid in meeting the demand for day-to-day cash. Shortage of working capital, at the very least, ties up management effort, delays expansion and product development, results in slow payables with attendant poor trade credit ratings, curtails present operations, and impedes general ability to progress. The most serious consequences of lack of working capital are insolvency and bankruptcy.

The chief means of evaluating working capital is to calculate the amount of sales per dollar of working capital. Merely divide sales by the working capital. For example, a company with $500 million in sales and $100 million in working capital would have $5 net sales per dollar of working capital ($500,000,000 ÷ $100,000,000).

Companies enjoying a rapid turnover of inventory will have high sales per dollar of working capital. Companies that must hold their inventories for long periods will have lower sales per dollar of working capital.

The proper amount of working capital varies by volume of sales and type of business. As a general rule, companies that sell nondurable goods such as food or apparel enjoy a rapid turnover of inventory. Hence, they will have a high ratio in the range of $8 to $10 of sales per dollar of working capital. But companies that hold their inventories, such as some industrial companies, fall in the area of $4 to $6 of sales per dollar of working capital. Businesses that sell technical instrumentation and related products with very low turnover of inventory track at a little over $3. If the company you're looking at fails to meet these standards for its industry, walk on by.

Also note the growth or decline of working capital over the years. A corporation's working capital is increased by net income, cash flow from provisions for depreciation and depletion, and injection of monies from the sale of assets or stock. The first two sources are generated from continuing operations and are important to a careful investor. On the other hand, the sale of stock or an asset is a temporary measure.

Working capital is decreased by the amount invested in new equipment and plant or paid as dividends. If working capital is declining, it could be a message that the business is eating capital faster than it can produce income. Unlike people, when this happens, the corporate entity gets thin, not fat. Thin people may be nice to be around, but believe me, it's not pleasant being around stock investments in financially thin corporations.

The information necessary to determine how the changes have occurred appears in a financial statement following the P&L and balance sheet. This statement normally carries the title Cash Flow from Operating Activities, Statements of Changes in Financial Position, or Source and Application of Funds. This statement is covered later in the chapter.

Return on Invested Capital
The percentage earned on invested capital is a true test of a business. This is not a P&L profit margin, but a measure of how

much the company has earned on each dollar that was invested in the business. It reflects both the efficiency of the operation and the way the company is capitalized (the amount and composition of investment).

To find the return, begin by making two easy calculations:

1. Take net income before taxes, and add back the interest expense as identified on the P&L.
2. Find invested capital at year-end. Ordinarily, this figure is clearly identified at the bottom of the right-hand side of the balance sheet. But just in case it isn't, it is the sum of the bonds, preferred stock, common stock, paid-in surplus, earnings surplus, and reserves.

You now have: (1) what the company earned after all expenses (salary, material cost, etc.) but before taxes and interest expense on borrowed money and (2) the total amount of money invested in the company.

Next take the adjusted net income (item 1), and divide it by invested capital (item 2). This is the return on invested capital.

If a company has $100 million of invested capital and earns $15 million before interest expense, it returns 15 percent on invested capital ($15,000,000 ÷ $100,000,000). This is the minimum percentage return I would require of any company I choose to invest in. It means that the business earns considerably more than the cost of borrowed money or the returns available on quality money instruments such as AAA-rated bonds and government securities. Thus, it can generate a profitable return with the money it borrows. Anything less than a 15 percent return on investment capital is lowering your standards and incurring additional risk.

Debt-to-Equity Ratio
In the 1980s the financial world was inundated by leveraged deals. (Leverage in financial circles is synonymous with debt.) Known mostly as leveraged buyouts (LBOs), these transactions were thinly disguised financial schemes to buy something of value with currency of questionable or no value. That currency was low-quality bonds known as "junk bonds." Junk bonds became synonymous with the megabuck wheeling and dealing of Wall Street's financial titans. A frenzied financial community underwrote and

distributed junk bonds to the public while corporate America loaded up its balance sheets with these "investments."

In truth, these were nothing more than high-yielding, high-risk, and nonrated bonds. They were bought by greedy investors after they had been schmoozed into a false security of flying with the eagles. To this extent, the 1980s were an emblem of wretched excess. Well, the junk bonds lived down to their name, and the soaring eagles went to the ground as overweight turkeys! The bloodletting continues as of this writing.

As that financial fiasco illustrates, there is only so much debt a company can handle relative to its equity. Businesses don't have the federal government's luxury of tapping into the population's pocketbook to support its spending spree. The company you own stock in, unlike our esteemed government, must pay the tab (interest and principal).

To judge what is an appropriate degree of debt, calculate the amount of a company's debt relative to its equity. To do this, take the total long-term debt outstanding (again on the right-hand side of the balance sheet ledger), and divide by the sum of that debt and total shareholders' equity (preferred stock, common stock, surplus, and reserves). For example, if long-term debt is $50 million and shareholders' equity is $125 million, divide $50 million by $175 million (the sum of $50 million and $125 million), equaling 28.5 percent. Hence, debt is 28.5 percent of the company's total invested capital.

A debt-to-equity ratio of up to 40 percent is acceptable. Above that level, the company runs the danger of becoming too highly leveraged. At 60 percent there is too much leverage, and the company risks being caught up in a destructive borrowing binge.

STATEMENTS OF CHANGES IN FINANCIAL POSITION

Following the balance sheet and P&L in the annual report are several statements of changes in financial position. These show changes in cash flow and in retained earnings and shareholders' equity. The titles may vary by company, but their meaning is clear. Each provides an accounting of changes in the respective areas for the fiscal year.

FIGURE 1-7

Boonton Electronics Corporation
Consolidated Statement of Cash Flows

For the Year Ended September 30,

	1988	1987	1986
Cash Provided By/(Used For) Operations:			
Net Income	$ 831,665	$ 618,893	$ 281,750
Charges/(Credits) to Income Not Requiring Cash:			
Depreciation	432,747	399,514	392,918
Other	(863)	36,139	38,722
Decrease/(Increase) in Current Assets:			
Accounts Receivable	408,887	(1,394,525)	216,117
Inventories	(532,682)	(754,892)	(198,057)
Other Current Assets	5,045	98,890	106,016
Increase/(Decrease) in Current Liabilities:			
Accounts Payable	(445,050)	641,606	(45,145)
Accrued Liabilities	95,973	264,296	42,978
Total Cash Provided By/(Used For) Operations	795,722	(90,079)	835,299
Cash Provided By/(Used For) Investment Activities:			
Additions to Fixed Assets	(179,630)	(273,564)	(265,668)
Deposits	(25,000)	0	0
Other	(8,050)	(8,050)	(8,766)
Total Cash (Used For) Investment Activities	(212,680)	(281,614)	(274,434)
Cash Provided By/(Used For) Financing Activities:			
Increase/(Decrease) in Bank Loans	(25,000)	25,000	0
Payments on First Mortgage	(200,000)	(200,000)	(200,000)
Borrowings on Officer's Life Insurance	0	30,484	0
Proceeds From Issuance of Common Stock	20,938	14,350	0
Purchase of Treasury Stock	(254,870)	0	0
Total Cash Provided By/(Used For) Financing Activities	(458,932)	(130,166)	(200,000)
Increase/(Decrease) in Cash and Cash Equivalents	124,110	(501,859)	360,865
Cash and Cash Equivalents at Beginning of Period	15,187	517,046	156,181
Cash and Cash Equivalents at End of Period	$ 139,297	$ 15,187	$ 517,046

Changes in Cash Flow

The statement of cash flow is sometimes labeled Source and Application of Funds. An example is the statement for Boonton Electronics Corporation shown in Figure 1-7. Here an investor can trace precisely where the company obtained cash and how the company used the cash item by item. This statement concludes with a net increase or decrease in the company's cash position for the fiscal period. Thus, reading the data, you can trace the flow of corporate monies in and out of the company.

It is important to identify where the cash flows from and how it is applied to enhance the company's business. It is desirable to see cash flowing from operations. Cash injected from the sale of an asset may be favorable, but it is a nonrecurring and nonoperational event. Also, if a company is financing its growth strictly from operations, it may be able to fund future growth without needing costly outside financing. On the other hand, a negative cash flow (more cash being spent than being generated) would indicate that at some future point, the company will need outside financing if it is to expand. Hence, this financial statement is must reading, particularly in conjunction with the financial ratios and measurements covered earlier.

Changes in Retained Earnings and Shareholders' Equity

Similarly, as shown in Figure 1-8 (page 48), the Statement of Changes in Stockholders' Equity for Boonton, investors may note the increase or decrease in these important items. Increases in retained earnings benefit the company and the shareholder. Similarly, shareholder equity, as covered earlier, is one important measurement of a stock's value. Track increases or decreases through this statement. A reduction in these two items is a negative; you want to see them growing.

Earning Power

When analyzing all these documents, remember that the most important role in security analysis and the determining factor in a stock's price is ultimately earning power. This is the earnings that may be reasonably expected over a period of time. Obviously it is desirable that a company show growth in gross and net earn-

FIGURE 1-8

Boonton Electronics Corporation

Consolidated Statement of Changes in Stockholders' Equity

For the Year Ended September 30, 1988, 1987 and 1986

	Common Stock		Additional Paid-In Capital	Retained Earnings	Treasury Shares, at cost
	Number of Shares	Par Value			
Balance September 30, 1985	1,479,485	$ 147,948	$ 4,308,054	$ 2,541,757	$ 0
Net Income				281,750	
Balance September 30, 1986	1,479,485	147,948	4,308,054	2,823,507	0
Exercise of Stock Options	3,450	345	14,005		
Net Income				618,893	
Balance September 30, 1987	1,482,935	148,293	4,322,059	3,442,400	0
Purchase of Treasury stock					(254,870)
Exercise of Stock Options	5,150	516	20,422		
Net Income				831,665	
Balance September 30, 1988	1,488,085	$ 148,809	$ 4,342,481	$ 4,274,065	$(254,870)

ings. So when conducting your study, assign more weight to earning power than to the other financial considerations discussed in this chapter.

CONCLUSION

You now have the basic knowledge for analyzing the key data about a company. In reading financial statements and attending material, you must consider various factors. By examining them, you can reach an informed opinion as to the company's present position and future potential.

All the ratios and evaluations applied to the financial reports are interrelated. A system of checks and balances is at work. This chapter has concentrated on the key measurements of a company's worth and stature. They are more than enough. Applying additional ratios would be redundant. Do your analysis, but avoid overanalyzing.

There is ample evidence to demonstrate that an individual investor, with a little work and discipline, can beat the market and the "experts" on a reasonably regular basis. Use the methodologies described. But don't abandon the standards of evaluation because you "feel good" about a stock for whatever reason. This will defeat the purpose of the entire fundamental approach, and you will probably join the silent majority of stock market losers.

The process of stock selection is multilayered. The fundamental approach, albeit a key one, is just one of the tools used in reaching an investment judgment. To be most effective and to maximize the rewards while avoiding the pitfalls, you must avail yourself of the other proven stock-picking and valuation methods presented in this book. As with fundamental analysis, you may master these tools easily. If you make the effort to do so, you will have a winning edge.

2

FOOTPRINTS IN THE SAND

AN INTRODUCTION TO
TECHNICAL ANALYSIS

———————————————————————— David Krell

THE STOCK MARKET IS A COMPLEX AMALGAM OF EMOTIONS, feelings, and opinions. In its totality, the stock market reflects the combined aspirations of all its participants. However, just as there are fads, trends, and cycles in fashion, entertainment, and most other emotionally influenced pursuits, so they appear in stock prices.

Successful investing in the stock market entails a wide variety of skills. Patience, discipline, and intuition are frequently considered among the most important. While certain skills come more naturally to some individuals than to others, successful trading is a learnable skill. However, acquiring that skill requires an investment of time and effort. Unfortunately, many individual investors plunge into the stock market totally unprepared for what the market is likely to deliver, so they are surprised by the difficulty of succeeding.

The views expressed in this chapter are solely those of the author as an individual, and not in his capacity as an employee of the New York Stock Exchange.

Chapter 1 looked at the fundamental gauges of a company's financial health insofar as they can be used to predict the likely direction and rate of change in the common stock's price. This chapter will focus upon technical, rather than fundamental, analysis.

Technical analysis seeks to identify the major trends in force in the marketplace and to harness that knowledge into a logical, methodical approach to investing. This chapter examines a variety of methods used to identify trends and evaluate the sentiment of the marketplace, and it looks at a number of techniques for charting trends and interpreting those charts.

Technical analysis assumes that all existing knowledge about the prospects for a company's earnings, products, management, competitive position, dividends, and the like are *already* reflected in the price of its shares and in the volume of shares trading. As a consequence, the technician assumes that the fundamental information is incorporated in the current price of the shares. Certainly surprises in any of these major categories will influence the price and volume of the shares, but this additional information will be so quickly assimilated into the price and volume pattern of the stock and the market that from a practical point of view investors may confine their "homework" to the technical interpretations of price and volume.

While the preceding description of technical analysis and technical philosophy are accurate, many investors are somewhat uncomfortable ignoring the fundamentals when looking for successful investment vehicles. These investors use technical analysis and fundamental analysis in tandem. If the fundamentals predict a bright outlook for a company, they seek confirmation of this prediction in the stock's volume and price. Conversely, they look to technical analysis to provide an early-warning signal of something going wrong that may not have yet shown up in the fundamentals. There is, of course, nothing wrong with this dual approach; for you it may be the most successful of all.

Technical analysis is used more frequently to evaluate and predict patterns over short and intermediate durations than to find trends over the long term. Basic changes in a particular industry or company may take years to evolve, especially in mature industries. This is particularly the case in industries where product introduction and acceptance is lengthy. In younger industries influenced by quick technological innovation, or in industries that could be influenced by a change in consumer purchasing habits, such basic changes are much more rapid. Technical analysis can be especially effective in spotting changes in investor expectations in these more volatile stocks and industry groups. Later in this chapter, we will consider several examples of such cases.

CHARTS AND THEIR INTERPRETATION

In its earliest years, technical analysis consisted mostly of charting the price movements of individual stocks. While modern technical analysis in the United States dates back to the 19th century, in several other countries historical evidence suggests that plotting the price of commodities has been actively practiced for several hundred years.

The purpose of plotting prices on a chart is to be able to relate the present price to the historical record. The chart is like a road map or navigational chart. Just as a ship's navigator identifies the ship's position on a maritime chart in order to determine the best course for sailing the vessel, so the chartist plots the position of a stock in order to determine his or her current position as it relates to the past.

The historical record is important to the chartist because one of the main tenets of technical analysis is that human emotion permeates the movement of stocks. Since technical analysis assumes that the entire spectrum of human emotion and all present knowledge are concentrated in the single element of price, the historical perspective provides a valuable insight into what investors were willing to pay for the security.

Medicine in general and psychology in particular require a thorough knowledge of the history of a patient before the practitioner can analyze the symptoms and initiate a specific therapy. Similarly, a thorough knowledge of the price history of a stock can improve the investor's ability to predict the stock's price in the future. By analyzing the price behavior in the past, the technician is hoping that the human elements that influenced its behavior will be repeated and that this will become more transparent on a chart. While it is not realistic to expect events to be repeated identically, just having a sequence of similar patterns recur is enough to provide the technical analyst with a good estimate of future performance.

TYPES OF CHARTS

Technical analysts primarily use two types of charts: bar charts and point-and-figure charts. Bar charts are more popular and are constructed using the high, low, and last sale price of a stock or an index. These charts can be used to plot daily, weekly, or monthly statistics. With the recent advances made in communications, bar charts have also been adapted to plot intraday price movements of stocks, indexes, and commodities.

Figure 2-1 (page 54) is a daily price chart of IBM stock. Each bar in the middle of this graph spans the range of prices at which IBM stock traded for a day. The dash in each bar represents the closing price for that trading session.

A point-and-figure chart is somewhat more difficult to use. In a point-and-figure chart, only price *changes* are plotted, while *time* and *volume* are ignored. In any given day, if the price of a stock were to fluctuate back and forth, there would be several entries for that day. In later periods, if the price were to remain stable, there would be no entries at all. In this way, point-and-figure charts are able to distill trends in price movement occurring over long periods. Figure 2-2 (page 55) illustrates how a point-and-figure chart can condense the price activity of four years into a single chart. While some of the nuances are lost, the long-term pattern is clearly apparent.

Point-and-figure charts are primarily useful in identifying likely areas of resistance or support. Because these charts are not as popular as bar charts, the rest of this chapter will concentrate on bar charts.

PRICE HISTORY

Chartists attempt to discern trends and patterns from the price history of a stock. For example, in Figure 2-1, line AB is an *uptrend line*. To draw an uptrend, the chartist connects the first

FIGURE 2-1

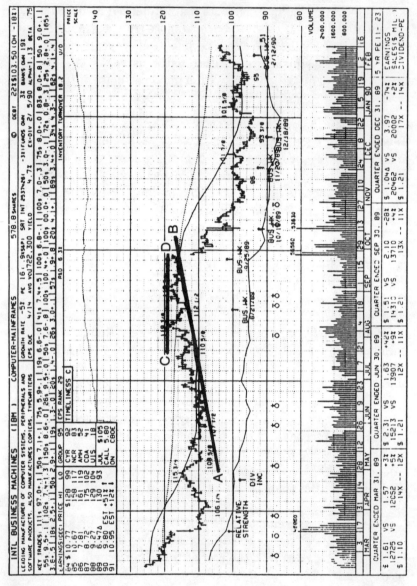

FIGURE 2-2

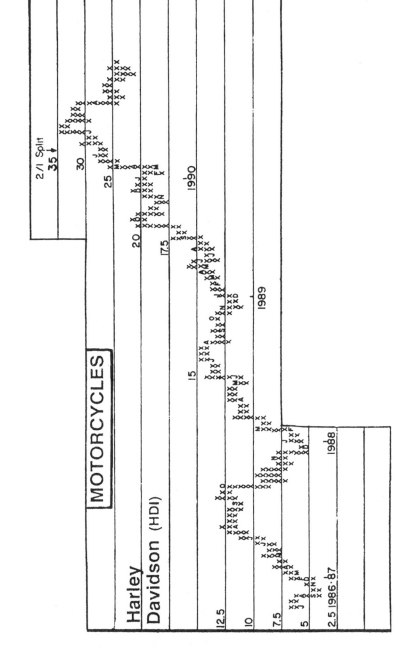

two or three significant points where the stock price stopped a
pattern of declines. In this instance, the chartist connected the low
points in mid- and late June, as well as the late-July decline.

To test whether a trendline accurately portrays price movement,
see whether later prices bounce off the trendline rather than pene-
trate it. If so, this test corroborates the existing trend of the stock.
Trendline AB passed this test in mid-August; prices did not break
through until the last week of September.

After a prolonged advance, price movement encounters resistance as the supply of stock becomes equal to or exceeds the
demand for it. When this occurs, prices move sideways, as in zone
CD. Line CD, which connects the high of early August and early
September, is called the *resistance line* or *zone*. This type of zone
depicts periods in which prices move sideways. For example, the
rally from the August pullback shown in Figure 2-1 was too weak
to exceed the highs of 118–119 reached in early August.

Whenever the intermediate-term trendline is decisively broken,
as in early September in Figure 2-1, the trend begins moving in
the opposite direction. When, as in the example, an upward trendline is broken, the trend of the stock is said to be down.

Downward trends frequently occur at sharper angles than rising
trends. This is because stock prices fall faster than they rise.
Human emotions influence the ebb and flow of stock prices and
often manifest themselves in irrational behavior whenever investors are stimulated to act out of fear. People are better able to
control their instincts to buy than to sell. While greed governs the
decision to purchase a security, it is fear that drives someone to
sell. When fear simultaneously inflames a large group of investors,
the usual outcome is panic selling. This places a sudden wave of
selling pressure on a particular stock, causing its price to plunge.

While the decline of IBM during late September–November
would not be characterized as a panic-selling wave, it nonetheless
illustrates that the decline was far quicker than the preceding
advance. Adding fuel to falling prices was the increase in volume
during the initial phase of the break in the trend in October.
Volume is an important ingredient to follow. Whenever a trend
break is accompanied by an increase in volume, the significance of

the break increases, as does the importance of the change in direction.

Downward trendlines connect the high prices of a stock and highlight the prices at which the stock encountered resistance when it attempted to rally. For example, IBM quickly receded from 112 in late September to 96 in mid-November. A short-term rally to 100–101 then ensued. This in turn was followed by a further decline in mid-December to 93. Trendline EF is the sharp trendline hugging the steep decline from 112 to 96. The wider trendline EG defines the longer-term downtrend from 112 to 93.

Prices find support when they successfully test a rising trendline. Thus, for IBM toward the end of December, the decline in share prices decelerated. That is, prices stopped going down as rapidly as they had fallen during the previous three months. Indeed, beginning on the first trading day of 1990, IBM's price spurted up and within a week was challenging 101, a level previously not seen for a full month. The subsequent pullback to 95 in late January provided the springboard for an outsized rally to the 106 level in early March. With the trend then in an upward direction, no significant price deterioration would be expected unless the new support line GH was decisively penetrated.

Investors can benefit from knowing when a major shift in trend has occurred. At these junctures, they can decide to enter into a trade. If the trend has shifted into a downward direction, they may elect to liquidate an existing position or to sell short (described in Chapter 10). Contrarily, they could decide that it is time to purchase when rising prices have broached a major downward trendline.

It is important to recognize that a trend-following approach to investing, such as the one using trendlines, will never enable the investor to buy at the very bottom or sell at the very top. Nevertheless, it will provide the investor with a mechanism to identify major changes in trends. If followed with care, it will prevent the investor from staying with an investment whose advance has run its course.

PATTERNS AND FORMATIONS

Chartists use numerous patterns and formations to identify rever-

58   David Krell

FIGURE 2-3

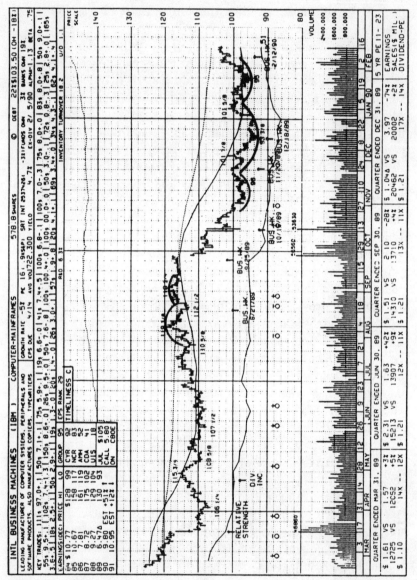

sal patterns and continuation patterns in stock prices. Two of the most important reversal patterns are illustrated in Figure 2-3.

Double Tops and Double Bottoms

The double top is a frequently seen pattern in which price action is confined to a rather narrow range after an advance of some duration and magnitude. Also, due to an approximately equal distribution of demand and supply, the price has trouble advancing further. The pattern that then develops resembles a double mound with a valley in the middle. Normally, the second mound, or top, is the more significant formation to recognize, since it points out that the price action was insufficient to surmount the previous peaks. Also, volume is often lower during the formation of the second top than the first.

Thus, IBM share prices rallied from 107 in the middle of June to 119 by early August. In mid-August prices experienced a normal pullback, which was followed by a resumption of the uptrend. However, volume began to falter, and the rally lacked much momentum to surmount the price levels of early August. During September prices meandered in a narrow range with a downward bias. This price action produced the double top of August–September.

The double top of August–September was also important because it coincided with a break of the uptrend line, discussed earlier.

Similar price formations could occur near bottoms, in which case they are called double bottoms. The only difference between double tops and double bottoms is that volume increases during the formation of the second bottom, while it contracts during the second top.

Head-and-Shoulders Formations

Another important pattern that often signals a reversal in prices is the head-and-shoulders formation. Head-and-shoulders formations may occur at major tops or major bottoms. When they occur at bottoms, they are called inverted heads and shoulders. An example of an inverted head-and-shoulders formation is the pattern traced by IBM from November 1989 to January 1990 in

FIGURE 2-4

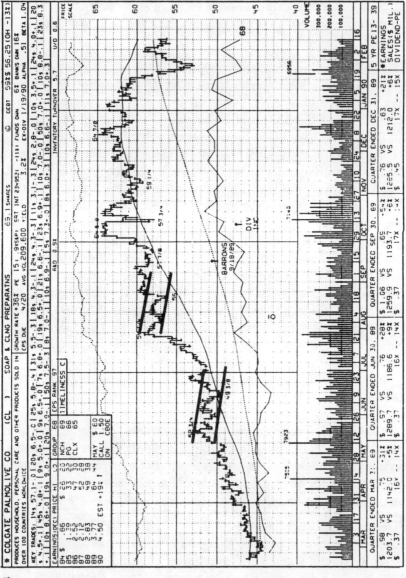

Figure 2-3. The left shoulder developed in November from 96 to the neckline at 101. The stock then declined to a new low of 93, forming the head of the pattern, followed by a rally to the neckline at 101. The subsequent pullback to 95 and reaction rally to the neckline completed the pattern.

An added benefit provided by head-and-shoulders patterns is that they allow the investor to estimate the potential rise or fall in the price of the shares when the neckline is penetrated at the end of the formation. Normally, the minimum target from the breakout point at the neckline is equal to the distance from the head to the neckline. In Figure 2-3, the distance between the head (93) and the neckline (101) is equal to 8 points. Thus, the target in this case was for IBM to rally to 109 (101 + 8).

Continuation Patterns
Numerous other patterns and formations typically accompany major tops and major bottoms. The ones described here are only two of the more popular. Moreover, a wide variety of patterns and formations are used to identify junctures where stocks are likely to continue an existing trend. These are called continuation patterns.

Continuation patterns are sometimes referred to as consolidation areas or zones. These are periods of movement counter to the general trend. Chartists view these as rest stops in a specific trend.

Flag Formations: Figure 2-4 contains two examples of flag formations within the confines of an uptrend. Flags are examples of consolidations or pauses during an established trend. These patterns look like flags when the trend is up. When the trend is down, they are in opposite form. Just before the formation of a flag consolidation, there is normally an above-average price move. In Figure 2-4, for example, the stock had an above-average rise during the month of July, increasing from 50 to 59 in four weeks. Moreover, volume increased during the advance in July to above-average levels.

It is essential that during a consolidation, volume decline from its high level of the prior advance. For example, during the flag consolidation in August, prices moved in a direction counter to the prior uptrend, and volume contracted. This supports the case that the pattern is a consolidation of the uptrend or a continuation pattern, rather than a change in direction or the beginning of a reversal pattern.

Flag formations and their near cousins, pennant formations (which are flags with nonparallel consolidation patterns), occur most often after a sharp run-up in the price of a security. The consolidation phase following the steep advance serves as a pause to refresh before prices continue to rise.

While the example in Figure 2-4 identifies a flag formation for a rising stock, flags and pennants also occur with descending stocks. However, a flag for a down-trending stock will have the consolidation pointing upward, in a direction counter to the downtrend in the stock.

Price Gaps: Price gaps on a bar chart are points at which there was no trading activity in a stock. This occurs when there is no overlapping of prices from one trading day to another. Normally this occurs infrequently. When it does take place, it is a significant event.

An example of a gap in the price of IBM's stock appears in Figure 2-5. This gap in late September occurred after a lengthy consolidation of more than two months. The gap between 112 and 116 broke away from the double top formation of August–September and represented the beginning of a declining phase in IBM share prices. This breakaway gap was considerably important as it led to a major correction in the stock's price for the next few months.

MOVING AVERAGES

To eliminate less important price movements and to smooth the fluctuations in the price of a stock, the technical analyst often averages out the daily price movements by combining several days or weeks of a price action into a single value. This value is then plotted on a chart. Doing this over a period of time generates a smooth line showing the general trend of a stock.

For a simple 10-day moving average, the technical analyst would add the closing prices of a particular stock for the prior 10 days, then divide the sum by 10. For example, assume that the closing prices for the past 10 days were as follows:

FIGURE 2-5

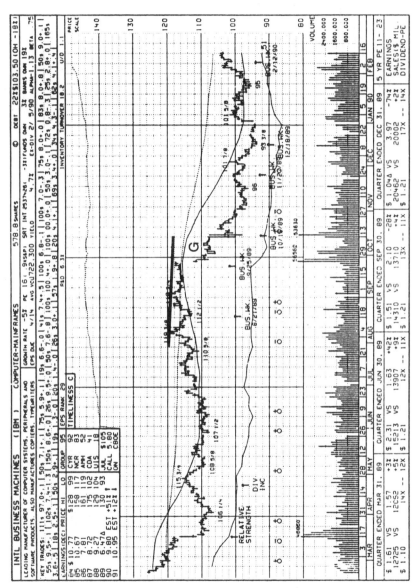

FIGURE 2-6

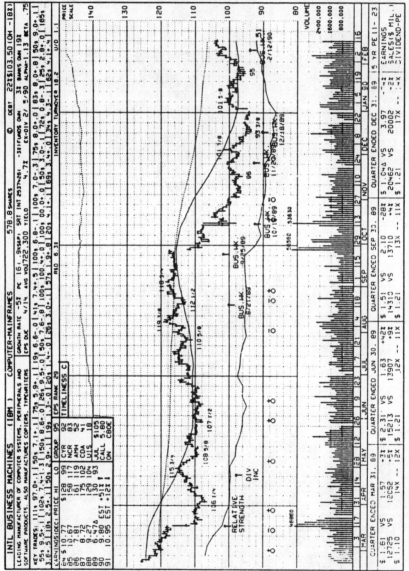

Day 1	28
Day 2	28½
Day 3	28¾
Day 4	28¼
Day 5	28½
Day 6	28¾
Day 7	29¼
Day 8	29¼
Day 9	30
Day 10	30½

When we add the prices for the 10 days and divide by 10, we get a value of 28.98. This is the 10-day average price for this stock. On the 11th day, we would repeat the same process but would omit the price of the first day.

The same method could be used to calculate moving averages of longer or shorter durations. The longer the time span of a moving average, the smoother is the line that results from plotting the average. Shorter moving averages are normally used by traders, and longer-duration moving averages are used by investors.

Figure 2-6 illustrates two moving averages for IBM. The solid line represents the 50-day moving average price, while the dashed line is the 200-day moving average price. Notice that the 50-day price movement is sharper than the 200-day moving average price.

Investors use moving averages in several ways. Longer-term investors might elect to wait to buy a stock until the daily stock price moves above the longer-term, 200-day moving average. Or they might wait until the shorter-term, or faster-moving, average rises above the longer-term, or slower moving, average before they buy.

Traders, in contrast, may not want to wait as long as investors for the longer-term moving average to be penetrated. Instead, they may buy when the daily price rises above the line for the 50-day moving average. This would result in many more trades than would be triggered by using a longer-term moving average, but for a more active trader, it may be a more desirable approach.

Using shorter-term moving averages presents problems as well. One of the more hazardous is an increase in the number of times the daily price penetrates upward through the moving average,

FIGURE 2-7

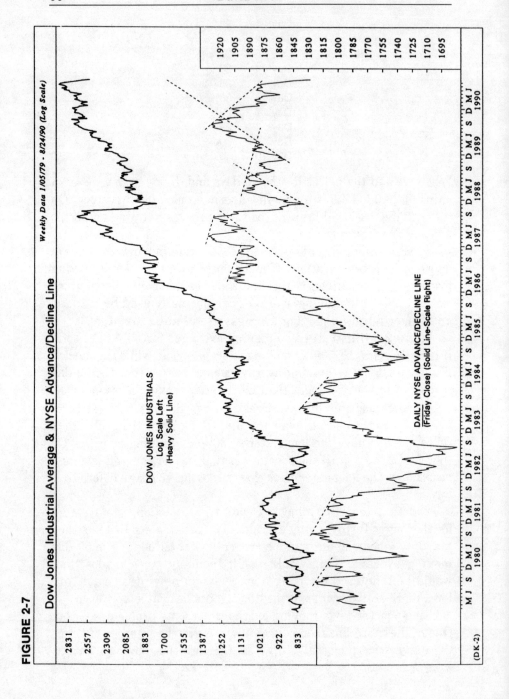

Dow Jones Industrial Average & NYSE Advance/Decline Line

Weekly Data 1/05/79 - 8/24/90 (Log Scale)

DOW JONES INDUSTRIALS
Log Scale Left
(Heavy Solid Line)

DAILY NYSE ADVANCE/DECLINE LINE
(Friday Close) (Solid Line-Scale Right)

(DK-2)

providing a signal for a purchase, then moves back down through the moving average. That pattern occurred with IBM's stock in January 1990. As Figure 2-6 shows, IBM moved up smartly through the 50-day moving average during the first week of January, but by the end of the month, the daily price crossed below the moving average. This whipsaw could result in numerous trades that may not yield any profits when the small gains or losses are added to the total commissions paid for the transactions.

THE ADVANCE-DECLINE LINE (BREADTH)

When looking at the overall price action in the stock market, the technical analyst needs to ascertain the quality of the advance or decline in prices in order to better forecast its trend. One way to do this is to measure "breadth" by counting the number of issues that are advancing relative to the number of issues that are declining. When more issues are advancing than declining, the technician views this as positive for the trend. When more issues are declining than are advancing, it is negative for the trend.

Breadth is recorded on a chart with an advance-decline line (A/D line). The A/D line is a cumulative total of the net number of advancing stocks versus declining stocks (normally for the New York Stock Exchange). For instance, if on Monday the number of advancing stocks were 800 and the number of declining stocks were 600, the A/D Line would be increased by 200. If on Tuesday the number of advancing stocks were 300 and the number of declining stocks 700, the A/D line would be decreased by 400. Figure 2-7 shows a sample A/D line.

A simple explanation of the logic of this indicator is that the price action in one of the major market barometers, such as the Dow Jones Industrial Average or the S&P 500 Index, may be unduly influenced by a few strong or weak stocks. These may mislead the technician into falsely interpreting the overall direction of the market. For instance, assume that one stock in the Dow has had a strong upward thrust, advancing handsomely while most of the other component stocks languished or encountered price erosion. In that case, the Dow could be advancing while most of its component stocks were declining. Just monitoring price action with this average would point to a rosy picture. However, close examination of the breadth of the Dow would show that the upward move was due to the price action of just one component while the others were declining.

While the A/D line often follows the price trends in the market, price trends and the A/D line sometimes diverge. At these junctures the analyst must determine whether the price action is strong enough to move without breadth moving in the same direction. Many technical analysts are skeptical of price movement without the confirmation of breadth. Some would not enter into a position unless one were in lockstep with the other.

MARKET SENTIMENT

Besides the observable evidence in the marketplace—trends, patterns, formations, and moving averages—the well-rounded technical analyst is also concerned about the psychological state of the market. Are most participants optimistic or pessimistic? Are they bullish, bearish, or just standing on the sidelines?

To assess this state of mind, the technical analyst weighs a number of indicators that have been designed to follow the sentiments of the participants in the market. Among some of the best known indicators of market sentiment are the put/call ratio, the newsletter editors' percentage of bulls and bears, and the mutual fund cash position.

PUT/CALL RATIO

The put/call ratio is the ratio of the volume of put options to the volume of call options. These options (described in Chapter 6) give their holders the right to sell the underlying security at a specific price during a specific period of time (put) or to buy the underlying security at a specific price during a specific period of time (call). When investors are buying puts, they are bearish on the market or the stock. Since they have the right to sell a stock at a given price, their put should rise in value if the share price of the underlying stock declines. Conversely, investors buy calls when they are bullish on the market or the stock. The call price should increase as the share price increases, and they will profit when the stock's price rises substantially.

When an overwhelming number of puts is bought relative to calls, it indicates a bearish feeling on the part of options traders. Normally this occurs at or near market lows. Historically, investors feel comfortable in buying puts when the market (or the stock) is in a downtrend. Most investors feel most pessimistic about the market's price expectations at or near the bottom. The technical analyst wants to know when such a condition exists, because it frequently indicates that the market has had an extended move to downside. At these times the technician may wish to take a contrarian view. That is, he or she may wish to buy stocks despite the widely prevailing bearish sentiment among options traders, on the assumption that the pessimism has already pushed the prices as low as they will go. In that case, the technical analyst has assessed that the majority opinion cannot be correct and is acting counter to the prevailing sentiment.

The generally accepted threshold levels are 1.3 and 0.7. When the put/call ratio is above 1.3, it may indicate a buying opportunity, since sentiment is largely bearish. When the put/call ratio is 0.7 or lower, it may indicate a selling opportunity, because overwhelmingly more calls than puts are being purchased. From time to time, some financial newspapers include a graph of the put/call ratio.

BULLISH AND BEARISH
INVESTMENT NEWSLETTER EDITORS

The percentage of bullish and bearish editors of investment newsletters is one of the oldest and most original methods of depicting market sentiment. This indicator was invented by Abe Cohen of Investors Intelligence approximately 25 years ago, and it's had an excellent track record.

Each week a large number of the most popular investment newsletters are polled about their attitudes toward the stock market. Historically, when an overwhelming majority of editors have been bullish, say, more than 70 percent, the market has had relatively little further potential to rise. On the other hand, when the vast majority of editors have been bearish, an advancing market condition has followed. This is another of the contrary sentiment indicators which generate signals to act in the opposite direction of the general sentiment.

There are good reasons why this indicator has worked so well in the past. Investment newsletter writers are cognizant of the need to be in tune with the market; otherwise their subscription rates decline. Therefore, they frequently are trend followers of the market. When the market is in a strong uptrend, we're apt to see more investment newsletter editors as bullish. Contrarily, when the market is in a prolonged decline, more of them become cautious, since recommending bullish investments is not palatable for their readers. Consequently, when taken as a group, investment newsletter editors are usually very bullish at market tops and very bearish at market lows.

MUTUAL FUND CASH POSITION

The cash positions of mutual funds are normally high when stock fund managers are bearish. In other words, when a fund's manager is pessimistic about the future performance of the market, he or she will convert more of the fund's assets into cash or equivalents to avoid taking a loss when stock prices fall. As a result, high cash positions usually occur closer to market lows than to market highs. At market peaks, cash positions are frequently very low.

This is another gauge of the general mind-set of the market. When cash positions are low (at stock market highs), there is too little fuel to keep an advance moving. The advance then stalls. On the other hand, when cash positions are high (at market bottoms), much of the selling that resulted in the expanded cash position has already taken place. The high cash position also provides potential demand for stocks whenever the stock market reverses its downward trend.

Mutual fund cash positions are deemed to be high when they exceed 11 percent of total portfolio assets earmarked for equity holdings. Mutual fund cash positions are considered low when they are below 4 percent of such portfolio assets.

CONCLUSION

Technical analysis is a logical and comprehensive approach to understanding the stock market. It can be used by short-term traders as well as investors to better select the times of their purchases and sales.

Technical analysts use a variety of methods to identify, buy, and sell signals. The few highlights in this chapter provide only a "tasting menu" of the broad array of tools available to the technician.

3

BEAUTY AND THE BEAST

Finding Bargains in Basement Stocks

———————————— Peter J. DeAngelis, CFA

THE FAIRY TALE OF BEAUTY AND THE BEAST PROVIDES A GOOD analogy for the world of individual investing. The beauty on Wall Street is the "special situation" investment opportunity. The special situation is an investment that offers a unique combination of values, breakthroughs, and otherwise extraordinary potential. The opportunities dazzle the investor. But upon close inspection, the companies, like the fairy tale beauty, are immature. They are strung out, undercapitalized, thinly staffed, unprofitable, or characterized by a host of other difficulties. Yet from among this group will spring tomorrow's corporate titans offering superior technologies, services, and products.

The beast is the infamous "low-priced stock." Like the man-beast of the fairy tale, the investment is judged by its appearance (the low price). It is shunned and regarded with suspicion by the institutional and individual investor alike. However, many a low-priced stock conceals growth, assets, income, innovations, and otherwise laudable values well in excess of the low price assigned the stock by the market. Often, although not always, a special situation is a low-priced stock.

In other chapters, experts provide invaluable insight and advice on the investment process, including successful techniques and how to be your own security analyst and investment adviser. This chapter offers a practical road map to identify what I label "neglected bargains among basement stocks." The aim is to show how you can score impressive gains on a small capital outlay by observing a few cardinal rules. These rules are based on finding special situations and low-priced stocks that are true bargains.

THE SPECIAL SITUATION AND THE LOW-PRICED STOCK

Special situations and low-priced stocks have a number of characteristics in common:

- *An operating entity*—These aren't start-ups, development-stage companies, or concept businesses, but ongoing operations complete with revenues and assets. In other words, they have substance and staying power.
- *Operating in an uptick or turnaround industry*—There's no percentage, and rarely a profit, in fighting a downtrend.
- *Operating with profits or with evidence of near-term profitability.* They have a clear potential for rising future earning power.
- *A special fundamental attraction*—The word is *fundamental*. These aren't masquerading fads. Items that qualify as an attraction would be a patent, a special process, a technological edge, and an innovative or proprietary product line or special service.
- *Low price*—The stock should sell for less than $10 a share.
- *A positive (supporting or strong) technical price chart.*
- *Enough stock shares*—The shares should trade in sufficient volume to provide adequate marketability. This is an important factor for two basic reasons.

    First, thinly traded low-priced issues characteristically have wide spreads. The spread is the gap between the bid price (offer to buy) and asked price (offer to sell). A wide spread makes it difficult to buy and sell the stock profitably. For example, if a stock has a bid price of $2 and an asked price of $3 or even $2.50, the spread is too much. This is because an investor normally would buy on the asked side of the market and sell on the bid side

of the market. An investor who purchased the stock at the asked
price would have automatically paid 25 to 50 percent more than
the stock could be sold for. With so wide a margin, the "easy
money" or "cream" is gone, and the investor's opportunity for
gain is sharply reduced. In this example, an acceptable spread
would be 2 bid, 2⅛ asked—a ⅛ spread. The largest acceptable
spread in this instance would be ¼.

Second, the market in the special situation or low-priced stock
should be broad enough that when it is time to sell, it is relatively
easy to find a buyer at the market price.
• *Minimal institutional holdings*—A sudden change of heart or
calendar quarter–end window dressing could unexpectedly
pound the price of an early special situation or low-priced stock
into the ground. At best, the holder of this stock wants the institutional investors who are buying to purchase this stock. So don't
follow the institutions in. It rarely works.
• *Innovative and proven management skills.*
• *In certain cases be acquisition candidates*—This is desirable if
the capital cost of entering an industry, entering new geographic
markets, or augmenting existing size is so large that it is more
advantageous to acquire a company than to make the attempt
independently.

It is extremely unlikely for all these characteristics to describe
any one selection. But companies that meet a majority of these
criteria have outperformed the market in the past, and I believe
will continue to do so in the future.

ATTRACTION OF THE SPECIAL SITUATION AND LOW-PRICED STOCK

Expectations of quick riches are epidemic on Wall Street. There
are over 50 million stockholders in America, and at least a quarter
of them are long-shot players far more interested in "making a
killing" than collecting dividends combined with modest gains.
What individual investor, from the most experienced to the new-
comer, hasn't conjured up expectations of big payoffs on small
stakes? Quick riches are the stuff that dreams, the American
dream, are made of.

Sometimes those dreams come true. In addition to the much-
heralded past successes such as IBM, Xerox, Polaroid, Boeing, and

Eastman Kodak, many lesser-known successes of recent years have gained as sensationally. Several examples of these unsung heroes are cited later in this chapter. All of these stocks at one time were special situations or low-priced stocks, and they later generated capital gains of 2,000 percent or more!

Yet today low-priced stocks, like the individual investor for which this book is written, are for the large part neglected. Individuals are encouraged to invest in the seasoned "brand names." The whole field of special situations and low-priced stocks has been neglected by the professionals, allegedly because of perceived speculative risks, thin markets, and lack of information. The major stock exchange firms have studiously ignored and overlooked this category of investments. More often than not, a broker of a major firm will chide the individual investor's inquiry about one of these companies and counter by recommending a seasoned blue chip or the in-house recommendation.

Why? Because there isn't any percentage in it. In other words, there isn't the potential commission business to justify the analyst's or broker's time, to say nothing of creativity, to research and recommend one of these stocks. It is simply easier to sell a brand-name stock than shares in a smaller company.

To be sure, there is a place for blue chips and mutual funds, but not to the total exclusion of potential fortune-building stocks. At this juncture in the investment cycle, there has been an unmistakable preference for—or, more appropriately, flight to—safety and quality by risk-averse investors. They have incorrectly perceived sanctuary to be in the blue-chip and core stocks, even though history shows that size and past laurels of the giant corporations hardly make them safe harbors.

Investor caution has in large part caused the stock market's present realignment, producing a severe dichotomy. The undervaluation of secondary stocks is near, if not at, historic lows. The special situations and low-priced stocks have measurably lagged the market throughout the past five to six years. This is in stark contrast to the larger capitalization issues, which continue to be bid up to lofty levels.

Excessive valuations of the brand-name stocks has accomplished two things. One is the two-tiered market. This imbalance can trigger a number of events. The market's definition of what is acceptable may broaden to include selected groups of special situations and low-priced stocks for their appreciation potential. In this case, this group should play a major-league catch-up ball game. More likely, the risk/reward imbalance will favor the special-situation/low-price group to the extent it attracts a meaningful number of investors. These investors will seek superior returns in these stocks, which are substantially more attractively priced and less heralded, rather than in the prestigious and high-priced alternative, blue chips.

The lopsided market has also brought about a less pleasant condition. With each move higher, the unhealthy gap between the brand-name group and secondary tier increases, as does the risk. The risk in the gilt-edge arena should not be ignored. It would not require much of a trigger to correct the imbalance. It is not likely to be a soft landing, whereas the special situations and low-priced stocks, by virtue of the valuation deviation, would likely represent a safe harbor. Ironic!

Today, more than ever before, there is a broad, open field of compelling values awaiting harvest by the discriminating investor. Accordingly, most investors' portfolios should set aside some portion for special situations and low-priced stocks. The whole field is exciting, and fortunately, timely selections can pay off handsomely. Oh, yes—in time these bargain stocks may grow up to become premier equities.

PORTFOLIO STRATEGY

The character of the market for special situations and low-priced stocks is such that it is prudent to devote only a portion of an investment portfolio to this area. This is true for a number of reasons. For example, these stocks typically do not pay a dividend, and if they do, they provide only a very modest return on investment. The "float" (common shares outstanding and freely trading) on these stocks is likely to be limited compared to most of the New York Stock Exchange brand-name securities. Hence, trading volume may be light, and the investor's ability to buy and sell (liquidity) somewhat restricted. Also, these stocks, by their very nature, are aggressive investments. Therefore, depending upon the individual investor's financial circumstances and goals, 10 percent to a 20 percent maximum portion of a portfolio should be dedicated to special situations and low-priced stocks.

Owning these stocks adds zest to the entire investment experience and, with good fortune, dollars to the portfolio. But this program isn't just a one-time exercise that an investor can do and then forget. The special-situation and low-priced stocks that perform best in a given time will become a growing portion of the portfolio. As a result, the mix of investments will change. It is essential to review the portfolio periodically to return it to its original proportions.

The point of investment diversification is to mix investments that don't move in tandem. The basic objective is always to have a segment of the portfolio do well. In effect, diversification ensures that part of the portfolio has a winning strategy by including different types of investments.

STOCKBROKERS

The broker and the firm (in that order) you deal with concerning special situations and low-priced stocks is most important. Picking a broker is second only to selecting the stock itself. While the major investment firms may fill the bill with a broker willing to assist, the reasons just discussed make it highly unlikely that this broker's firm will support him or her.

My own preference is for an established, full-service regional stock exchange firm. Such a firm is more in tune with the needs of the individual investor ("retail" client), in contrast to the major firms, which cater to institutional customers. The regional organizations provide not only reliable quotes and executions and impressive solvency, but also extensive information and service useful in making timely decisions about securities, companies, and industries.

Compared to choosing a broker, selecting a firm is easy. Make your choice as carefully as you would pick a physician. The broker is essential to your financial health. Remember, the stock selection is yours, but the execution and the flow of market information are in the broker's hands. You are one step ahead by picking a reputable firm. You'll have no guarantee that the brokers there are up to high standards, but at least you are on the correct turf.

Meet the broker, get referrals, and if possible check out the broker's credentials and tenure with the firm. Never, never, purchase a stock on the strength of a cold phone call from a stranger. Academic? Basic? Hell, no! I've known captains of industry to invest not inconsequential sums of money in situations presented over the phone by perfect strangers.

THE MARKETS WHERE THE BARGAINS ARE TRADED

To trade any class of securities, it is essential to have a marketplace where issues are regularly bought and sold in an orderly and controlled environment. The ideal market is one in which the trading is active, the spread between bid and ask is narrow, the daily volume of shares traded is substantial, transactions are promptly reported, and records of stock price activity are published daily in financial media.

The best-known market is the New York Stock Exchange (NYSE). Next to it in size is the American Stock Exchange (AMEX). All domestic publicly traded securities not traded on these exchanges are labeled "unlisted" and are bought, sold, and quoted "over the counter" (OTC).

Although many people think the largest securities markets are the NYSE and AMEX, the OTC market is actually larger. It includes trading of most government securities, corporate bonds, preferred stock, and the common shares of about 14,000 banks, as well as many large insurance companies. In the common stock sector of the OTC market, about 20,000 issues are traded and quoted with some frequency. The majority of special-situation and low-priced stocks are traded over the counter. However, the NYSE and the AMEX have some noteworthy candidates.

The market for OTC companies is provided by "market makers." A market maker is a broker willing to bid on or to offer a stock for immediate purchase or sale. The bid and asked prices are set by the forces of supply and demand. The more interest there is in a stock, the more actively it is traded. The greater the trading activity, the more market makers. The more market makers there are, the more competitive the market and the narrower the spread.

As discussed earlier in this chapter, it is to the investor's advantage to have an active market with narrow spreads.

The bulk of the OTC shares are traded and quoted by the National Association of Securities Dealers Automated Quotations (NASDAQ). NASDAQ is an electronic system that automatically lists the volume and price of the last transaction for a given stock and provides information such as last sale, volume traded, current bid and asked prices, and market makers. Thus, the OTC market is not a place, but a network of transactions. NASDAQ-listed companies are divided into three groups, for which trading data are published daily in the *Wall Street Journal* and *New York Times*:

1. NASDAQ National Market.
2. NASDAQ National List.
3. NASDAQ Supplemental OTC List.

An important distinction to be made in the OTC marketplace is between those shares traded as just described versus the approximately 7,000 stocks tabulated in the "pink sheets." The pink sheets, which are published daily by NASDAQ, list each stock in alphabetical order. Opposite the listing is the name of the broker or brokers making a market in the stock.

These pink-sheet markets are characterized by abnormally wide spreads and are inhabited by the treacherous penny stocks. Most firms, whether with national exchanges or regional houses, will make markets in selected pink-sheet stocks. Avoid the exclusive pink-sheet, penny-stock brokerage firms, especially those with a short operating history and no seats on listed exchanges. These firms are the breeding ground for the infamous penny-stock frauds that have plagued the individual investor over the years.

SPOTTING SPECIAL SITUATIONS AND LOW-PRICED STOCKS

Special situation is a frequently used, misunderstood, overdefined, and abused term on Wall Street. It is usually quickly applied to the stock of any company that has been left at the gate in the present lopsided market and is often used with no consideration of the fundamentals that distinguish true special situations from the mob of cheap imitators. The true special-situation stocks are not high-risk speculations. True, they are smaller companies than the gilt-edged corporation of the blue-chip stock. However, smaller companies are just as likely, or more so, to be driven by earnings acceleration and compelling concepts built upon innovation and expansion.

There's no such thing as a free lunch. You're going to have to put in some work to spot these stocks. Select a retail broker as discussed, but don't expect the broker or analyst to recommend special situations or low-priced stocks. Be your own security analyst. Follow a few simple commonsense procedures, and it should work well.

The golden rule of investing is "Be informed." Swear off investing on tips, hearsay, gossip, hunches, fads, fashions, and emotions. Those who place their faith in such have fleeting success, if any, and usually move on to other misadventures. It's beneficial to be current on the financial markets in general. There's no better place to begin than the pages of the nation's financial publications such as the *Wall Street Journal, New York Times, Barron's, Forbes, Financial World*, and *OTC Review*. Also, while the brokerage firm may not recommend lower-tier stocks, information on them may be available in the broker's libraries, which typically subscribe to investment services such as Value Line and Standard & Poor's, as well as computer data-retrieval systems. Finally, as mentioned in Chapter 1, a simple phone call or letter to any reputable publicly owned company will secure the latest in financial reports, press releases, and the like.

In the search for the special situation and low-priced stock, move from the general to the specific. Look for a stock selling in the single digits and a company with some special allure. Simplistically, by scanning stocks trading on the NYSE, AMEX, and OTC, you can identify stocks selling for less than $10 per share. Compile a list. Then determine whether these low-priced stocks also qualify as special situations.

Stocks that are low-priced and also special situations fall into two prime categories. The first consists of stocks that stand out because the company's hard values exceed the stock's price in the market. The second category is more esoteric and includes stocks that are exceptional because the company is innovative, serves specialty markets, or is in a transition that looks favorable.

SUPERIOR VALUE RELATIVE TO PRICE

These are five ways to assess whether a company's value exceeds the price of its stock:

1. Asset values.
2. Intrinsic value.
3. Trading range stocks.
4. Revival/Lazarus (bankruptcy and reorganization) stocks.
5. Yield.

The stock should be superior in at least one of these categories.

Asset Values

To compare price with asset value, consider visible and not so visible assets. As Chapter 1 explained, some asset values are accurately reported, and others are understated on the balance sheet. You can benefit if you can spot some undervalued assets, but they must be tangible. For example, look for undervalued real estate holdings; even positions in publicly owned and traded shares of other corporations; unrealistic book value of "hard assets" or severely discounted stock market valuation of stated assets; stand-alone divisions whose potential independent values in the event of sale, merger, or public offering would greatly exceed the present value of the entire company in the stock market; plant or equipment replacement value well over the carrying amount on the balance sheet; cash-rich and otherwise liquid assets; and loss carryforwards.

These asset items appear in public documents such as the company's annual report and financial filings with the Securities and Exchange Commission. All these documents are on file and available either by request to the company or in your broker's library. Remember, you have to do some work! Simple research such as the perusal of the annual report and the footnotes to the financial statement, as discussed in Chapter 1, can reveal otherwise obscure asset values. The everyday stock guide and Standard & Poor's tearsheets that are available list book value. And don't forget the financial newspapers. For example, the April 10, 1989, edition of *Barron's* featured a full-length article on cash-rich companies, complete with statistics on market price, cash per share, P/E ratio, price/book value ratio, and more. Eleven of the companies had single-digit stocks! There are even low-cost subscription services among financial newsletters featuring the very thing you're looking for.

Test the asset values of companies on your list of low-priced shares publicly traded. If the value of a company on any one or combination of the assets mentioned exceeds the value that the market has placed on the whole company, then the stock is a strong candidate to be a special situation. (To determine the value of the company in the market, multiply the current price of the stock by the number of shares outstanding.) However, the company must be sound operationally. Don't invest in discounted assets on a sinking ship unless a liquidation is anticipated. Even then, that's another game, and your time is better spent elsewhere. You're in business if you've discovered a low-single-digit stock of a company whose business is firmly established and where the asset value per share substantially exceeds the market value.

This works best for stocks with a low price per share. While the relative values are identical, an observation of market action reveals that under normal trading conditions, a $5 stock with an $8 asset value is more likely to pay off than a $50 stock with an $80 asset value. Don't try to reason it out. Chalk it up to investor psychology.

Your goal is to invest successfully by recognizing stocks whose value is now discounted and therefore likely to eventually move higher. A stock priced in the low single digits is probably at its low. Since you are bottom fishing for a discounted value of an established company, your risk is largely that the stock will fail to gain, not that its price will decline.

Also, as a bonus, your investment stands some chance of being the target of a takeover. This is because those looking for a takeover candidate often judge companies by the same guidelines. And in this day of acquisitions, friendly and hostile, it's no secret that a company is usually acquired at a handsome premium over its prevailing stock market price.

Intrinsic Value

Every corporation has an intrinsic value—a value that reflects its essential nature. Don't confuse intrinsic value with stated net tangible worth (book value), even if that worth is adjusted to reflect today's value in the marketplace. Intrinsic value is tied to the company's existence. Assets aside, just what is an existing business in place worth? The answer depends upon the type of investor. To someone in the same industry, for example, it's worth more than to someone in another business. To an entrepreneur, the company has a worth as an operating base upon which to build.

Determining intrinsic value is not a precise science. But by using some commonsense guidelines, you can determine whether a company is so undervalued that it is trading below its intrinsic value. For example, a medium-sized service company with approximately $18 million of revenue and a modest profit has no "hard book" worthy of mention. But it holds a solid market share in its geographic area and has managed to grow revenues at 8 percent to 10 percent yearly. By traditional analytical standards, its price/earnings ratio is not low, yet the company is capitalized at a modest $4 million in the stock market. That's only 20 percent of revenues! At this writing, this is a true story. All things equal, do you think this company is trading a wee bit below its intrinsic value? You betcha!

There is a kicker, too. Once again, the viability of such a company as an acquisition candidate is high, particularly to someone in the same industry. The capital cost of entry into an industry, entry into new geographic markets, or significant growth makes it advantageous and less risky to "buy in" via an out-and-out takeover or joint venture.

If values seem totally out of proportion to stock price, study the financial statements closely, looking for hidden weaknesses. Be certain the business is viable and not a "buggy whip" enterprise. Search the footnotes, especially those dealing with legal obligations and liabilities. Public companies are required by law to fully disclose material facts. They are audited by accounting firms, and the board of directors must sign off on all such matters. With the possible exception of outright fraud, it's all there for your information. If, after investigation, you find no flies in the ointment, you may well have identified a special situation.

Trading Range Stocks

Trading range stocks are shares of companies whose profit levels seldom move dramatically but swing in cycles over several years. These stocks generally enjoy active daily markets with high volume. They are well worth considering because of their stable earnings coupled with trading ranges that afford opportunities to buy and sell within their established ranges.

Look for Low Prices: To research such a beast, begin by scanning transactions of low-single-digit stocks (those selling at $5 a share or less). Lower priced stocks attract a wider following among traders, irrespective of the stocks' fundamental value. Traders like them because they trade quickly in fractions of a point, which represent a significant percentage move and, thus, the opportunity for a large percentage gain. For example, if a $4 stock moves $.50 (½ point) a share, this represents a 12½ percent move. Thus, in the section of *Barron's* devoted to the week's largest percentage gainers (stocks), you will find many low-priced issues.

When surveying the OTC market for trading range stocks, it's best to remain with the National Market System, where there is prompt and relatively accurate reporting of price and volume. Focus on the most actively traded issues, and ferret out a dozen or so in the low-priced range that finished on an uptick. This simple exercise identifies the low-priced stocks that are attracting the most players. Activity (daily volume) and sponsorship (uptick prices) are valuable guidelines to a performing low-priced stock.

Turn your attention to the historic price swings (readily available in the S&P tearsheets or in long-term stock price charts at the brokerage house). Emphasize the bottom level. If the stock is near its historic low or some distance from the upper price range achieved in past cycles, then proceed to the next step. (If the shares are trading at $5 or less, the odds are that you have already screened out the trading range stocks near the top of their price cycle.)

Examine the Fundamentals: I'm a fundamentalist at heart—never have or ever will buy on faith or chart patterns alone—so it'll come as no surprise that I advise you to next take a sweep at the fundamentals. Employ some of the fundamental analysis tools covered in Chapter 1. However, look for negatives rather than positives. If you fail to find any, you may have scored a low-priced stock trading opportunity.

Next, by reviewing historic prices and fundamental patterns, discern the current phase of the trading range shares under consideration. Active trading range stocks generally go through four phases:

1. *Accumulation*—When shares are scraping bottom following liquidation.
2. *Markup*—When perceptive buyers already have been buying and have fueled the market for the stock into an up cycle.
3. *Distribution*—When the market nears or achieves a cyclical crest and profit taking has begun.
4. *Liquidation*—When the most adroit traders have exited and sellers dominate the market, causing downward momentum to the low point in the stock's price cycle.

Consider purchasing only if the stock's price is at or near its historic bottom and if it is in the accumulation or early markup phase.

Look for Potential "Bounces" at Year-End: There is a popular year-end investment calendar sport that qualifies as a trading range stock event. It is the "January effect" or "the dead-cat bounce." Both terms refer to the tendency of battered stocks to rise once tax selling is completed. The theory is that at year-end investors, individual and institutional alike, will shed stocks they have lost money on so that they can apply those losses to reduce their tax obligations on stock market profits. The effect of this selling is exacerbated by the year-end window dressing of professional portfolio managers. This is the time when they clean house of losers before they issue their annual reports, which make the portfolio public knowledge. The increased supply of stocks that results from all that selling depresses prices, which then bounce back somewhat when things return to normal in January.

To find "bounce" candidates, hunt among the major stock price losers of the year. Lists of the top gainers and losers are constantly being published throughout the year, especially in December. For example, each December most of the major financial publications publish a roster of extremely depressed stocks, complete with helpful statistics. In 1988 this roster listed over 40. The majority were low-priced stocks selling at single-digit prices.

Like all programs of this nature, this technique is not 100 percent reliable. You must undertake further research before making a commitment. Of prime importance is to exclude firms with major losses, weak balance sheets, poor market liquidity, and long-term debt/equity ratios of 50 percent or more.

Revival/Lazarus Stocks

The Bible identifies Lazarus, the brother of Mary and Martha, as someone who was raised from the dead. Thus, Lazarus stocks or revival stocks refer to the issues of companies devastated by disaster, insolvency, or bankruptcy. A number of these will miraculously come back to life—usually by the route of a Chapter 11 (voluntary) reorganization but occasionally merely by the injection of new capital or a timely merger.

Investors have made fortunes in defaulted and reorganized businesses. The fortunes made on defaulted railway securities from 1933 forward are legends in our time. For example, shares in the New York, New Haven, and Hartford; the St. Louis, San Francisco; the Chicago, Rock Island, and Pacific; the Chicago, Milwaukee, and St. Paul; and the Boston and Maine all sold at very low prices at one time, yet all scored comebacks and made spectacular gains. Chicago, Milwaukee, and St. Paul became Chicago Milwaukee Corporation. Under Chapter 11 the company became cash-rich from the proceeds of its divestitures and the prudent management of the remaining operations. The common shares rose from a low of 4 to a 1984 peak of 176.

Bankruptcy Equities: Declaring bankruptcy under Chapter 11 of the Federal Bankruptcy Code is different from Chapter 7 bankruptcy. Chapter 7 is an involuntary action, usually resulting in liquidation and proportionate distribution of the firm's assets to its creditors. Companies voluntarily enter Chapter 11 with the goal of returning to normal operations following consolidation and lump-sum settlement of the combined claims of creditors, lawsuits, and other obligations.

History is packed full of modern-day examples of revival through Chapter 11. An excellent case is Toys "R" Us. This toy store chain was spun off from the bankruptcy of Interstate Stores back in 1978. Out of a classic failure and reorganization under Chapter 11 came the development of a sensational retailing success. Today there isn't a parent or a child in the country who doesn't know of these stores. The company is the leading discount toy supermarket. For 1989 the company reported annual sales of $4.8 billion and a net income of $321 million. Trading on the NYSE (symbol TOY), the stock has performed spectacularly. Adjusting for a series of 3-for-2 stock splits and dividends in 1986, 1989, and 1990, Toys "R" Us recovered from being a penny stock selling at $0.29 a share and reached a high of $35 per share in 1990. A 12,000 percent gain from low to high—all this from the ashes of insolvency!

A current example still unfolding is Manville Corp., a multibillion-revenue diversified mining and forest products company, which took a dive into bankruptcy in 1982. Manville was the subject of massive asbestos-related lawsuits. The company sought protection under Chapter 11 from an estimated minimum aggregate liability of $1.9 billion. At the time of the bankruptcy, the stock had fallen to a low of $4 from a high more than 10 times that price. On November 28, 1988, Manville emerged from Chapter 11 following the implementation of a restructuring plan that included formation of a trust to pay personal injury claims. The company has survived to generate over $2 billion in revenues, and its stock (symbol MVL) trades actively on the NYSE. Manville Corp. resumed trading in November 1988 at about $6.25 a share, and it moved within a year to approximately $10.50 (up nearly 70 percent). At that time bottom fishers hauled in a respectable profit from low to high.

At this writing, the stock is down to 4¾. It is perceived differently by outspoken investment professionals. Some consider it a sound long-term value, while others have serious reservations concerning the adequacy of the funds set aside for settlement of its lawsuits. The jury is still out, and only time will tell whether Manville is again a Lazarus stock opportunity.

Bankruptcy Debt: While this chapter is exclusively concerned with common stocks, it would be derelict not to mention the senior debt of bankruptcy filings. The holders of senior securities dictate the reorganization terms. In the case of Manville, for example, its bankrupt bonds proved to be the most rewarding, as was the case with the bankruptcies of Allegheny, Texaco, LTV, and Wickes. A recent university study confirms this. The study examined 17 major companies that underwent bankruptcy during 1982 and 1988. Purchasing their debt one month after bankruptcy filings and holding it for one year produced an average return of 30 percent. The source of information on Chapter 11 debt issues is the same as the source for common stocks—the traditional financial reports aided by documents required to be filed with stockholders concerning the bankruptcy proceedings. All are available from the public sources identified in Chapter 1.

A Caveat: Hunting for "good" bad companies is a legitimate program for finding special situations and low-priced stocks. Some bankruptcy equities will perform brilliantly. However, not all companies emerge from bankruptcy, and not all that do reward shareholders. Many companies do not survive but are liquidated for pennies on the dollar to creditors, and stockholders may be wiped out. Don't expect to perform in the market by blindly purchasing issues of bankrupt companies. Once again, you must research your choice and pick carefully among the bones. In these cases, the better risks are larger companies with a lot of assets still in hand. In addition to the aforementioned source materials, there are services dedicated to this area.

Revival Without Bankruptcy: The revival category of special situations and low-priced stocks is also populated by securities of troubled companies that only skirt bankruptcy and later on reward patient shareholders. Companies often obtain laudable results from substantial injections of capital combined with motivated management that upgrades operations while implementing operating efficiencies. Modern-day examples are Chrysler and Lockheed Corp. Chrysler rose from a distressed price of $1.50 a share in 1982 to a subsequent high of $48.00 in 1987. The recovery of Lockheed's stock price was nothing short of miraculous. It gained from its $7.00 low in 1980 to a 1985 high of $68.00 and traded in the 60s for the next two years.

Hindsight is always 20/20. Nevertheless, even in their worst moments, it was clear that both Chrysler and Lockheed were not likely to be permitted to languish and die. Survival of some sort was definitely in the cards. Yet the stock prices foretold the worst possible scenarios. Venturesome bottom fishers taking positions in these two early mainstays of American industry were amply rewarded.

Note, however, that the bottom fisher must stay alert and informed. Why? Because time and conditions change. Once revived, a Lazarus stock will perform. But that isn't any guarantee of its future prospects—only its near-term outlook. Most of all, the investor must be willing and agile in taking profits at the first sign of weakening fundamentals (Chapter 1) and/or technical position (Chapter 2). For example, while the early investor had major winnings from an investment in Chrysler (the low was 1⅝), there were pitfalls in holding too long. The high in 1989 for Chrysler stock was 29⅝, and the high in 1990 was 27⅛. But at this writing the stock has plunged to a low of 12¾.

Nevertheless, comebacks are a fertile field for harvesting special situations and low-priced stocks. The financial headlines are replete with news of companies in financial difficulty. When interest rates rise again or the economy slows significantly, troubled securities could be in abundance—especially in companies that have issued high-yield "junk" (nonrated) bonds.

Target those where the damage to the share prices is already fully evident. Then move forward by researching the data using the sources enumerated in this chapter and throughout the book. The raw data used to identify the candidate issue may not reveal the complete picture of the company's fortunes—or misfortunes. Look for bailout proposals and corporate partnering that would provide the necessary cash transfusion.

Yield

The subject of yield should be self-explanatory. However, for reasons unknown, investors typically overlook yield opportunities among special situations and low-priced stocks. There are double-digit cash yields available among stocks with single-digit prices.

Screening for yields on these stocks is comparatively easy. Subscription services available directly or through your broker compile yield data. Of course, the broker may have research available, and his or her firm may actually subscribe to the very services you require to complete a shopping list.

Qualifying yield choices for special situations and low-priced stocks involves three elements. First and most important is to determine the safety of the dividend payout. The payout is the ratio of cash dividends to actual and forecast earnings. For example, a $.75 dividend on earnings of $1.50 would equal a 50 percent payout, and a $1.00 dividend would represent a 66 percent payout. As a general rule, do not purchase a yield issue of a special-situation or low-priced stock if the payout exceeds 65–70 percent. Always look to the current operations and earnings trend to determine the outlook for continued dividend flow.

The second element in qualifying yield choices is to pick the yield stock at the top of the yield curve (i.e., when yields are highest). Getting a feel for the interest rate outlook is not difficult. The financial community abounds with experts, as does the Federal Reserve.

Third, if possible, choose a company with some prospect of improvement in long-term earnings, no matter how modest. If there is a "kicker" in terms of some special feature that could transform the business later on into a more dramatic operation, all the better.

The purpose is obviously to pick, at the top of the interest rate cycle, a high, safe yield with the prospect of modest future enhancement. If interest rates decline, the stock should respond favorably by increasing in price as it adjusts to the market conditions. Should the market discover the stock, then too a favorable adjustment is likely. Given no change in prevailing interest rates, the modest increase in the cash payout is likely to provide some appreciation while the investor is compensated with a good income flow.

Growth stock analysts will tell you that a growing company's earnings are best applied to internal investment to fund the company's future. Therefore, they will argue that a growth company will not pay much in the way of cash dividends. And this is correct—for a growth company. While special situations and low-priced stocks often develop into emerging growth companies, which in turn may become established growth companies, they should not be confused at this stage of their respective development. The yield stock you are seeking here is a special-situation or low-priced stock with a safe, high cash return. For example, if the prevailing near-to-intermediate yield is in the range of 7.5 percent, then a return of 9–10 percent in a low-price issue meeting the aforementioned criteria would qualify.

DISTINCTIVE ADVANTAGE IN THE MARKETPLACE

The second prime category of stocks that are low-priced and special situations consists of stocks that stand out because there is something distinctive about the company. This distinctiveness may be apparent in four ways:

1. Leading edge/innovation.
2. Niche market.
3. Metamorphosis.
4. Comparative market measurements.

Leading Edge/Innovation

The expression "You'll know it when you see it" is somewhat apt with regard to identifying leading-edge or innovative companies. A small to modest-sized company with a product innovation, new technology, service—something heretofore not on the scene but now making its debut—is the trademark of the special-situation, low-priced stock in this category. Interestingly, many of the major inventions and breakthroughs we enjoy today have their origin in independent or smallish firms. Tremendously successful companies and dramatic stock performance in this decade exist among stocks that many in the financial community have never heard of. Yet the gains have been in multiples of 1,000 percent.

The pitfalls are the false starts, scams, and otherwise doomed hopefuls. To avoid such traps, fall back on fundamentals—revenues, assets, profits, balance sheet, and management. Applying these basic yardsticks will eliminate the puff and leave the field populated by companies with bona fide operations and the necessary financials and organization to succeed. This is not to say that an operating company meeting the test on these criteria cannot be a fraud. It's just less likely to be so if there is already a sound business foundation.

A late-1989 story comes to mind of a low-priced stock of a firm with $20 million in revenue and very modest profits. This company claimed to have a coating product that would prevent almost any material from burning. Videotapes depicting product testing were distributed widely. From its $3 price threshold, the stock roared up over sixfold in eight weeks' time. Then the company came under investigation, and the stock pulled back considerably to near 10 from the high of almost 20. The many who rushed in before even reading the financial statements, believing there was no time to confirm the product or the stock's value, made the most basic errors—bought late and high, and sold low. The day after Thanksgiving, November 24, 1989, the company was served a grand jury subpoena. Trading was suspended. When trading resumed, the remaining shareholders had a post-Thanksgiving Wall Street turkey. The stock collapsed another 4½ points from the already depressed level! At this writing, the remaining stockholders are "sucking wind." The moral of the story is that you must always push aside the hype to clearly identify a special-situation or low-priced stock, and that there is always time for sound research.

Determining which company is a legitimate hopeful and which ones aren't requires a bit of work. A leading-edge technology that has just been developed may be verified by customers, competitors, or independent studies. This verification should be undertaken against a backdrop of the typical financial data sources. Remember, the key ingredient is to select a low-priced stock whose price is already supported in part (if not whole) by the present levels of operations. At all times, a low or negative definable risk coupled with large potential reward is a desirable feature in evaluating the support for the issue's price.

A vital characteristic of the special situation and low-priced stock is that there is a clearly defined underlying value supporting the stock price. This floor should be close to the current market price. Thus, the balance of risk and expected return is most favorable. On the upside, such a floor indicates considerable potential for appreciation. On the downside, the risk is essentially a failure to gain. The combination of value and price provides a "heads I win, tails I don't lose" situation. This is what imparts the "special" to the term *special situation* and separates it from the speculative element normally identified with single-digit stocks.

Niche Market

A group I always favor among smaller OTC issues is companies serving niche markets. Industries and industry leaders emerge and evolve in various manners. Many progress from an orderly development of a product or service; others have their origin in making a technological advance or providing for some special need. Often these companies are relatively unknown and, in the process of financing their research and development as well as operations, have become public companies.

Stages of Development: These companies normally spring from seedlings among the previously described pink-sheet companies. Special-situation and low-priced stocks in these companies generally go through six stages:

1. *Entrepreneurial*—This is the formative stage, where the innovator(s) conceive and develop the initial business plan. This is the company's birth. There is little more than the vision of its founder(s) to drive it. The business concept is vague, and the company is little more than a research and development operation. It is typically labeled a "development-stage company."
2. *Venture Capital*—This is when the business has evolved to a "start-up company." Its product is usually a prototype. Capital infusions come from an aggressive, high-risk venture capitalist. These are the high rollers playing the odds of making one major score from a host of long shots.
3. *Public Funding*—This is when the company may raise funds by an initial public offering (IPO) of stock or, for an existing public company, the sale of additional shares to the public (secondary offerings). Many of these offerings are marred by excessive capitalization (too many common shares authorized and outstanding). Offered at low prices or even at fractions of a dollar (penny stocks), these offerings lure investors in low-priced stock. The low price of the stock is relative to the number of shares outstanding. To the uninitiated investor who doesn't take the time to study the prospectus, the low price can give the illusion of a bargain, when in fact it has no relationship whatsoever to fundamental values.
4. *Early Market Development*—This is the stage when the niche company has made it to operational status and is selling in its

very special marketplace. The true special-situation company should have already turned its first modest profit and achieved initial acceptance in the industry. Early, speculative stock price excesses have succumbed to reality, and the stock price should be in the range of an attractive special-situation, low-priced stock.

5. *Growth*—This stage represents the exploitation of the niche market. The company penetrates the market and establishes leadership. Its revenue and earnings growth accelerate. The advance in the stock's price is most pronounced at this stage.

6. *Maturity*—This is when the niche market is nearly or fully developed. Imitation may be the most sincere form of flattery, but it also means keen competition with the ancillary pressures on pricing, marketing, and operating and manufacturing costs. Growth slows, profit margins narrow, and income is harder to come by. The stock stabilizes or declines.

Clearly, the fishing hole for a special-situation, low-priced stock in a niche market is stage 4, early market development. At this stage, the niche has been established, business is profitably under way, market development and penetration have just begun, and severe competition has yet to develop. Best of all, success has not been prominent enough to attract the investment community at large. The next stage of growth will do that and in the process should reward those who made an early investment.

Conversely, it is prudent to consider cashing out at or near the final maturity stage. Unless there is a compelling reason, sale of all or part of the stock at that point is advisable.

Case Study: Dranetz Technologies: While the logic behind this chapter is that there are always ample fortune-building special situations and low-priced stocks going wanting, pontifications on the subject can be ponderous—or, put another way, talk is cheap. Therefore, I offer the following case history of a present-day spectacular success—Dranetz Technologies, Inc.—as documentation. Like the legends of yesteryear such as IBM, Polaroid, and Xerox, this lesser-known company achieved amazing success in recent years.

Dranetz, based in northern New Jersey, was founded on a financial shoestring in 1960 by two entrepreneur/innovators, Abe Dranetz and Irv Backinoff. Its products are precision electronic instrumentation equipment for computer service organizations, electrical power companies, and producers of communication equipment. The company serves a need that its founders perceived early and met.

Dranetz followed the path just outlined. It began with an initial investment of the founders and some venturesome investors. It became a modest operating company and completed an initial public offering in the late 1960s. True to form, the stock declined from the public offering price and languished for several years into the mid- to late 1970s. By then the company had developed its product and defined its niche market. Its products became the industry's standards of excellence, and the company rose from an obscure, small, nominally profitable business of less than $2 million in revenues to a peak of almost $30 million with net earnings of $4 million.

The company's operating progress was matched by its incredible financial strength. The debt-free company built not only earnings but a cash and equivalent position equal to over a third of revenues ($10 million)! Trading over-the-counter, this stock first came to my attention as a Dowbeaters® choice in May 1978, when it traded at 5¾. At that time, the stock had several of the outstanding characteristics of an attractive special-situation and low-priced stock. With over $1 in cash per share of stock, it was already debt-free and posting impressive earnings growth. Its product was the technological leader and had moved to the forefront of a developing (niche) industry. Dranetz Technologies' stock was a clear choice.

Adjusted for subsequent stock dividends and splits, the price rose from the equivalent of $.50 a share to a 1983 high of more than $18—a 3,600 percent advance. At that time, its stock was held in prestigious institutional investment portfolios such as mutual funds and the like. To put this into perspective, a $1,000 investment in 1978 would have appreciated to a maximum of $36,000 in only five years. Imagine what a $10,000 investment did. It appreciated to $360,000—an achievement that would be the envy of a brand-name company many times its size.

If an investor had not been so nimble as to sell around the 1983 top, the years that followed provided enough opportunity to cash out at a gain of more than 2,500 percent. With approximately five million shares outstanding, the stock traded mostly in the double digits right up to the time of the company's August 1988 cash sale to the Hawker Siddeley Group PLC at $10.50 per share. So, if an earlier investor never made the decision to sell, it was made for the investor at a price 2,100 percent higher than in 1978.

Metamorphosis

The special situation and low-priced stock classified as a metamorphosis is different from a corporate turnaround or a Lazarus stock. A metamorphosis is a change of physical form, structure, or substance. When a corporation transforms its business, there are clear signals and often open communication with its shareholders concerning the alteration. With regard to a special situation and low-priced stock, the metamorphosis is preceded by an uninspired business or a declining industry. Ideally, the company has lost most of its following in the financial community, the stock has declined to single digits and is trading below hard book value per share, and the remaining shareholder base is largely complacent.

Left to its own devices, such a company will drift for an indeterminate time until it either falls on its sword or is picked off in an acquisition. Ordinarily, given the absence of any evidence to the contrary, it is best to pass by such a company. The only prudent time to invest is when (1) the stock trades at an obvious value relative to assets, yield, earnings, revenue per share, breakup value, and other measures, and (2) the stage has been set for change. The latter condition is critical.

Signs of Change: The precursor of change is telegraphed by any number of events. Most common are a wholesale change in top management, a major change in stock ownership, concentration of stock holdings, private placements or injections of capital by prestigious investors and investment bankers, sale of mainstay divisions, and an active program of investor/stockholder communications. In other words, there will be ample evidence of an "out with the old and in with the new" syndrome. These and other events will build the balance sheet during this time.

It is necessary to enter the metamorphosis early. Once the players have established their respective positions in the company ownership and have made the first few early moves, the stock price should begin to positively reflect the change. The easiest and the safest (lowest-risk) gain is always that first move off dead center. It is the cushion and fuel for an individual investor's staying power.

Case Study: Union Corp.: A modern-day example of a metamorphosis special-situation and low-priced stock is Union Corp. Throughout 1984 and most of 1985, Union Corp.'s six million common shares (symbol UCO) traded on the New York Stock Exchange mostly between $4 and $5 a share. The company's tangible book value in 1984 was $4.78 a share, and sales were $139 million. The company's financial condition was sound, with a 2.9 ratio of current assets to current liabilities. Current assets totaled $81.5 million, of which $23.2 million was in cash. For income tax purposes, the company had an available loss carryforward of approximately $10 million to apply against future profits.

My service, Dowbeaters®, picked up on the stock in April 1984. Although Union Corp.'s business was deadly dull and largely stale, it was a valuable dinosaur. As a cyclical conglomerate, it offered additional attractions to the already mentioned conspicuous ones. The company's major parts (including equipment manufacturing, industrial components, resource recovery, and electronic components) were worth more than the whole. Also, hidden among this mishmash and accounting for 6 percent of revenues was a financial services division engaged in credit collection services for national and local companies.

In 1986 and 1987 came the classic signal. Ownership and, subsequently, management of the company changed dramatically with the private placement of a large block of stock and accompanying options to a prestigious New York investment banker. The asset redeployment that began with this event was completed in May 1989 with a $69 million sale of the manufacturing operations. The cash raised from that final sale, together with proceeds from similar moves earlier, provided funds for developing the financial services group. That group generated 41 percent of the fiscal 1989 revenues of $131 million and over 60 percent of the $7.2 million in pretax profits.

With the metamorphosis completed, the stock moved to a high of 26⅝, and it trades, at this writing, at 24¼. This represents a gain of well over 100 percent annually since 1985. Here then is a clear example of an unknown, low-priced NYSE stock that for a period of time went begging despite the blatant values present and change under way. A diligent reading of the financial media such as the *Wall Street Journal*, annual reports, and shareholder releases would have telegraphed this pearl to any hunter of special situations and low-priced stocks.

Comparative Market Measurements
The traditional analytical methodology used to identify worth relative to established values in the marketplace can also pinpoint special situations. As described in Chapter 1, the ratio of stock price to net earnings per share, sales per share, return on capital, balance sheet, technical charts, market capitalization versus assets/gross revenues, and book value per share are all standard yardsticks by which to compare the relative worth of stocks.

These measurements are common fare among investors. Compare one company against the norm in the stock market and against industry averages. If the numbers vary significantly in favor of the special-situation, low-priced stock, chances are you have fought the major portion of the battle to identify a sleeper.

Note that the characteristics of various special situations and low-priced stocks frequently overlap. This is not only OK but desirable. It is best to have as many of the criteria as possible in play at any given time.

4

ALL DEBTS, PUBLIC AND PRIVATE

Selecting and Managing Debt Issues

Van W. Knox III

For most of us, the concept of debt has from earliest childhood been overlaid with extremely negative connotations. We hear talk of the national debt more as a national disgrace than as a legitimate means of financing economic growth. From Shakespeare's *Hamlet* ("Neither a borrower nor a lender be; / For loan oft loses both itself and friend") to Henrik Ibsen's *A Doll's House* ("There can be no freedom or beauty about a home life that depends on borrowing and debt") to the words of John Ruskin ("Borrowers are nearly always ill-spenders, and it is with lent money that all evil is mainly done, and all unjust war protracted"), our literary and cultural heritage is full of admonitions to avoid debt like the plague.

The notions of scandalous bankruptcy, personal ruin, and even debtors' prison are held out as dire warnings to those who succumb to the temptation to borrow. The possibility of default and complete loss of investment are counter-inducements to the greed of those whose investments in junk bonds have been so much in the news in the past year or so. Borrowing money from banks is

frequently an embarrassing and frustrating process, carrying
with it the presumption that we somehow shouldn't have to be
borrowing in the first place, and being turned down for a loan
inevitably carries with it the implied stigma that we are not good
enough for the lender.

In actual fact, however, *prudent* debt is an absolutely essential
part of the financial foundations of capitalism and underlies America's rise to economic preeminence among nations in the modern
world. The evolution of virtually all industrial progress—from the
first stage of the invention or development of an innovative concept
to the final stage of widespread customer acceptance and use—
almost inevitably relies at least partially upon the ready availability of financial resources in the form of seed equity *and* borrow-
ings to finance product development, the generation of manufacturing capacity, and the underwriting of initial expenses for
marketing and distribution.

Debt financing is no less relevant and important in the case of
existing, established businesses. The availability of credit to finance growth in inventories, to expand or improve production
facilities, or to increase efficiency via computerization of accounting and control procedures has enabled American industry to
react swiftly and aggressively to changes in the competitive marketplace, and to maintain leadership once achieved.

Why, then, does debt have such a bad name, from the point of
view of the borrower *and* the lender? The answer, clearly, is one of
degree. *Some* debt is usually necessary and desirable, while *excessive* debt can drive an otherwise viable company (or individual, for
that matter) completely out of business. From the lender's perspective, the appropriate level of lending (or investing, as we shall see)
is that which produces the optimum blend of risk and return
consistent with the lender's outlook for interest rates, economic
growth, and the particular company, project, or product being
supported by the borrowed capital.

This chapter considers the primary form of investable debt
instruments: bonds. It describes the way they work, the important
characteristics of different kinds of bonds, and the six key variables you need to evaluate when considering bonds as components
in your portfolio.

WHAT ARE BONDS?

A bond is simply a promissory note, or an IOU, sold by the borrowing entity in order to raise cash. It states the amount being borrowed (face value or principal), the length of time before repayment (maturity), the interest to be paid (coupon), the underlying collateral, if any, and any call features, explained later in this chapter.

It may be sold at par (100 cents on each dollar of the face value) or at a price either higher or lower than par. The price of a bond will, in fact, fluctuate to some extent throughout its life, in reaction to changes in the then-prevailing interest rates. However, the issuer is always expected to redeem the bond at par upon maturity.

A bond may be bought when originally issued. It may also be purchased at any point throughout its life in the so-called "secondary market," which is maintained by brokers and bond dealers. Many of the bonds of the largest corporations are listed for trading on the major exchanges.

Unlike common stock, which represents ownership of the entire underlying corporation (equity), a bond is an instrument of debt. The bond represents only an obligation to repay the face amount of the bond, plus any interest due for the time the bond is outstanding. If the issuing organization goes out of business and its assets are liquidated, the bondholder generally has priority over the stockholder in receiving payment. Some companies issue several classes of bonds, each of which has a designated priority of claims against assets in the event of default. U.S. government debt, backed by the full faith and credit of the U.S. government, is considered to be free of any risk of default.

TYPES OF BONDS

Debt instruments may be issued by the federal government, corporations, and state and local governments. This chapter considers those issued by the U.S. government, commonly called "Treasuries," and those issued by corporations, or "corporates." State and local authorities may issue tax-free municipal bonds, which are discussed in the next chapter. *All* these instruments share many of the investment considerations discussed here.

TREASURIES

The U.S. government operates by taxing its citizens and corporations, then redistributing this money through the various spending programs created by federal legislation (such as defense, Social Security, and Medicare). To the extent that the government operates under a deficit (that is, spends more than it takes in), it must raise additional funds to operate the government—and refinance its existing debt—by selling debt instruments. These promissory notes are issued by the Treasury Department and are bought by corporations, financial institutions, and individuals alike.

There are three main types of Treasuries: *bills* (or T-bills, as they are usually called), which have maturities of one year or less and are most commonly issued with maturities of three months or six months; *notes*, which have maturities of two to ten years; and *bonds*, which have maturities greater than ten years.

Apart from the maturities, the only difference in these instruments is that T-bills are bought and sold on a discount basis, rather than actually paying interest. That is, a $10,000 T-bill with a stated yield of 6.5 percent and a maturity of one year will actually be issued at a price of $9,350 and redeemed one year later for the full face value of $10,000. Note in this case that the actual yield is *not* 6.5 percent, but is just over 6.95 percent (interest of $650 on an investment costing $9,350).

Treasuries with longer maturities (notes and bonds) pay interest semiannually. Their purchase and sale prices are quoted as a percentage of par value, using the somewhat arcane practice of giving the price in increments of $\frac{1}{32}$ of a percentage point. To complicate this still further, these quotations are written as though in decimal form. For example, a written quotation of 99.15 means "99 and $\frac{15}{32}$ percent of par," or $99,468.75 for a $100,000 bond.

T-bills are issued in minimum denominations of $10,000 and increments thereafter of $5,000. Treasury notes and bonds are issued in minimum denominations of $1,000.

All Treasuries are issued in registered (also called "book entry") form, which means that no actual certificates are issued to the purchaser. Rather, the Treasury Department keeps a record of the name and address of the owner of the bond. It sends interest payments directly to the owner. In the same way, repayment of principal is mailed directly to the owner of record at maturity.

Treasuries are normally available in all maturities from one week to thirty years in the secondary market maintained by U.S. securities dealers.

The easiest way to purchase or sell any Treasury instrument is through a securities broker, who will normally charge only a nominal fee for this service. Investors may also purchase Treasuries directly from a Federal Reserve bank or branch (at no additional fee), by filling out the necessary paperwork. T-bills are sold by the government each week; Treasury notes and bonds may be purchased at quarterly auctions in February, May, August, and November. The Federal Reserve will not buy back its own securities, so investors may sell existing Treasuries before maturity only in the secondary market.

The primary advantage of Treasuries over other forms of debt lies in the absence of any credit risk. That is, Treasuries are considered to be risk-free investments in terms of the timeliness of interest payments and the certainty of repayment of principal upon maturity. Thus, for investors concerned about the safety of their principal, Treasuries provide complete liquidity and total peace of mind. A further advantage, particularly to investors in states and localities that tax income at high rates, is that interest earned on all Treasuries is exempt from state and local taxation.

The primary disadvantage of Treasuries is that, because they lack any risk of default, the yield needed to attract buyers is lower. Therefore Treasuries may pay a lower yield than that available on other bonds, which may have *very little* credit risk.

CORPORATES

Most corporations from time to time require infusions of additional money beyond that generated in the normal course of business. For example, corporations need extra cash to expand their existing activities, to enter new markets, or to acquire other businesses or business assets. Normally they raise this cash in one of two ways: by issuing and selling new shares of stock (equity), or by borrowing the money (debt). Businesses borrow either by tapping into lines of credit from banks or other financial institutions, or through a bond offering.

While some bond offerings may be purchased in their entirety by a single institution or syndicate of institutions, an enormous amount of debt in the form of corporate bonds is available to the individual investor. These bonds become available either as a result of the initial offering of the bond by the sponsoring underwriter, or through a secondary market maintained by both the New York and American stock exchanges, as well as a huge unlisted (over-the-counter, or OTC) market in which your broker will help arrange a purchase or sale of corporate bonds.

Prices of corporates are normally quoted as percentages of par. For example, 99.375 means $993.75 for a $1,000 bond. The minimum denomination of most corporates is $1,000. As a practical matter, however, most corporates trade in lots of 10 bonds ($10,000).

The major difference between corporates and Treasuries is risk. While all Treasuries are considered risk-free, corporates entail *some* risk of default. At one extreme is the exceedingly small risk on bonds issued by the largest and most financially solid corporations (such as IBM, General Electric, Exxon, and many of the regional Bell Telephone companies). At the other extreme is the considerable risk of default on many of the junk bonds issued in connection with the leveraged buyout craze of the 1980s. Thus, the financial health of the issuing corporation is an important measure of a bond's risk.

The degree of security or protection for the investor also depends on the type of bonds the corporation issues. The least protection (and, thus, the highest degree of risk) is offered by bonds called *debentures*. These are simple promises by the corporation to pay the interest and principal, and they offer no collateral as security against the loan. Certain debentures may be specifically designated as *subordinated debentures*, meaning that owners of these debentures stand behind holders of other debentures in the priority of their claim against assets of the corporation in the event of default.

A *mortgage bond* is secured by a claim against real property owned by the corporation. Again, there may be priorities within this subclass as well, with bonds designated as first mortgage bonds, second mortgage bonds, and so on.

Still higher up the ladder in terms of freedom from credit risk are the *collateral trust bonds*. These are corporate bonds that have been guaranteed by the stock and/or bonds of another corporation, in addition to representing a claim against the assets of the issuing company. This is often a case in which bonds of a subsidiary company are collateralized by the assets of the parent company as well. The highest form of collateral trust bonds are those, sometimes called *guaranteed bonds*, in which the payment of interest and principal are guaranteed unconditionally by a totally unrelated (and usually much bigger) corporation.

Generally considered to be the most secure form of corporates are the *equipment trust certificates*, which are bonds backed by specific pieces of equipment (usually the equipment purchased with the proceeds of the bond offering). These bonds are often issued by airlines, railroads, and other companies that have huge inventories of such equipment, which is essential to their business.

Given the possibilities, it is easy to see that different bonds, even issued by the same corporation, may have different risks involved. Consequently, they may offer investors quite different rates of interest to compensate for the varying risk levels.

Evaluating and Selecting Bonds

In evaluating every bond, whether Treasury or corporate, taxable or tax-free, six key variables will determine whether or not a particular bond is suitable for inclusion in your portfolio. These variables are quality, yield, maturity, liquidity, call features, and price. While each refers to a distinct characteristic of a bond, each is related to, and partially reflects, all the others. Thus, in an obvious example, you would expect the price of a lower-quality bond to be lower, and/or the yield higher, than on a higher-quality bond, all other things being equal. Fully understanding each of the key variables will enable you to find the bonds best suited to your unique situation and needs.

A fundamental characteristic that is essential to understanding and evaluating all six of the key variables is that a bond will pay a *fixed* dollar amount of interest throughout its entire life, regardless of what happens to interest rates in general. Thus, as interest rates in the overall economy move up and down, the value of the fixed stream of income produced by the bond will change as well, shifting the price at which a seller is willing to sell that income stream and a buyer is willing to purchase it. The extent to which a change in current interest rates will affect the price of a bond depends on the nature and interrelationship of the six key variables.

QUALITY

A bond's quality is the degree of freedom from risk that the issuer will be unwilling or unable to make timely payment of interest or, in the worst case, will default on the principal repayment as well. As previously noted, all Treasury debt is considered to be the highest quality available, free from any credit risk. Quality of corporates depends not only on the underlying financial strength of the issuing entity, but also on the various types and classes of other outstanding debt that may precede the bondholder in a claim against assets in the event of default.

Fortunately, from the point of view of the individual investor, the credit quality of most individual bonds is easy to determine from the rating given to it by one of the bond-rating services (Standard & Poor's and Moody's being the two largest and best known). The analysts of these services are constantly reviewing the various elements and developments that affect each bond's creditworthiness. The services assign the bond one of nine ratings, ranging from AAA to C. The highest four ratings (AAA, AA, A, or BBB by Standard & Poor's; Aaa, Aa, A, or Baa by Moody's) are considered to identify bonds that are "investment grade" and can be bought by banks and other fiduciaries. Grades lower than BBB or Baa are considered "speculative," and belong only in the portfolios of sophisticated investors who are actively managing their bond portfolios on a daily basis and who recognize and accept the possibility of default in such issues.

The ratings of bond quality are published monthly by Standard & Poor's and by Moody's. Copies of these guides can be found in any broker's office or in the public library. If you are a relatively good customer, your broker may even regularly provide you with a current copy of either of these two guides, or at least give you his or her old copy each month when the new one comes in. These guides provide a wealth of information in addition to the quality ratings on each bond, including the call provisions, if any, and whether the bonds are traded on an exchange.

Bond yields are inversely proportionate to the credit quality of the issuer. Thus, Treasuries offer lower yields than *any* corporates of similar maturity and call features. Likewise, higher-rated corporates will provide lower yields than will issues with a lower rating. As a practical matter, AAA-rated issues normally suffer a bigger drop-off in yield than is justified by the difference in quality between them and AA-rated issues, because many investors are unwilling to sacrifice any quality whatsoever and will purchase only AAA bonds, regardless of yield differentials.

YIELD

Simply stated, yield refers to what the bondholder is paid to compensate for the use of his or her money each year. Thus, a bond with a $10,000 face value and a coupon of 8.5 percent, purchased upon original issue at par and held to maturity, will pay the holder $850 per year throughout the life of the bond, and the yield is 8.5 percent.

Current Yield

Assuming that this bond was issued several years ago, however, and that current interest rates have risen to 9 percent from 8.5 percent, the value of the bond may have fallen to around 96.75 (or 96.24 if we are talking about a Treasury). This price decline would reflect the fact that an annual income stream of $850 is no longer competitive, at a price of $10,000, to alternative investments available to the investor. What, then, is the yield of the bond at its current price of 96.75? The calculation of interest paid ($850 per year) divided by the new price to be paid for the bond ($9,675) shows that the bondholder will receive a *current yield* of just over 8.785 percent.

Yield to Maturity

This does not tell the entire story, however, since at maturity the bondholder will receive $10,000 for a bond he or she paid just $9,675 to purchase. The additional $325 is also a form of interest paid for the use of his or her money, and is reflected in a calculation called *yield to maturity*.

This calculation determines the average annual change expected in the price of the bond for it to reach par at maturity (assuming no further changes in interest rates), and treats this as an additional element of annual interest. Specialized financial calculators can easily compute the yield to maturity on any bond, given the price, coupon, and maturity.* Alternatively, your broker should be able to tell you the yield to maturity on any bond you are considering as a purchase. Keep in mind that yield to maturity, not current yield, reflects the total annualized return available from a bond.

If the price of a bond is near par, the difference between current yield and yield to maturity will be small. On bonds where the coupon yield significantly differs from currently prevailing interest rates, however, the difference may be quite large. The most extreme example of this can be found in zero-coupon bonds, which pay no current interest whatsoever. Rather, these bonds are sold at a substantial discount from par, and the entire yield consists of the appreciation in price between the original discount and the redemption value at par upon maturity. Originally, these bonds offered a way to defer income taxes, since no yield was actually generated until maturity. However, the IRS currently requires payment of income taxes upon the imputed income (also called "phantom" income), which the government now holds is actually being earned, although it is not paid to the holder. Clearly, this turns an advantage of these bonds into a distinct disadvantage, except in certain circumstances.

Yield to Call
Still a third concept of yield, called *yield to call*, is important for bonds that the issuer may redeem (call) at some point before the bond's stated maturity. The calculation of yield to call is the same as that for yield to maturity, except that the call premium (if one exists) and call date are used in place of par value and maturity date. This yield may be important when dealing with bonds with significant call features, discussed later in this chapter.

MATURITY
A bond's maturity—the length of time remaining before the issuer redeems it—has implications along three different lines. Each

---

*The formula to calculate yield to maturity is:
Yield to Maturity = Stated Interest Amount ± Amortization of Price Discount or Premium divided by Current Bond Price + Par ÷ 2

implication arises from the fact that the bond is producing a fixed income stream that will not vary over the life of the bond.

Maturity and Volatility

First, the maturity of a bond will to a large extent determine the volatility of the bond's price. If an investment-grade bond is to be redeemed in just a few months, it really doesn't make much difference what the coupon of the bond provides as current yield—the price of the bond will remain very close to par, since even a slight variation in price would substantially change the yield to maturity on an annualized basis. Conversely, a bond that does not mature for 20 or more years will be highly sensitive in price to any shift in current interest rates. That is because the price difference required by the marketplace to equalize the yield to maturity is to be absorbed over such a long period of time. All other things being equal, the yield to maturity is the point of comparison, and if the maturity is longer, far greater price movements will be needed to bring the yield to maturity into balance.

A simple comparison clearly demonstrates the effect of differing maturities upon price volatility. Bond A and Bond B are considered to be of equal quality, and both carry coupons of 7 percent. In an environment where interest rates call for a yield to maturity of 8.5 percent, Bond A, which matures in four months, will have a price of 99.48, while Bond B, which matures in 20 years, will be priced at 85.69. However, if interest rates call for a yield to maturity of 9 percent rather than 8.5 percent, the price of Bond A will change only slightly, to 99.32, while Bond B's price must drop to 81.60 in order to produce an equivalent yield to maturity.

Maturity and Reinvestment Rate Risk

The second implication of a bond's maturity is the consideration of reinvestment rate risk. On a bond with a longer maturity, the interest will be paid at the rate determined by the price and the coupon over the full life of the bond. With a shorter-term bond, the funds made available upon maturity will be available for reinvestment, but at what rate? If rates have gone down since the purchase of the shorter bond, the funds can be reinvested only at a lower rate, so the longer bond will produce the superior yield. If rates have gone up, the reverse is true. Thus, the investor's outlook for the future course of interest rates must play a part in the choice of the most appropriate maturity.

Maturity and Inflation

Finally, any determination of appropriate maturities for bonds to be included in an investment portfolio must take into account the anticipated rate of inflation. In periods of high inflation, the fixed stream of income generated by a bond will be robbed of its purchasing power. The longer the term of the bond, the greater the effects of compounding upon this theft of purchasing power. Remember that $100 in annual income, after 20 years of inflation at just 3.5 percent per year, will buy only $49.04 of goods and services!

This in itself does not necessarily mitigate against long bonds in favor of short ones, because a steady rate of inflation will erode the purchasing power of all fixed-income securities at the same annual rate, regardless of a bond's maturity. Rather, it points out the damage that inflation can do to all investments that produce the same interest yield, year after year. It also highlights the fact that long-term commitments to bonds are much less desirable when future levels of inflation are anticipated to be high.

LIQUIDITY

When bonds are purchased or sold in the secondary market, they are generally quoted on a "bid/asked" basis. That is, a dealer will state the price at which he or she is willing to purchase a particular bond from you (the bid) and a higher price, at which he or she is prepared to sell the bond to you (the asked, or offered, price). The difference between these two prices, known as the spread, represents the profit to the dealer, which will also cover the cost of maintaining this bond in his or her inventory.

Treasuries and bonds issued by major corporations are generally in greater demand and trade much more frequently than those of smaller entities. This difference in liquidity will often result in much smaller price spreads for those bonds, since dealers are less anxious about having to keep the more liquid bonds in inventory for any extended period of time. The most liquid bonds (apart from Treasuries) are those listed for trading on the New York and

American exchanges, where they trade in very much the same way as do common stocks. In fact, your broker can give you instant quotations on these bonds directly from his or her quotation machine, whereas on unlisted bonds, your broker must telephone dealers who make a market in those bonds in order to obtain pricing information.

There is nothing inherently less desirable about an unlisted bond from the point of view of risk or yield if you buy the bond with the goal of holding it until maturity. However, the original purchase price of such a bond is likely to be somewhat higher—and the eventual resale price somewhat lower if you sell the bond before maturity—than would be the case for a more liquid bond. In addition, you can sell a listed bond in a matter of minutes, whereas selling an unlisted bond may take several days if the broker solicits prices from a number of dealers.

CALL FEATURES

Many bonds, whether Treasuries, corporates, or tax-free municipal bonds, contain a feature that is very advantageous to the issuer and very disadvantageous to the investor in these bonds. These are the provisions for calling the bonds for redemption at some point before the stated maturity date of the bond. Thus, if interest rates decline significantly at some point in the life of the bond, the issuer may reserve the right to pay off the bond, usually with the proceeds of a new bond, which will be issued at the new, lower interest rates then prevailing. Calling the bonds in this situation lowers the issuer's cost of borrowing the money and leaves the hapless bondholder with the principal and accrued interest, but able to invest those funds only at the current (i.e., lower) rate available.

Not only do these call features provide for early redemption of the bonds if rates go down, they also provide an effective cap upon the price of a bond the investor has purchased when rates are high. Such a bond might have generated a significant capital gain when lower prevailing rates made it relatively more valuable. However, this value is limited by the fact that the issuer can call the bond (at par or at a slight premium) at any time in accordance with whatever call provisions are in the original bond indenture. Thus, higher-coupon bonds may be priced at what appears to be a very attractive yield to maturity, since the pricing is actually based on an assumption that the bond will be called in well before the maturity date.

Not all bonds have call provisions. Many Treasuries (although not all, especially in the longer-term bonds) are noncallable. Other bonds may have deferred call provisions, which is to say that there is a specified time period during which the bonds are not callable. In addition, call provisions may require the issuer to pay a premium of as much as 5 percent (or, rarely, even more) on top of par value if the bonds are called. The most commonly encountered call provisions provide for a period of noncallability followed by a first call date at a slight premium (say, 102), followed by a second call (usually at par) at a later threshold date.

Noncallable bonds, being more attractive to investors, generally provide somewhat lower yields than do bonds with various types of call provisions. The important things to keep in mind are that call provisions may have a definite effect upon the value of a bond and that brokers will sometimes not be completely familiar with the call provisions of bonds they are telling you about unless you ask them specifically.

A final consideration regarding call provisions on bonds: Clearly, if two bonds are callable at only a slight premium in the relatively near future, a bond selling at or near par will have a much more stringent cap upon its future price performance if interest rates go down than will a higher-coupon bond that is selling at a significant discount to par. If an investor is purchasing bonds not only for steady income but also as vehicles for capital gains in anticipation of lower interest rates, the investor can at least partially offset the limiting effects of call provisions by carefully manipulating a number of the other key variables in picking which bonds to purchase.

PRICE

The amount by which the price of a bond differs from the bond's par value represents the adjustment necessary to bring the bond's yield to maturity into balance with returns on alternative investments, adjusted for differences in risk, maturity, liquidity, and the investor's outlook for inflation and the direction of interest rates. Whether or not a bond is more attractive, or less attractive, at a given price also depends upon several other considerations concerning the investor's own financial situation, rather than the bond itself. For example, consider two hypothetical bonds; both are of comparable quality, neither is callable, and both have remaining maturities of 10 years. Bond A, with a coupon of 6 percent, is priced at 85.18. Bond B, with a coupon of 10.25 percent, is priced at 113.81. At these prices, *both* bonds generate a yield to maturity of 8.2 percent. What situations would call for the purchase of Bond A, and under what circumstances would Bond B be preferable?

Tax Considerations

At maturity, the price of both bonds will be 100. Thus, there is a built-in capital gain for Bond A, taxable only upon maturity. With Bond B, there would normally be a capital loss upon maturity. Depending upon an investor's anticipated financial situation, one or the other might be preferable. With Bond A, the investor defers part of the total yield (and the taxation) until he or she receives the gain upon maturity. With Bond B, the current income and taxation are accelerated (in the form of higher interest payments received), then partially offset by the capital loss upon maturity. For an investor who expects some change in income patterns (for example, as a result of retirement or substantial income from other sources), one or the other bond will make more sense.

Note also that the IRS allows an alternative method of taxing the income from bonds purchased at a premium. Currently an investor may elect to treat the excess income received each year as a partial return of capital. This lowers the cost of acquisition to par up on maturity and eliminates the residual (deductible) capital loss, but it shelters the excess interest income from income taxes each year the bond is held. While the rules for calculating how much of the interest can be sheltered are somewhat complicated, it is very often in the bondholder's better interest to have a sheltered stream of income rather than a capital loss.

In any case, the fact that a bond is trading either below par or above par is not in itself necessarily favorable or unfavorable. However, a price discount will result in the bond's generating a total yield with a quite different structure—with quite different tax implications—than for a bond selling at a premium.

Another consideration for an investor using bonds as a vehicle for capital gains is that if interest rates are lower in the future, a lower-priced bond will achieve greater capital gains than will a higher-priced bond with the same yield to maturity. This is because the lower-priced, lower-coupon bond provides a greater portion of the total yield to maturity in the form of price appreciation than does the higher-priced, higher-coupon bond. In the case of the hypothetical bonds described earlier, if after one year both bonds are to be priced to yield 7.2 percent to maturity instead of 8.2 percent, the price of Bond A will increase by 8.18 percent, to 92.15, whereas the price of Bond B will increase only 5.3 percent, to 119.95.

Duration

A related concept is that of a bond's "duration," a term that has a special meaning to professional bond traders and fixed-income money managers, but that need not be of concern to individual investors unless they are working with extremely large amounts of money. Duration of a bond refers to the average length of time until all payments resulting from holding that particular bond to maturity are dispersed (in other words, the average length of time required to receive all interest payments plus the principal). Bonds that are paying a high coupon rate and are trading at or above par will have a shorter duration (you get more of your money sooner) than will bonds that carry a lower coupon rate and are trading at a discount to par.

Zero-coupon bonds are the ultimate example of long-duration bonds. The investor does not receive *any* money back until the very end of the bond's life.

Duration is useful in comparing the risk among widely differing bonds. It is also used by pension fund managers and insurers to match anticipated cash flow requirements for pension payouts and so forth with cash they will receive from their bondholdings.

Conclusion

Bonds are somewhat more complex than may at first appear to be the case. Nonetheless, at least some portion of almost all investors' portfolios should be allocated to these investment vehicles. Carefully selected and monitored, they can provide a steady stream of secure income, as well as potential for capital appreciation.

THE LAST HURRAH?

THE UNIVERSAL APPEAL OF TAX-EXEMPT SECURITIES

Arthur K. Carlson

TAX-EXEMPTS ARE SECURITIES ISSUED BY GOVERNMENT BODies at the state, local, and territorial level, and normally occur in the form of bonds. Income from all state and local issues is tax-exempt at the federal level, but is exempt from state taxation only in the state that originally issued the securities. Territorial issues from Puerto Rico, the Virgin Islands, Guam, and the Northern Marianas are federally tax-exempt and are also exempt in all 50 states.

WHY TAX-EXEMPT SECURITIES?

These securities largely constitute the vehicle that is used to finance highways, airports, hospitals, schools at all levels, and many more public services. As a result, these issues benefit all citizens. A further, indirect, benefit is that municipalities can finance these projects at significantly lower costs than if they borrowed the money. The reason is that buyers of the bonds will accept a lower rate of interest income (and thus the interest expense to the municipalities) on a tax-exempt basis than if the interest were subject to income taxation. Table 5-1, for example, shows equivalent yields of taxable and tax-exempt income to taxpayers in Hawaii.

115

TABLE 5-1

ESTIMATED TAXABLE EQUIVALENT YIELDS FOR 1989 IN THE STATE OF HAWAII

State Taxpayer Status	State Taxpayer Income	Federal Tax Rate	State Tax Rate	Effective Combined Tax Rates
Married	$11,000–21,000	15.0%	8.25%	22.01%
Filing	$21,000–29,000	15.0	9.25	22.86
Joint	$29,000–30,950	15.0	9.75	23.29
Return	$30,950–41,000	28.0	9.75	35.02
	$41,000–74,850	28.0	10.00	35.20
	$74,850–177,720	33.0	10.00	39.70
	Over $177,720	28.0	10.00	35.20
Single	$10,500–14,500	15.0%	9.25%	22.86%
Return	$14,500–18,550	15.0	9.75	23.29
	$18,550–20,500	28.0	9.75	35.02
	$20,500–44.900	28.0	10.00	35.20
	$44,900–104,330	33.0	10.00	39.70
	Over $104,330	28.0	10.00	35.20

State Taxpayer Status	Tax-Free Yield								
	5.0%	5.5%	6.0%	6.5%	7.0%	7.5%	8.0%	8.5%	9.0%
	Taxable Yield Equivalent								
Married	6.41%	7.05%	7.69%	8.33%	8.98%	9.62%	10.26%	10.90%	11.54%
Filing	6.48	7.13	7.78	8.43	9.07	9.72	10.37	11.02	11.67
Joint	6.52	7.17	7.82	8.47	9.12	9.78	10.43	11.08	11.73
Return	7.69	8.46	9.23	10.00	10.77	11.54	12.31	13.08	13.85
	7.72	8.49	9.26	10.03	10.80	11.57	12.35	13.12	13.89
	8.29	9.12	9.95	10.78	11.61	12.44	13.27	14.10	14.93
	7.72	8.49	9.26	10.03	10.80	11.57	12.35	13.12	13.89
Single	6.48%	7.13%	7.78%	8.43%	9.07%	9.72%	10.37%	11.02%	11.67%
Return	6.52	7.17	7.82	8.47	9.12	9.78	10.43	11.08	11.73
	7.69	8.46	9.23	10.00	10.77	11.54	12.31	13.08	13.85
	7.72	8.49	9.26	10.03	10.80	11.57	12.35	13.12	13.89
	8.29	9.12	9.95	10.78	11.61	12.44	13.27	14.10	14.93
	7.72	8.49	9.26	10.03	10.80	11.57	12.35	13.12	13.89

In addition to benefiting the community at large, tax-exempts constitute the cornerstone of many investment portfolios. They are also instrumental in long-range tax planning.

CREATION OF TAX-EXEMPT SECURITIES

When a state legislature or other government body determines that a public project is necessary, it must decide how to pay for it. To make that decision, the legislators must answer a series of questions:

1. How much will the project cost?
2. How will the cost be financed? Out of general state (or local) funds, or through the sale of tax-exempt securities?
3. If out of general funds, will taxes be increased?
4. If through a bond issue, how will it be repaid?

It is through the answer to the fourth question that tax-exempts come into being.

These securities generally fall into one of two categories—general obligation bonds or revenue bonds. General obligations are issued to provide financing for tax-supported projects such as water and sewer facilities, school improvements, and roads. These are backed by the full taxing power of the issuing municipality, regardless of the ultimate financial viability of the specific project being financed. Therefore, they are widely regarded as the safest and strongest of all tax-exempt securities.

Revenue bonds are used to finance airports, toll roads, hospitals, and other projects that generate revenue as part of their operations. These bonds are backed by the earning power of the specific project for which they are issued. Therefore, they carry significantly higher risk that unforeseen developments might threaten the municipality's ability to pay interest and principal on a timely basis.

Whichever type of tax-exempt it selects, the issuing authority will work with an investment banking firm to prepare a prospectus. A prospectus outlines the proposal in detail and is required for issuance of public bonds and other types of municipal financing.

When the government body and the investment banking firm (underwriter) agree on all terms of the proposed issue, including size, interest rate, and maturity, the banking firm buys the issue from the state, thus giving the state its needed funds. The banking firm then resells the bonds to the public. The underwriter thus undertakes the risk of being able to sell all of the bonds and, if successful, will earn its profit. When the sale is completed, the bonds will be in the marketplace along with billions of dollars of other issues available for purchase or sale for investment purposes.

RISK FACTORS

In terms of quality, tax-exempt securities are generally regarded as second only to U.S. government direct obligations (Treasury securities), which places them among the safest investments available. It would be a mistake, however, to buy tax-exempts blindly, because, as with all investments, their quality ranges from extremely high to marginal. Thus, careful selection is necessary.

Many issues are graded by rating agencies and research facilities of brokerage and underwriting houses, and the grading data are available to the investor for help in the selection process. Many investors choose to engage professional management by buying shares in mutual funds that specialize in tax-exempt investments and provide quality selection, maturity, geographic diversification, and constant supervision.

UNDERLYING PHILOSOPHY

If you regard investment instruments as a set of tools to accomplish your goals, there is little philosophical difference between the investor and the skilled craftsperson, whose collection of professional tools enables him or her to build or repair items in his or her chosen field. In a similar way, the investor should carefully select the tools that will help most in achieving his or her objectives and, like the skilled craftsperson, will find that the highest-quality tools will provide the best performance.

As this section will show, tax-exempt securities are important tools in the construction of an investment portfolio. More specifically, tax-exempts are appropriate for the key facets of long-term financial planning and tax planning.

Long-Term Financial Planning

In long-term financial planning, high-grade tax-exempt securities almost always combine well with other investment instruments. They meet the objectives of almost all classes of investors, whether they are planning for children or planning for catastrophic medical care:

- To provide for a child's college education.
- To reduce annual tax bills.
- To increase interest yield compounding tax-exempt income.
- To combine with high-grade growth stocks for balanced investment approaches.
- To combine with money fund investments, both taxable and tax-free, in the same manner.

Young Marrieds

Tax-exempt securities provide a number of benefits to young couples. When mixed with high-quality growth stocks, tax-exempts provide a growing nest egg for future needs. They also help hold down tax bracket exposure. If the couple needs additional income, they can divert the tax-free income from tax-free reinvestment to other uses that are more important at a particular time. For example, they may want to use some of the income toward the down payment on a house.

Middle Years

People in their middle years are usually at their peak in earning power, so finding wise investments and minimizing taxes are especially important at this time. Tax-exempt securities provide a separate and independent resource that can grow rapidly as people make tax-free reinvestments. Tax-exempts also tend to hold down tax bracket exposure.

Tax-exempts are a prime example of the power of interest compounding when interest payments are allowed to be reinvested. It is especially important that some of this interest income be tax-exempt during the peak earning years.

By investing in tax-exempts, the holders build confidence in their future. This confidence arises from their independence from relying solely on a pension fund and Social Security for retirement funds.

RETIREMENT: THE GOLDEN YEARS

There is no better time than retirement to be in control of your own destiny. Retirees who have invested wisely avoid the harrowing insecurity of depending upon others whose money management skills may be deficient or on the whims of politicians who certainly have other concerns besides your retirement needs.

For retirees, minimizing taxes is often not as important as maximizing income. However, a good tax-exempt portfolio can be gradually rolled over into higher-yielding taxable securities. This is often a wise move if lower earnings upon retirement bring lower tax rates.

TAX AND OTHER CONSIDERATIONS

If there ever was any doubt that people should be in control of their own affairs, it certainly was dispelled when Congress in its infinite wisdom elected to pass the ill-fated Medicare Catastrophic Care Supplement. This, in its adopted form, was a true catastrophe for all responsible senior citizens, as the resulting firestorm of protest to Congress revealed. The measurement of who must pay this tax began with the historically infamous "adjusted gross income" of the IRS. If it had not been repealed, this tax would have become so serious and repugnant that adjusted gross income could very well have been renamed "Madame Guillotine" on the basis that it provided a feeding frenzy for tax-hungry political individuals and entities responsible for taxation.

Surely the foregoing events, together with current accounting procedures used for Social Security and the taxing authorities' invasion of the Social Security area in general, should spur responsible investors to protect themselves by holding down adjusted gross income. An important way to do this is through the use of tax-exempt securities. Such an approach seems almost the only way to hang onto one's income and avoid becoming a ward of the welfare system later in life.

MARKETS

By and large, almost every investor should consider longer-term investing in tax-exempt municipals. However, tax-exempt markets are among the most difficult to operate in. Therefore, trading should be done only by highly skilled professionals.

The reason for the complexity of tax-exempt markets is that tax-exempts are issued by individual state, county, and local governmental entities, who sell the securities to finance public needs, then pay them off over a period of time from general tax receipts or revenues derived from the specific improvements. Although some issues measure in many millions of dollars, most are relatively small. Even those considered large are small in terms of the mega-billion-dollar taxable issues sold to the public by the U.S. government and by industry through large bond and stock issues.

As a result, the market features a large number of lightly traded, relatively small issues that often have wide spreads between the bid to purchase and the offer to sell at any specific time. Indeed, they often do not have any quote at all on a given date. These markets therefore are more like a jungle than the very orderly bid-and-ask process that exists in primary stock markets.

Another problem for the average investor involves the trading unit. Each unit is generally five $1,000 (par amount) bonds. This means that a single trade will cost about $5,000. Since this money is all in one issue, the investment will lack diversification.

Finally, the investor must determine the investment's quality. Fortunately, many (not all) tax-exempts are rated in one of the nine rating categories by the leading bond rating agencies. Ratings range from AAA, which is best, through C, which is lowest. Figure 5-1 shows the rating categories of Moody's Service. There are additional rating services such as Standard & Poor's and Fitch. Their ratings generally are similar to Moody's Service in format and requirements.

Buying only rated bonds would leave out many good unrated bonds that are available but that do not carry a rating because the issue is small and thus not widely available for trading. Here again, the services of professional investment specialists can help you find good-quality bonds at reasonable prices.

WILL THERE BE A LAST HURRAH?

Some people believe that the right to issue tax-exempt securities is provided for in the U.S. Constitution. However, the Supreme Court

FIGURE 5-1

MUNICIPAL BOND RATINGS*

Investment Grade	Prime	Aaa
	Excellent	Aa
	Good	A
	Average	Baa
	Fair	Ba
	Poor	B
	Marginal	Caa
	Default	Ca
		C

*Moody's.

has determined that this right does not appear to be provided, but that neither is it denied.

As a practical matter, however, it does not seem likely that the U.S. government will attempt to deny tax exemption on these issues, because the entire current financing structure could very well collapse under higher interest costs at the state level. States would be furious at the loss of self-determination, and Congress would be saddled with the entire cost of the nation's infrastructure (bridges, highways, airports, hospitals, and the like). This would cause a truly monumental addition to the federal budget and debt structure. It seems highly likely that there will *not* be a "last hurrah," but rather there will continue to be a universal appeal for these investments.

MECHANICS OF INVESTING

PLANNING CONSIDERATIONS

For many generations young people have been counseled wisely that the only things certain in life are death and taxes. Less well understood, but prevalent for periods of time during all history, is inflation, which is well on its way to joining death and taxes as the third major element that must be included in life's planning.

We all understand the mortality of humans, although we still cannot accurately forecast any specific person's life span. Therefore we must make all plans assuming a long life or using actuarial tables. In any event, there are limits. Even if those limits are extreme in some instances, investors can plan with enough skill to cover most eventualities.

In the case of taxes, however, the problem becomes much more intense. Even though we live in a republic where voters presumably are in control, taxing processes have become extremely complex because there are so many taxing bodies, because tax systems tend to be interrelated, which causes unrecognized "double taxation" situations, and because government rightly or wrongly concerns itself much more with spending than with saving. These comments are not intended to attempt to pass judgment on these conditions, but simply to recognize the facts as they exist and as they determine how one must invest to maximize protection and income. Plans to accommodate the tax system are extremely difficult to create because many taxes are adjusted (as often as yearly), and when public pressure mounts, entire revampings take place. These changes can render an individual's planning obsolete literally overnight.

The final consideration, inflation, is probably the most insidious of all because it comes at the investor in so many forms:

- *Currency inflation*—where government increases currency in circulation without adequate backup of hard reserves (gold, bullion, etc.).
- *Wage inflation*—where rates of pay advance faster than offsetting efficiencies (productivity).
- *Product price inflation*—where the price of a product rises faster than the underlying price of raw materials and labor.
- *Tax inflation*—where tax rates are increased on the same size asset base or where related taxes are increased or usual deductions are disallowed without an offsetting reduction in taxes due.
- *Excessive government employment*—sometimes known as empire building. Often employees cannot be redeployed because the "Peter principle" has taken effect. (The Peter principle occurs when employees have advanced beyond their capabilities. At this point they should not be promoted, and usually demotion is not an available option.)

There are other examples, of course, but these certainly reveal the problem of inflation and the difficulty of restraining it once it has gotten under way. It takes real courage on the part of business-people and especially on the part of public officials and elected representatives to contain or to cure the problem. Instead, they tend to avoid any unpleasantness until the last possible moment—usually when there is little choice left.

PROBLEMS AND OPPORTUNITIES OVER A LIFE SPAN

Planning holds the key to reducing many stress items that are relatively common at various key points in a lifetime. The following represent some of these instances.

Birth

When a child is born, it is helpful if the parents or grandparents have accumulated some zero-coupon tax-exempts that are coming due in time to help with medical expenses not covered by insurance and to help offset the loss of income if the mother stops working or to pay for child care if she resumes her career. Also, this is a good time to begin acquiring equities to grow into a college fund.

College

The time when a child leaves home to attend college is frequently a difficult one. School costs and living costs escalate every year, and students want many nice little extras that are costly. A portfolio of tax-exempts at this time would enable the parents to hold down their adjusted gross income during those years, when every penny counts. This is even better if the parents have successfully accumulated a high-grade stock portfolio in time to give it to their college student.

Marriage

Parents who expect to help finance their children's weddings certainly need to plan ahead. Some wise investing can also enable them to provide a gift or contribute to a honeymoon or boost the new couple toward a good start in life.

Also, at the time when the children become adults, one's income is probably nearing its peak, and taxes have to be a principal concern. Thus, building investments with an eye toward death, taxes, and inflation is the best route to take.

The Middle Years
The relatively high income typical of the middle years means that investing should focus on earning tax-free income, adding to quality growth stock holdings, and seeking out quality investments that can reduce taxable income through means other than tax-exempts (for example, through depletion or depreciation). As your income peaks, you are probably developing lifestyles that you would like to continue, at least in part, when you retire. Consideration should be given to this desire throughout planning.

This age period is becoming more important all the time because of changes in tax laws and the addition of taxes never levied until recent years. Taxation of the elderly has reached proportions never before experienced, and this is best addressed in the middle years, when it is possible to obtain some protection by recognizing the problem early.

Thus, planning is crucial in the middle years. It all comes down to two simple guidelines:

1. Maximize tax-exempt income.
2. Generate constructive controlled deductions.

The Golden Years
The retirement years really can be golden! This time is when planning is all supposed to come together. But for those who haven't planned, retirement can be a nightmare. Many problems of the elderly have been brought on by changes in tax laws:

• Marginal tax rates are confiscatory for those who choose to continue to work.
• Largely because of tax rates, over 80 percent of all men and more than 90 percent of all women over retirement age are choosing not to work and are living on smaller incomes.
• Pension income is taxed.
• IRA income is taxed.
• Any catastrophic government insurance will result in significantly higher taxation.
• For people eligible for the alternative minimum tax calculation, social security benefits are taxed.
• Surviving spouses and/or children can have serious financial problems if not protected against death and inheritance taxes.

At this time when income may be more needed than anyone can anticipate, a good portfolio of tax-exempts and high-yielding short-term U.S. Treasuries (the latter acquired through conversion of growth stock accumulated in earlier years) will provide a nice addition to basic income.

MAXIMIZING TAX-EXEMPT INCOME

About the only game left in town after the income tax revisions of the 1980s is tax-exempt securities. For reasons discussed earlier, it is reasonable to expect this form of investment to continue to be available and to expect that it will draw more and more investors. As a matter of fact, tax-exempts may become to the bond market what quality growth stocks have been to the stock market.

It surely is quite reasonable to start portfolio building for any age spectrum with tax-exempt securities and quality growth stocks. Any basic account of this type can be fleshed out or tailored to the express needs of an individual or institution by adding other types of securities or investments specifically suited to the account's needs. Needless to say, you must be clear about your objectives before you start. Also, review your objectives periodically for any change so that the account can be adjusted to meet specific needs.

Conditions of Tax-Exempt Investing

Not all municipal bonds are tax-exempt. The Tax Reform Act of 1986 has made some municipal-type securities taxable. These are to be avoided, except where they fit specific account needs. Taxable securities are defined and listed as such.

Make every effort to find securities exempt from both federal and state taxation. As mentioned earlier, in any given state, only securities issued by instrumentalities of that state are tax-exempt. However, securities of Puerto Rico, the Virgin Islands, Guam, and the Northern Marianas are exempt from federal taxes as well as from taxation in all states.

Exercise great caution in managing tax-exempt securities. They are more difficult to hold and to trade. Some of the specific problems are as follows:

• Tax-exempt securities pay interest semiannually, and most pay at approximately the same time (June 30–July 1 and December 31–

January 1). This creates a peak and trough income flow that is not readily adjustable.

- To diversify, you must buy an assortment of issues, most of which are subject to prerefunding and call. (Prerefunding occurs when new funds are raised and held to pay off bonds as they become available; a call is the bond issuer's payment for all or part of the issue before maturity.) If you miss a call notice, you can lose as much as six months' interest.
- Events such as missed calls generally occur when you hold "bearer" bonds. These are not registered, so the issuer does not know who holds them and cannot directly advise the holder that there is an outstanding call.
- In addition, with bearer bonds, you must exercise a great deal of care to protect them, as they are fully negotiable (for sale in the hands of anyone who holds them). Coupons must be clipped, safeguarded, and tendered through the paying agent every six months. This in itself is pure drudgery. Clearly, registered bonds are more convenient and definitely safer.
- Because issues tend to be local and often of small to medium size, many issues do not trade regularly; when they do, they may not be publicly reported. This makes it difficult to establish their price for sale or purchase or estate valuation. It also tends to develop wider spreads between bid and asked quotes whenever you enter the marketplace. Therefore, tax-exempts tend to trade further off the direct relationship to interest rate structures than do heavily traded securities in the same market.
- To further complicate ownership, it is sometimes very difficult to get enough financial information to underscore a good judgment to buy or to sell. This is especially true when trading in the secondary, or resale, markets. It is even more difficult to obtain interim information to review your original decision from time to time.

How to Approach the Market for Tax-Exempts
In light of all the difficulties, how should the average investor approach the market? There have been three principal ways: using an individual approach for individual securities, using a brokerage account to hold individual securities, and using a bank trust-type account.

Individual Approach for Individual Securities: To follow an individual approach, set yourself up with the best advisory sources you can get and concentrate on only the best-rated securities. You will have to build your personal affairs around the constraints just listed so that your finances run smoothly.

It is difficult and expensive, even for a highly skilled professional in the business, to conduct a tax-free investment program in this manner. You really need every source of service that brokers and investment bankers have available in their business to apply to your account alone. Considering all the management pitfalls, this approach seems to be the least cost-effective.

A Brokerage Account to Hold Individual Securities: You probably will be paying brokerage fees to conduct your trading as an individual, so you could have your broker take over administration of your tax-exempt bond holdings and perform all the necessary services. Don't give the broker discretionary power over your account, but just use the account as a safe place for him or her to keep your holdings, collect interest, respond to calls, and alert you to new opportunities and/or changes in the situation with your existing holdings. Not only will this arrangement protect your securities, but it will also hold your securities in a form that is readily available for trading and will have the advantage of built-in safeguards against missed calls and missed coupon clipping. You also will have a working relationship with a major trading firm acting on your behalf, and your broker probably can locate securities available for sale or buyers seeking specific issues for purchase to help develop the highest-quality portfolio for your needs. Generally, your broker will be alert to opportunities on a continuing basis, rather than being in or out of the market at any given time.

Considering all these benefits, this approach is generally cost-effective. Many brokerage firms assess no additional fees to hold your securities in "street" name—that is, to hold them in a pooled account in the broker's name. In other cases there may be a modest additional charge.

A Bank Trust-Type Account: The most formal arrangement you can have is a trust-type account at a bank. It carries the additional protection of being grounded in a body of fiduciary law. It also is the most expensive by quite a margin, because of the additional safeguards. Trust accounts come in many forms and can be tailored to achieve your objectives. Direct account management is generally reasonably good, and the bank communicates with brokers and investment bankers on a minute-to-minute basis during the trading day so they can generate very good industry data to support their trading and account management functions.

Of course, this arrangement has the big advantage of providing a fiduciary approach to estate planning. In other words, it provides for management of accounts under fiduciary law, which is much more protective of the customer.

GENERATING CONSTRUCTIVE CONTROLLED DEDUCTIONS
While generating constructive controlled deductions is an important part of business and estate planning, it is not germane to the general subject of investing in tax-exempt securities. Suffice it to say that it is a tax-planning item that you should approach with a good accountant at your side. It principally concerns real estate investing and individually owned businesses, and it features such tax items as depreciation and depletion.

TAX-EXEMPT MUTUAL FUNDS:
WAVE OF THE FUTURE

Over the past 10 years or so, a newer form of tax-exempt ownership has exploded onto the scene. This is the tax-exempt mutual fund. It comes in a number of forms that have evolved as investors' needs have become more apparent and they try to adjust to changing economic conditions, rising tax rates, and persistent inflation.

The punishing marginal tax rates noted earlier certainly are creating an unfair burden for older taxpayers, who as a group are seeking help to shelter as much of their fixed income and assets as possible. Actually, as all citizens become more aware of the havoc that has evolved as our tax system is repeatedly "refined," they are seeking protection as best they can. The need for tax-exempts is reaching into lower tax brackets, and the demand has taken yields down to where they are now closer to those on U.S. government securities than is normal. At the same time, people need professional help to manage their affairs. Mutual funds provide this help, especially for the average citizen who has trouble understanding and keeping current under our ever more punitive tax laws.

It is always important to review the fund's performance and to see its portfolio. To do this, inquire at your broker or obtain the most recent copy of the fund's offering prospectus from the issuer. There is no substitute for quality. This becomes especially important if the fund has a larger than usual percentage of revenue-based bonds that cannot generate income through the tax base, as is the case with general obligation bonds. On the other hand, well-selected revenue-based bonds do often provide a higher yield and thus are attractive.

As of this writing, there are four basic types of tax-exempt mutual funds: general, short-term general, individual-state, and individual-state short-term.

GENERAL TAX-EXEMPT MUTUAL FUNDS
A general tax-exempt mutual fund is one that holds tax-exempt securities generally and offers tax exemption under federal income tax laws but only partial state tax exemption in any given state. This means that only income from those tax-exempt securities held in the fund issued by your home state plus the territories of Puerto Rico, the Virgin Islands, Guam, and the Northern Marianas would be exempt from your state income tax.

SHORT-TERM GENERAL TAX-EXEMPT MUTUAL FUNDS
Short-term general funds differ from general funds only in that they are very short-term and serve as depositories for funds awaiting reinvestment in other tax-exempt areas or for funds in trust estates awaiting distribution or reinvestment. Their nature is transient, but their continuing volume is such that the size of these funds has been growing quite steadily. Interestingly, local governments have used them for temporary fund-raising, often before a major financing, and they regard this facility as a natural adjunct to the financing process.

INDIVIDUAL-STATE TAX-EXEMPT MUTUAL FUNDS
Another name for individual-state tax-exempt mutual funds is "double tax-exempt funds." This really is a misnomer but is in-

tended to describe a security that is exempt from both federal and state income taxes. These funds are very useful for taxpayers who live in a state where a fund of this type is available. Quite a few are already in existence, and more are coming as investment service providers are able to identify attractive states and generate the capital necessary to start up a new fund.

Individual-state tax-exempt mutual funds are also helpful to states seeking local funding for public projects. This is especially true where individual issues are small enough that the state is able to reduce expenses by avoiding underwriting costs initially and avoiding the cost of rating coverage on a continuing basis. For taxpayers and other citizens of an individual state, this fund provides more efficient financing for meritorious public projects. At worst, these projects might otherwise not be done. At best, they would be rolled into some other type of general financing, where funds might be diverted if the principal project covered by the new issue ran into sizable cost overruns—a condition that is all too prevalent today.

Some of these state funds use the best local investment advice available (banks or other advisers), since the organizing group—which may or may not be local—wants to get the best continuing advice possible. The value of this approach becomes apparent when good unrated issues come along and must be evaluated thoroughly with a knowledge of history and current firsthand experience. This fact is not lost on state governments that are constantly seeking the best fund sources available, nor is it lost on investors who are seeking the strongest and safest tax-exempt investments possible.

INDIVIDUAL-STATE SHORT-TERM TAX-EXEMPT MUTUAL FUNDS

An individual-state short-term fund is very similar to a general short-term fund except that it is confined to investment in municipal securities of one state plus the territories. They are excellent short-term (as much as possible) tax-exempt bridge-type investments—that is, they take the investor from cash to a longer-term investment—and are attractive to bank trust divisions and local investors. They are also attractive to local political entities seeking short-term funds for public projects that will be funded later on a long-term basis or will be paid off directly with the proceeds of taxation.

These funds are relatively new in their present format. However, investors have received them so well that they are likely to continue to increase in number and in size. They are, in effect, the newest medium designed to satisfy specific investment and financing needs in the short-term marketplace.

Supply of Tax-Exempt Securities

Although it is unlikely that Congress will pass any legislation to eliminate tax-exempt financing, no discussion of this subject would be complete without a review of the potential supply of tax-exempt securities. This is especially true in view of the obvious desirability of this type of instrument to individual and institutional investors and to the various public financing entities.

Financing for Infrastructure Needs

A major source of the need for tax-exempt securities is the enormous deficit that has been accumulated in the nation's infrastructure. The U.S. Department of Commerce estimates that, as a percent of gross national product, annual outlays for public projects have declined from 2.3 percent to 1.0 percent. Expenditures have declined from $62.8 billion annually to $44.7 billion adjusted for inflation. At the same time, not only has the infrastructure been wearing out, but it has also suffered from natural disasters such as the earthquakes in San Francisco, the hurricane in Charleston, and tornadoes in many areas.

Estimates of the cost to get the infrastructure back into acceptable condition range as high as an additional $100 billion annually for an indefinite period into the future. In essence, the federal, state, and local governments must make up for the decline in maintenance and construction that has been going on since the 1960s.

For these needs alone, there clearly will be a more than adequate supply of securities, unless budget pressures cause further delay. Such pressure is not likely, however, because legislators will respond to public demand. Public outcry is becoming very clear in the areas of highways, mass transit, aviation, water resources and supply, and waste disposal and treatments.

Highways

Evidence of the need to rebuild the nation's highways includes collapsing bridges, inability to handle growing traffic volume, and, perhaps worst of all, serious deterioration of the highways most recently constructed under federally assisted programs. Bonds sold for this purpose are expected to be mostly general obligation issues, repaid out of tax income.

Mass Transit

With regard to mass transit, the problem is twofold. Most existing systems are suffering severe obsolescence in both technology and passenger-carrying capacity. New systems, particularly the light-transit types, are needed to speed up movement of individuals and to help fight pollution in densely populated areas. Most issues in this area are likely to be tax-supported, as they are unlikely to be self-supporting except, under very broad interpretations, where the benefits of reducing the cost of pollution are included in total benefits.

Aviation

In the area of aviation, it appears that private airlines have done a reasonable job in upgrading equipment and systems since deregulation. However, the broad availability of low-cost air transport has attracted record volumes of passengers, which has led to a significant increase in flights. This has jammed airways over principal airports, where air-traffic control and ground facilities have not kept pace. Very large expenditures must be made to bring these services up to standard. Bonds to finance these needs most likely will be the revenue type supported by fee structures paid by airlines and, in growing instances, passengers.

Water Resources

An ever-increasing number of cities are looking for additional sources of water. Total water use appears to increase virtually very year, regardless of how strongly communities pursue water conservation. In some areas, a relatively light drought can be serious. Efforts to develop water resources center in three areas:

1. Trapping and holding water in lakes (dams where ecology permits) and reverse pumping from rivers to high basins for redistribution.

2. Drilling new aquifer resources and, in some cases, light desalinization of water lifted from very deep wells where the water is brackish. Actually, there is a pretty good supply of brackish water in the midcontinent.
3. Full desalinization. This has occurred mostly abroad to date but is likely to become more important in coastal and peninsular areas. To the extent that these services are publicly provided, the government will probably use tax-supported bond issues to finance the project. There are, however, private industrial water companies, and any financing of their ventures would be taxable.

Water Supply

As with water resources, the effort to build the water supply would be financed with either tax-exempt or taxable bonds. The main difference is that financing distribution of water from the source to the consumer in most instances is handled by local government. Of course, such financing provides for nontaxable securities.

Waste Water

The handling of waste water used to be called sewer service and was provided by local government. It is still provided by government, but the service has been widely expanded to filter, treat, and purify sewage water so that it can be substituted for primary water in operating industrial cooling processes, watering gardens and golf courses, cleaning streets, and other uses. This approach has only begun and is expected to expand greatly over the coming years as part of the overall effort to use natural resources more intelligently. These projects will undoubtedly be financed through issuance of tax-supported tax-exempt bonds.

Solid Waste

Probably the most immediate national problem is solid waste, and it is getting to be more widely understood. Simply stated, we are running out of places to dump garbage, and older dumps that had little or no design in construction are severely polluting the ground under the fill. Solutions to the problem include better design of landfills and the use of recycling.

Landfills: Landfills must be designed carefully to draw off polluting liquids for treatment and neutralization. This is a vast improvement over past methods and helps but does not eliminate the problem of finding enough dumping areas. Incidentally, dumping of wastes in lakes and oceans will be phased out and will add to landfill problems. Modern dumps will be built both publicly and privately and be financed on both a tax-exempt and taxable basis, depending upon which entity builds and operates the dump.

Recycling: Recycling is coming on strong. One way to recycle is to turn garbage into fuel. It has been determined that about 52 percent of the garbage stream is combustible, with a Btu content about the same as lignite (brown coal). Combustible garbage also has a low sulphur content, which is highly desirable for boiler fuel. Thus, if separated and briquetted, garbage could be a good fuel source as well as an aid in reducing the amount of waste needing disposal.

Of the remaining 48 percent of the garbage stream, over 40 percent can be separated and recycled—iron and steel magnetically for sale to mini steel mills, aluminum cans and trays by air separation, and bottles by hand. What is left—less than 5 percent—is mostly silica (sand) and can be disposed of economically.

If recycling is done in very large plants, it is likely they will be private and ineligible for tax-exempt financing. However, some public financing might be done. The major problem is that good recycling might produce more material than can be sold and absorbed by industry. But if costs are attractive, all of it will be used ultimately, and there will be a significant ecological gain from reducing demand on raw material sources.

Hazardous Waste
For handling hazardous waste, most financing will be private because of the nature of the business—a new science—neutralizing waste that can be dangerous to individuals or hazardous to our natural habitat. This waste includes concentrated acids, salts, heavy metals, and other items of this type.

OTHER USES OF TAX-EXEMPTS
There also is a small but growing trend for state and local governments to issue tax-exempt bonds in small denominations to boost general funds. Usually they are sold at discounts, as are E bonds (the predecessors of EE U.S. Savings Bonds), and accumulate

interest to maturity date. They are not very marketable and, of course, offer investors none of the protection that comes from diversifying investments.

There probably will continue to be a movement toward more revenue-supported tax-exempt projects, which are now probably in excess of 70 percent of all public works in this country. Therefore, to assess these projects and build a tax-exempt portfolio, research and quality judgments will continue to be important.

CAPITAL APPRECIATION

Besides income, tax-exempt bonds offer capital appreciation to investors who are willing to do their research carefully and who are close to the marketplace so that they can trade at a moment's notice. To benefit from appreciation, investors select issues, usually during periods of high interest rates, that have good quality but are trading at deep discounts because they carry a low coupon. Given time and patience, well-executed programs of this type are very profitable.

However, remember that under today's tax laws, the gain is taxable. As of this writing, such capital gains are taxable at regular income tax rates. A capital gain also adds to your adjusted gross income and, in turn, may force you into a higher tax bracket.

Capital gains give a lot of satisfaction when well done but are of no help to a program designed to maximize income by investing to hold down "Madame Guillotine's" effect on your long-term well-being. Remember, the rule is *defend your income against intrusion, and manage expenses to your benefit*. Given time, your program will work well, and you will be able to achieve financial independence.

6

AN INTRODUCTION TO EXCHANGE-TRADED OPTIONS

Cheryl Curley-Dukoff

AN OPTION IS SIMPLY A CONTRACT IN WHICH ONE PARTY grants another the right to either purchase or sell an underlying instrument for a specific price during a specific time. The underlying instrument may be a stock, bond, commodity contract (for example, oil, gold, currencies), or other investment vehicle.

Options trading is thought to have begun in Holland in the early 17th century. A sudden demand for tulips caused a surge of activity in this market. Dealers used call options, granted by the growers, to sell bulbs to speculators for future delivery. While this type of market became instantly popular, the marketplace was undisciplined. In 1636 it collapsed, causing the near demise of the Dutch economy, the effects of which were felt for many years thereafter.

Exchange-traded options were introduced in Chicago in the early 1970s, and U.S. interest in options was instantaneous. In the 1980s, the interest exploded as investors recognized that options offered them tremendous potential as a portfolio risk management tool. Today options are traded on a global scale, with participants using them for both hedge and speculative purposes. Options are traded on stocks, commodities, futures contracts, and cash indexes on over 50 exchanges worldwide and in the growing over-the-counter (OTC) market. Participants in the OTC market are primarily large institutions and banks.

This chapter provides a basic description of exchange-traded options. A glossary at the end of this book is useful for quick reference later. Every investor should acquire further knowledge of the subject before trading options, as they may not be suitable for everyone.

BASIC PROVISIONS OF OPTIONS

There are two types of options: calls and puts. As shown in Figure 6-1, a *call option* is the right to *buy* the underlying instrument on or before a specified date. A *put option* is the right to *sell* the underlying instrument on or before a specified date.

The price at which the underlying instrument may be bought or sold is called the exercise price or strike price. An option affords this right for a limited period of time. The date at which the option may no longer be exercised is the expiration date. (An option is either American, giving the buyer the right to exercise the option any time before expiration, or European, giving the buyer the right to exercise the option only on expiration day. Most listed options are American.)

In practice, very few options are exercised. If prices rise, the holder of a call option can sell the option back to the market at the higher market price. If prices fall, the holder of a put option can profit by selling the option back to the market at the higher market price.

The underlying instrument, exercise price, and expiration date are standardized by the exchange on which the option trades.

An advantage of options that accounts for their enormous popularity is that there are no margin calls for option buyers. Margin is a good-faith deposit made by the buyer to the broker in order to guarantee the fulfillment of contract obligations in adverse markets. A margin call is the broker's demand for additional margin funds when prices move against a trader's position. In the case of options, buyers pay up front and trade with their risk limited to the premium they paid for the option. On the other side,

FIGURE 6-1

OPTIONS: RIGHTS AND OBLIGATIONS

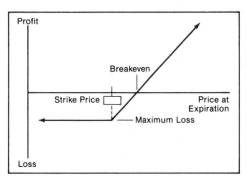

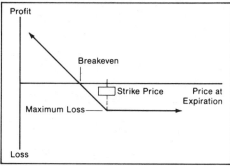

BUY CALL

Buyer has the right to buy the underlying instrument at the exercise price on or before expiration

Expect rising prices

BUY PUT

Buyer has the right to sell the underlying instrument at the exercise price on or before expiration

Expect falling prices

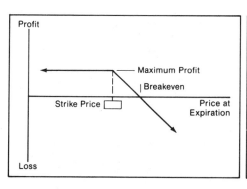

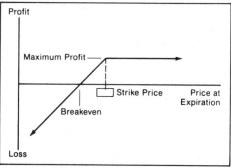

SELL CALL

Seller grants right to buyer, so has the obligation to sell the underlying instrument at the exercise price at buyer's option

Expect neutral/falling prices

SELL PUT

Seller grants right to buyer, so has the obligation to buy the underlying instrument at the exercise price at buyer's option

Expect neutral/rising prices

sellers of options must post margin, and their risk is unlimited.
The amount of the deposit is a percentage of the value of the
underlying instrument. This amount is set by the exchange on
which the contract trades. (In lieu of cash, sellers can meet margin
requirements by depositing U.S. Treasury instruments.)

OPTION PREMIUMS

The premium, or price, paid for an option is affected by five
factors: the price of the underlying instrument, the exercise price,
the time remaining until expiration, the volatility of the underlying
market, and interest rates. (Interest rates are a minor determinant
in the pricing of options on futures.) Furthermore, although cash
dividends on the underlying instrument are not a major determinant of option premiums, they can be important to the seller of an
option on a dividend-paying stock (more on this later).

  With options the challenge is to maximize the participation or
the protection while minimizing the cost. When buying options to
speculate on market direction, the challenge is to minimize the
premium paid while maximizing profit potential. When buying
options to hedge adverse market movement, the challenge is to
minimize the premium paid while maximizing the protection
from such a move. When selling options to either speculate or
hedge, the objectives are similar, but the challenge is to minimize
the risk while maximizing the premium received.

COMPONENTS OF THE PREMIUM

The premium can be separated into two components: intrinsic
value and time value. An option's intrinsic value is the amount that
an option buyer would receive as a result of exercising the option
and closing out the position against the underlying instrument at
the current market price. A call has intrinsic value only if its
exercise price is less than the current price of the underlying
instrument (meaning that the buyer has the right to buy below the
market). A put has intrinsic value only if its exercise price is
higher than the current price of the underlying instrument (so that
the buyer has the right to sell above the market).

  Often an option's price, or premium, in the marketplace is
greater than its intrinsic value. The additional amount of premium

over the intrinsic value is the extrinsic value, more commonly referred to as time value.

An option's premium is always composed of precisely its intrinsic and time value:

Premium = Intrinsic Value + Time Value

For example, if an XYZ $20 call is trading for $1.00 with the current price of the underlying instrument at $20.25, we know that the intrinsic value is $.25. Therefore, the time value must be $.75. The intrinsic and time values together must add up to the option's premium of $1.00.

An option that has intrinsic value is said to be in-the-money by the amount equal to its intrinsic value. If there is no time value, the option is said to be trading at parity. If an option has no intrinsic value, it is said to be out-of-the-money. As shown in Table 6-1, the premium of an out-of-the-money option consists solely of time value. Note that if a call is in-the-money, a put with the same exercise price and underlying instrument must be out-of-the-money. If a put is in-the-money, a call with the same exercise price and underlying instrument must be out-of-the-money.

Finally, an option whose exercise price is identical to the price of the underlying instrument is said to be at-the-money. At-the-money options have the greatest amount of time value.

TABLE 6-1

THE OPTION'S EXERCISE PRICE

Out-of-the-Money	At-the-Money	In-the-Money
Lowest absolute dollar price	No intrinsic value	Highest absolute dollar price
All-time value	Highest time value	Intrinsic and time value
Highest leverage	Reasonable leverage	Least leverage
Greatest participation/ least protection	Immediate participation/ protection*	Greatest Protection/ least participation

*Beyond the premium paid.

THE BLACK-SCHOLES MODEL OF OPTION PRICES

Since an option's price is a function of the underlying price, the exercise price, time to expiration, volatility, interest rates (and cash dividends), it is logical that a formula could be drawn up to derive an option's value from these variables. Fischer Black and Myron Scholes formalized this relationship in the Black-Scholes model, one of the first option-pricing models to be introduced.

Changes in the Premium

Options are multidimensional. Their prices can change in ways that may surprise even the most experienced trader. Fortunately, in addition to calculating an option's theoretical value, option-pricing models such as the Black-Scholes model also generate several numbers that are useful in estimating the direction and the magnitude of these changes.

Delta: The first mathematical derivative of the model is *delta*, which measures the expected change in an option's premium given a small change in the price of the underlying instrument. Delta is expressed as the percentage change in the value of the underlying instrument. In essence, it reflects the sensitivity of option premiums to movements in the price of the underlying instrument. Delta is dynamic; that is, as market prices of the underlying instrument rise or fall sharply, option deltas change.

In theory, an option can never gain or lose value more quickly than the underlying instrument, so the delta of a call has an upper bound of 1. In other words, a call option with a delta of 1 will behave similarly to the underlying instrument. If IBM moves up by $1, the call option will also move by $1. Similarly, a call with a delta of .50 will move by $.50 with a $1 move in IBM, and a call with a delta of .25 will move $.25 with a $1 move in IBM.

In theory, a call also cannot move in the opposite direction of the underlying instrument. Therefore, the call delta has a lower bound of 0. A call with a delta approaching 0 will move insignificantly, even if the underlying instrument makes a large upward move.

Puts have characteristics similar to those of calls, except that puts move in the opposite direction of the underlying instrument. When the underlying instrument moves up, puts lose value; when the underlying instrument moves down, puts gain value. For this reason, put deltas have negative values, ranging from 0 for deep out-of-the-money puts to −1 for deep in-the-money puts.

Gamma: The second mathematical derivative of the model is *gamma*, which measures the expected change in an option's delta given a small change in the underlying price. Gamma is measured in deltas per point change in the underlying price.

For example, if an option has a gamma of .05, then for each 1-point rise in the price of the underlying instrument, the option will gain .05 deltas. If the option originally had a delta of .25 and the underlying instrument moved up by 1 point, then the new delta of the option would be .30. Should underlying prices decline, the gamma is subtracted from the old delta to obtain the new delta. Like the delta, the gamma changes with changing market conditions.

Time

The more time remaining in an option's life (that is, the more time an option buyer has the right to exercise), the more value the option will have. More time remaining implies that an option has a higher probability of becoming in-the-money. The less time remaining in an option's life, the less value an option will have. Recall that an at-the-money option has the greatest amount of time value.

The rate of premium decay changes in relation to diminishing time remaining until the option contract expires. Premium decay per day is much more rapid on an option with two weeks left to expiration than the daily decay of an option with two months left to expiration.

The time decay factor, *theta*, is the first mathematical derivative of the model with respect to time. It measures the expected change in an option's theoretical value over a change in time. Theta is expressed in cents per day.

Theta provides option buyers with premium cost on a daily basis, and it provides option sellers with an indication of premium earned per day. An option with a premium of 1 and a theta of .25 will lose .25 in value per day and be worth .75 (1−.25) one day

later. Therefore, option buyers have a negative theta position because time works against them, and option sellers have a positive
theta position because time works in their favor.

Volatility

Another key factor in the pricing of options is volatility. Premiums
for calls and puts will increase as volatility in the underlying
market increases. They decrease as volatility lessens. The magnitude of volatility's effect on premium value depends on the amount
by which the option is in- or out-of-the-money.

Volatility has a more pronounced effect on premium value when
there is more time to expiration. Time provides a greater opportunity for volatility to influence the probability of the option moving
in-the-money and thus becoming profitable to exercise before expiration.

The standard deviation of return, or volatility, is used to measure risk. Two types of volatility concern the options trader: historical and implied volatility.

Historical Volatility: The most easily understood type of volatility
is historical. Historical volatility is an annualized measure of how
active a market has been over a period. It is calculated from the
movement of the underlying market price over a specified period.
The shorter the time period, the more emphasis that is placed on
recent price action. Common periods are 10, 30, and 60 days, but
any time frame can be used to calculate historical volatility.

Implied Volatility: The second type of volatility that the options
trader should be aware of is implied volatility. Implied volatility
represents a forecast of future price ranges. It has an advantage
over historically based estimates of market volatility. Historical
projections are necessarily backward-looking: to use them as a
forecast, one must assume that future price behavior will resemble
past behavior. Implied volatility, in contrast, is forward-looking by
design. It can be calculated indirectly by solving for volatility
using the known inputs to the model.

Numerous software packages allow traders to calculate implied
and historical volatility. Most brokerage houses also provide daily
volatility information.

Vega: The first mathematical derivative of the Black-Scholes model with respect to volatility is *vega*. It measures the expected change in an option's premium given a 1 percent change in the implied volatility of that option. For example, assuming an implied volatility of 15 percent and a vega of $25, if implied volatility increases by 1 percent to 16 percent, the option trader's position would increase in value by $25. If implied volatility decreases by 1 percent to 14 percent, the position would decrease in value by $25.

Risk-Free Interest Rate

The risk-free interest rate is generally understood to be the current rate of 90-day Treasury bills. These instruments are considered risk-free because they are backed by the full faith and credit of the U.S. government (see Chapter 4).

Higher interest rates imply slightly higher option premiums, while lower rates imply lower premiums. To understand why, consider an option as a substitute for an equivalent position in the underlying instrument. Since the purchase of stock requires an immediate cash outlay, an increase in interest rates will make call options on stock more desirable. By purchasing a call instead of a stock, on margin—that is, borrowing from the broker to purchase the stock—an investor can avoid the interest charges sometimes associated with carrying a stock position on margin. For example, the purchase of 100 shares of XYZ stock at $50 per share requires an immediate cash outlay of $2,500. However, the purchase of 1 XYZ call enabling the buyer to control the same 100 shares of stock may require an outlay of only $500. The remaining $2,000 can be invested in an interest-bearing instrument. In contrast, higher interest rates will make puts *less* desirable. By selling the stock short, an investor will earn the higher interest rate on the proceeds received from the stock sale.

Cash Dividends

Cash dividends can be especially important to the seller of an option. Option buyers discount (to varying degrees) the option premium by the amount of the upcoming cash dividend. Cash dividends tend to lower call option premiums, because the stock's price will be reduced by the dividend amount and the option buyer does not receive cash dividends. The larger the dividend, the greater the discount on the price of the call option.

The interplay of all these determinants can be quite complex. While a rising stock price should increase call premiums, decreasing time to expiration or volatility may drive call premiums lower. In other words, the buyer of an out-of-the-money call option may lose money even though the underlying market has risen, if time has eroded the value of the call or volatility has decreased.

SELECTION OF THE EXERCISE PRICE: ELEMENTARY STRATEGIES

The options trader has a great deal of choice. For example, with at least four different expiration months, each having 10 or more exercise prices available for both calls and puts, it is not unusual for an options trader to be faced with as many as 80 different options contracts. If we eliminate the inactively traded contracts, the choices are fewer, yet still extensive. With so many choices available, an options trader needs some logical method to decide which options actually represent profit opportunities. Which should the trader buy? Which should he or she sell? Which should be avoided altogether?

In theory, the choice of whether to buy (go long) or sell (go short) options depends on the relative prices in the marketplace. If options are "cheap," it makes sense to buy options. If options are "expensive," it makes sense to sell options. (In practice, the choice is a question of risk versus reward. Recall that option buyers trade with limited risk; uncovered option sellers trade with unlimited risk. Thus, the amount of risk the trader is willing to take will be a factor in determining whether the trader is a buyer or seller of options.)

The following sample investment strategies will illustrate some of these possibilities.

STRATEGY: BUY AT-THE-MONEY CALL

Example:	Buy 1 XYZ $20.00 call @ $1.00
XYZ Stock Price:	$20.00 per share
Maximum Risk:	$1.00 per share or $100.00 per contract
Maximum Profit:	Unlimited on the upside
Breakeven Price:	$21.00

Call buying is the simplest form of options investment, so it is the strategy most frequently used by the individual investor. The main attraction is leverage. One could potentially realize large percentage profits from only a modest rise in prices. The success of this strategy depends not only on the investor's ability to be right about the direction of the underlying market, but also on the magnitude and timing of the move.

Options strategies can be tailored to provide varying degrees of potential reward and risk in most market environments. For example, an out-of-the-money option generally offers both larger potential reward and larger potential risk than does the purchase of an at- or in-the-money call. Many option buyers tend to select the out-of-the-money option merely because it is cheaper. But as previously mentioned, absolute dollar price should in no way be the deciding factor. The out-of-the-money option requires a bigger move in the underlying market in order to be profitable. However, if this move is realized, the out-of-the-money option will provide the largest reward. (Your analysis should also consider the other factors that affect an option's value, namely, time and volatility.)

STRATEGY: OUT-OF-THE-MONEY COVERED CALL WRITE

Example:	Buy 100 shares XYZ stock @ $20.00
	Sell 1 XYZ $22.00 call @ $.50
Maximum Risk:	Unlimited on downside
Maximum Profit:	$2.50 per share or $250.00 per covered call
Breakeven Price:	$19.50

Covered call writing (selling) is a conservative strategy whereby the call writer owns the underlying instrument. (This is in contrast to the naked call writer, who trades with unlimited risk.) This strategy is commonly used in the stock market in order to maximize yield and generate some downside protection.

For example, a stockholder who writes (sells) a covered call is selling the buyer of the call option the right to buy shares of the stock the writer owns. If the stock moves sideways, the buyer will forfeit the right to exercise, the option will expire worthless, and the covered call writer will keep the stock and the premium, increasing his or her total yield.

FOLLOW-UP ACTION

Depending upon the movement in the underlying instrument, the covered call writer may take one of several follow-up actions.

When the underlying stock increases in price, the writer could "roll up" the calls by buying back the original calls and selling the same number of calls at a higher exercise price. The drawback with rolling up is that the writer incurs a debit, thereby raising the breakeven point and exposing the writer to a potential loss should the stock price retreat.

When the underlying stock declines in price, the writer generally "rolls down" the calls by buying back the original calls (presumably at a profit, since the underlying stock has declined) and selling the same number of calls with a lower exercise price.

As expiration approaches and the time value dissipates from a short call, the writer may "roll out" the calls by buying back the original calls and selling the same number of longer-term calls with the same exercise price. Rolling out generates a positive cash flow, so it simultaneously increases the writer's maximum profit potential and lowers the breakeven point.

Out-of-the-money call options offer the greatest upside participation in the movement of the underlying instrument. Conversely, because the seller of an in-the-money option receives a higher premium, this premium will offer the greatest protection against a decline in the value of the underlying instrument. Of course, depending upon the magnitude of the price decline, the protection offered by this strategy is limited.

STRATEGY: BUY OUT-OF-THE-MONEY PUT

Example:	Buy 1 XYZ $18.00 put @ $.50
XYZ Stock Price:	$20.00 per share
Maximum Risk:	$.50 per share or $50.00 per contract
Maximum Profit:	Unlimited on downside
Breakeven Price:	$17.50

Option traders often use the strategy of buying puts when they expect a price decline and/or rising volatility in an underlying market. Similar to the out-of-the-money call, the out-of-the-money put offers the trader both higher potential reward and higher potential risk than does the in-the-money put. (Recall that the risk of options buyers is limited to the premium paid.) If the underlying market drops substantially, the leverage from having purchased a cheaper put will be greater. However, should the underlying market decline only moderately in price, the in-the-money put will often prove to be the better choice.

STRATEGY: MARRIED OUT-OF-THE-MONEY PUT

Example:	Buy 100 shares XYZ stock @ $20.00
	Buy 1 XYZ $18.00 put @ $.50
Maximum Risk:	$2.50 per share or $250.00 per contract
Maximum Profit:	Unlimited on upside
Breakeven Price:	$20.50

The "married put" is the simultaneous purchase of an underlying market and a put option. It works as essentially a kind of term insurance policy on that market.

For example, a common concern raised by a potential stock buyer is "I like the stock, but I'm not sure that now is the right time to buy." The decision to do nothing may in fact be the best strategy; however, if the stock advances quickly, the investor may feel he or she has missed the move and that the stock is now too expensive. The married put strategy offers a viable solution to the problem of indecision.

The range of exercise prices offers the hedger (the market participant who owns the underlying instrument) flexibility in structuring protection against adverse price moves and participation in favorable price moves. For example, the in-the-money option will provide better protection against falling prices than will the at-the-money or out-of-the-money options. However, by virtue of its relatively large premium, the in-the-money put entails a greater insurance cost and therefore the least amount of participation should prices rise.

STRATEGY: SELL OUT-OF-THE-MONEY PUT

Example:	Sell 1 $19.00 put @ $.75
XYZ Stock Price:	$20.00 per share
Maximum Risk:	Unlimited on the downside

Maximum Profit:	$.75 per share or $75.00 per contract
Breakeven Price:	$18.25

The profit/loss profile of a put seller is the mirror image of the profile for the put buyer. Since the buyer of a put stands to profit if the underlying market drops in price, then the seller of a put will make money if the underlying market rises in price.

In return for assuming the obligation to buy the underlying instrument at the exercise price, the put seller receives a premium payment. This premium is the seller's maximum profit. It is earned if the underlying market remains above the exercise price and the put expires worthless.

The more aggressive trader may sell an in-the-money put in order to collect a larger premium. However, increased profit potential increases risk, and the in-the-money put seller will lose money more quickly than the trader who initially sold an out-of-the-money put.

Put selling is also a strategy used by stock buyers in place of a limit order (at a price below the current market price) as a method of attempting to accumulate a stock position at prices lower than today's market price. If the put buyer exercises the put, the put seller is obligated to buy the stock (at the exercise price less the premium received). Should the put expire worthless, the seller will have at least collected the premium.

COMBINATION STRATEGIES

The following strategies are more advanced, in that they involve more than one option position. All demonstrate the flexibility of options and can be used in a variety of market environments.

Strategy: Short Fence

Example:	Buy 100 shares XYZ stock @ $20.00
	Buy 1 XYZ $18.00 put @ $.50
	Sell 1 XYZ $22.00 call @ $.50
Maximum Risk:	$2.00 per share or $200.00 per contract
Maximum Profit:	$2.00 per share or $200.00 per contract
Breakeven Price:	$20.00

A strategy commonly referred to as a *fence* is particularly attractive to the hedger when premiums are "expensive" and volatility is expected to be steady to lower. The fence uses a short option position to subsidize the cost of purchasing an option, thereby reducing hedging costs. The trade-off is limited participation in favorable price moves.

Specifically, a short fence involves buying a put and selling a call, together with a long position in the underlying market. A long fence involves buying a call and selling a put, together with a short position in the underlying market.

Strategy: Long Straddle

Example:	Buy 1 $20.00 call @ $1.00
	Buy 1 $20.00 put @ $1.00
Stock Price:	$20.00 per share
Maximum Risk:	$2.00 per share or $200.00 per straddle
Maximum Profit:	Unlimited in either direction
Breakeven Price:	$22.00 and $18.00

At times, traders strongly anticipate that a particular market is about to make a substantial price move but are uncertain in which direction this move will occur. A *long straddle* is considered a long volatility trade because the trader earns profits when the market moves dramatically in either direction, and incurs losses in stable markets. The trade involves simultaneously buying an at-the-money put *and* call with the same expiration date. When the price of the underlying market rises, the long call increases in value, and when the price of the market falls, the value of the long put increases.

Long straddles are popular trades before industry meetings or before the release of new trade information—events that will likely have a significant impact on the market. Bear in mind, though, that the profitability of this strategy is tempered by the premiums that the buyer must pay.

When option premiums are high relative to an investor's expectations for price and volatility, *short straddles* become attractive. A short straddle is considered a short volatility trade because the trader earns profits when the market trends quietly sideways. Since the trade involves selling both an at-the-money put *and* call with the same expiration date, the short straddle may generate a large time value premium to the seller. Nevertheless, profits are

limited to the premiums collected, while risk is unlimited if volatility causes the market to move beyond the breakeven level (the
sum of call and put premiums). Recall that for this reason, options
sellers must post margin.

Strategy: Bull Call Spread

Example:	Buy 1 $20.00 call @ $1.00
	Sell 1 $22.00 call @ $.50
XYZ Stock Price:	$20.00
Maximum Risk:	$.50 (the initial net debit)
Maximum Profit:	$1.50 (the difference between exercise prices and the initial net debit)
Breakeven Price:	$20.50

An option spread is a combination of two or more options positions. Option-spreading strategies have two purposes. First, option
spreads may offer better profit potential than outright purchases
or sales of options. Second, many option spreads offer the ability to
define maximum risk on a given trade.

Bull and bear spreads, also known as vertical spreads, are
strategies used to take advantage of directional moves in the
underlying instrument. A bull spread is created by purchasing a
call (put) and selling another call (put) with a higher exercise
price. Typically, the expiration date is the same for both options.
The spread is bullish because a rise in the price of the market for
the underlying instrument will theoretically increase the value of
the spread.

A bear spread is created by purchasing a call (put) and selling
another call (put) with a lower exercise price. The expiration date
is the same for both options. The spread is bearish because a
decline in the price of the market for the underlying instrument
will theoretically increase the value of the spread.

Bull call spreads and bear put spreads are executed for a debit
that is the maximum potential loss. The maximum profit is the
difference between the exercise prices and the initial debit.

Bear call spreads and bull put spreads are executed for a credit
that is the maximum potential profit. The maximum loss is the
difference between the exercise prices and the initial credit.

Other spread strategies take advantage of flat markets. These are commonly known as horizontal, calendar, or time spreads. The most common type of horizontal spread involves buying a call (put) and selling a call (put) with the same exercise price and different expirations. When the long-term option is purchased and the short-term option is sold, the trader is long (initiated for a debit) the spread—that is, a net premium is paid. When the short-term option is purchased and the long-term option is sold, the trader is said to be short (initiated for a credit) the spread—that is, a net premium is received. Unlike the value of a vertical spread, where all options expire at the same time, the value of a time spread depends not only on movement in the underlying market, but also on the trader's expectations about future movement as reflected in implied volatility.

A Special Situation

Exchange-traded futures contracts are subject to daily price limits. For example, gasoline futures trading comes to a halt when prices rise (limit up) or fall (limit down) by $.02 in one day, the maximum allowable price movement. However, most options on futures contracts will continue to trade. This feature allows a trader to close out a losing futures position or add to a winning one by using options.

Here's how it works. Suppose you are long May gasoline futures and gasoline falls the maximum daily limit to $.64. Also assume that you don't want to risk that gasoline will move limit down again tomorrow. You would like to close out your long futures position but cannot sell because the futures market has reached its limit.

At first you may decide that the situation is hopeless and there is nothing to do but wait and keep your fingers crossed. But if a market is limit down for some extended period, the limit will be increased subject to individual exchange regulations. Thus, if the market for gasoline futures was limit down on the third consecutive day, the limit would be expanded to $.03, with no relief in sight.

Why not use options? You could buy a $.64 May gasoline put option for a premium of, say, $.03. Then you could exercise the put option and go short the May gasoline futures contract at $.64, and use the position to offset your long futures position. (While this approach may offer the futures trader a way out of a futures position, it may be costly, and a trader should compare premium versus risk.)

CONCLUSION

Options provide speculators and hedgers with the broadest possible range of opportunities for trading and risk management. Calls represent options to buy, while puts represent options to sell the underlying instrument. A long call position offers participation (protection) in a market characterized by rising prices and increasing volatility, while a long put offers participation (protection) in a market characterized by falling prices and increasing volatility. Both strategies are established at a fixed cost, offering limited risk and unlimited profit opportunity.

Selling put and call options generates income when prices are neutral and volatility is decreasing. Furthermore, puts can be sold in place of using a limit order to buy stock below the market. Covered call writing increases the total yield and provides limited downside protection.

The versatility of options is clearly demonstrated by the many combination strategies available. These enable the investor to tailor an investment to satisfy his or her profit objectives and tolerance for risk.

Remember, while options offer numerous opportunities for both profits and protection, these opportunities do not come without risk. Depending on the strategies employed, this risk can be significant. Before trading options, you should discuss your investment objectives and risk tolerance with an investment professional to determine whether options are suitable for you.

10 PRINCIPLES TO ENHANCE YOUR SUCCESS
IN OPTIONS TRADING

1. Seek out a broker who is knowledgeable in options.
2. Be prepared to lose your entire investment.
3. Set a realistic profit objective, and stick with it.
4. Be aware of the risk/reward characteristics of naked (or uncovered) options.
5. When selling options, be alert to the possibility that the buyer could assign an option to someone else.
6. Before executing a multisided options strategy, consider commissions.
7. When executing a combination strategy, execute the entire position at once; don't leg into the position.
8. In general, when selling options, sell near-term options.
9. In general, when buying options, buy deferred options.
10. Timing is everything.

7

ALL THAT GLITTERS
OPPORTUNITY FOR GAIN IN GOLD AND SILVER

Ira U. Cobleigh

"THE MOST FINELY SPUN THEORIES ON THE STUPIDITY OF THE gold standard, and all the clever satires on mankind's frenetic digging for the yellow metal, and all the ingenious schemes for creating a goldless money will never change the truly remarkable fact that, for thousands of years, men have continued to regard gold as the commodity of highest and surest worth and as the most secure anchor of wealth." These words by William Röpke in *Economics of a Free Society* set the stage well for a chapter on precious metals.

This chapter reviews the merits of gold as a haven for investment; supply and demand factors; and the recent trend of gold prices, which suggests that another powerful forward move in gold may occur in 1991–1992. If such a surge is in the offing, investors will do well to start building a shopping list soon.

GOLD

For years the American public was kept deliberately uninformed about gold. From January 1, 1934, to January 1, 1975, it was illegal for American citizens to own, or trade in, gold, except for jewelry, industrial and ornamental use, and coins of numismatic value minted before 1934.

During the period from 1934 to August 15, 1971, the gold price was stabilized at $35 an ounce by the U.S. Treasury. Paper dollars could be presented to the U.S. Treasury for an ounce of gold. But individuals were not permitted to make such an exchange—only central banks, and governments in settlement of international trade balances.

On August 15, 1971, President Nixon closed the gold window, and the dollar was no longer convertible under any terms. A free market developed, and gold moved up in the next two years from $35 to around $45 per ounce. This started a long upswing in the metal, which carried it to fantastic heights: $850 an ounce for gold on January 20, 1980 (and $48 an ounce for silver).

The huge speculative profits gleaned by perceptive "gold bugs" in that era sparked a broad interest in gold for gain. People still remember the swift fortunes made in gold during 1979–1980. Today many believe another gold boom lies ahead.

GOLD THROUGHOUT HISTORY

What is so wonderful about gold that it has been humankind's most cherished portable asset for over 6,000 years? First, gold is virtually indestructible. Ornaments placed in Egyptian tombs in 2500 B.C. were still in perfect condition when discovered by archaeologists in the 1920s. Gold coins recovered from sunken ships after 300 years glistened as though freshly minted.

Gold also can be conveniently stored and carried. It is impervious to rust and the elements. It is malleable, ductile, lustrous, ornamental. It is heat-resistant and an excellent conductor of electricity. Gold is also alleged to have therapeutic powers in lotions and baths.

Thus, when humans found gold, they found something special. The glitter of gold has proved eternally attractive. Gold's beauty and adaptability were early applied to personal adornments such as rings, bracelets, necklaces, chains, tiaras, earrings, and even gold wigs. Such golden ornamentation became the envied symbols of wealth and power in early societies.

Discovery of Gold

Sometime around 4000 B.C., farmers drawing water from the Nile noticed bits of yellow dust or an occasional yellow pebble in shallow water or on riverbanks. The dust they saw was gold, and those little pebbles were gold nuggets. The discovery of gold fascinated them and led to such an insatiable thirst for gold that men died for it and women were enslaved by it. Nations fought for it and became world powers by acquiring great gold stores through commerce, force, or fraud. Countries faded if they lost or dissipated their yellow treasure. Gold has exerted a pervasive influence on the course of history. It has come to represent elegance and quality in such phrases as *the Gold Cup*, *the Golden Age*, *the Golden Rule*, *gold records*, and *good as gold*.

Early in history gold became significant in the economy of nations. The potentates of Egypt, after gathering into their coffers the immediately accessible river-borne gold, sent out expeditions with labor forces (slaves) south into Nubia and Ophir to expose alluvial areas and to follow quartz veins down into the earth, to expand their hoards of gold. Early Egyptian governments controlled, regulated, and financed placer or shaft mining operators, or charged 10 percent royalties to individuals who panned for gold on their own account.

The search for gold spread from the Nile to the Zambezi, the Niger in Africa, the lower Euphrates, the Oxus flowing into the Black Sea (the Golden Fleece came from there), and, later on, the Pactolus in Asia Minor and the Guadalquivir in Spain (which supplied the Roman Empire).

On the other side of the world, the Chinese were working the Yangtze. Alluvial gold was washed down in streams from outcroppings of original quartz or granite formations in rock, which had been forced to the surface by repeated folding, cracking, and upthrusting of the earth's surface over millions of years.

Selection of Gold As Money

After 2500 B.C., trade between peoples in the Mideast and the Mediterranean began to expand as population became concentrated in large cities. Navigation and commerce grew. More advanced nations created enough wealth from agriculture, herding, or military conquest that they could afford foreign goods such as foods or luxuries. Merchants plied their trade from the gates of India to Mesopotamia and along the shores of the Mediterranean, marketing silks, spices, carpets, ivory, and more. They urgently needed a broadly acceptable medium of exchange. Barter was clumsy. It was unhandy to exchange, say, 100 bushels of wheat for an Oriental rug.

As a replacement for barter, and to provide a durable medium of exchange and a store of value, people used a variety of things as money: rocks, fish, shells, cattle, hides, ivory, grain, salt, beads, land, and women. Eventually they concluded that metals made the most practical money, and that gold was the best metal.

For over 3,500 years gold has been regarded as the basic monetary metal. Today over 42 percent of all the available gold in the world is kept as a reserve in the treasuries of central banks. The U.S. Treasury has the largest gold store in the world—261 million ounces (which it values at $42.22 an ounce).

No other commodity has been so widely accepted by people at all times, and in all nations, in settlement of debt or in exchange for goods or services.

The evolution of gold as currency was spread over hundreds of centuries. Around 3200 B.C. an Egyptian pharaoh, Menes, set an official value to 14-gram bars carrying his name. Then followed authorized Egyptian gold rings of standard weight. To King Croesus of Lydia belongs the credit of inventing the coin. In 550 B.C. he struck round coins shaped like lima beans from gold. These novel coins of uniform weight were honored throughout Asia Minor.

Minting of gold coins was soon copied by the Greeks. Cyrus the Persian started minting a coin, the daric, shortly after he had conquered Lydia and taken Croesus prisoner.

Alexander of Macedonia was avid for gold. His amazing conquests were due in part to his systematic confiscation of all visible gold from royal or government treasuries, from every nation he defeated. With these funds, he paid his troops, enriched his generals, and subsidized regional satraps.

Coinage expanded rapidly and led to a progression of famous gold coins: the aureus of Rome, the dinar of North Africa, Florentine florins, Venetian ducats, Spanish doubloons, British sover-

eigns, French napoleons, and American $5, $10, and $20 gold
pieces.

Gold has amply earned its reputation as the preferred monetary
metal.

THE GOLD SUPPLY

Gold has always been a scarce metal compared with iron, copper,
lead, zinc, and silver. It remains scarce, with only about 105,000
metric tons available above ground in the entire world. Yet it is the
best-preserved metal, with more than 90 percent of all the gold
ever surfaced available somewhere today—original or melted and
remelted.

Gold ore has been found on all six continents. First in Egypt and
mid-Africa, then the Black Sea area, Spain, Asia Minor, Mexico,
Russia, Australia, the United States, the Klondike, South Africa,
and Canada. The largest gold ore bodies in the world were located,
in the 19th century, in South Africa. Mines there today are the
largest and most important in the world. Each year, South Africa
supplies about 60 percent of the free world's newly mined gold.

The available supply of gold varies each year, depending on
several factors. These include the supply of newly mined gold, the
amount of gold recycled, and the portion of gold reserves that come
to market.

TABLE 7-1

WORLD GOLD PRODUCTION IN METRIC TONS

	1984	1985	1986	1987	1988
South Africa	683.3	673.3	640.0	615.0	615.0
Canada	86.0	90.0	107.5	120.0	138.5
United States	66.0	79.5	108.0	125.0	150.0
Australia	39.1	58.5	75.0	100.0	135.0
Papua New Guinea	18.7	31.3	36.1	42.0	48.0
Brazil	61.5	72.3	67.4	65.0	66.0
Other African countries	51.5	51.7	52.6	53.5	55.0
Philippines	34.3	37.2	39.9	43.0	46.0
Other countries	19.7	139.5	154.3	162.0	169.0
Total	1,060.1	1,233.3	1,280.8	1,325.5	1,422.5
Soviet bloc countries					350.0
China					200.0
Estimated world total					1,972.5

Newly Mined Gold

The most important factor affecting supply each year is the amount of newly mined gold. Table 7-1 breaks down world gold production by country.

As shown in Table 7-1, gold production (stimulated by an $850 an ounce price of gold reached in that year) has risen steadily since 1980. In the 1980s, gold has proved the most profitable metal to mine. Due to the superior profit margins, most of the capital devoted to mines worldwide has been concentrated on gold, rather than copper, lead, or silver mining. In 1988 there was a bulge in mined gold because of a stable price (around $400 an ounce) and advances in mine technology.

Traditionally, gold has been produced in four ways:

1. Panning by individuals (a tiresome process).
2. Placer mining, sluicing, or dredging gold from rivers or streams.
3. Shaft mining, using vertical shafts and entry from hillsides (adits).
4. Open-pit mining.

Panning was the method used at Sutters Mill, California (1849), and in the Klondike Gold Rush of 1898.

Shaft mining flourished in South Africa, where gold-bearing reefs of conglomerate ore, infused with a minute gold dust, spread out for miles around the present city of Johannesburg. No one recognized, in 1866, how fantastically rich and extensive this reef formation was. It did not lend itself to individual mining, as deep shaft mines were required, calling for large outlays of capital and large forces of manual labor. Soon groups of wealthy individuals, who had made fortunes earlier in diamonds, entered gold mining and formed substantial companies for that purpose.

Today a representative South African gold mine may cost $500 million before production, have a shaft two miles deep, and require an air-conditioning system that would serve the Empire State Building. Such a mine may produce a million ounces of gold a year at a cost of below $225 an ounce. Here shaft mining has become a science, and huge capital outlays are justified because of the ore capacity of deep mines and the level quality of ore surfaced.

Shaft mines are the major sources of gold production. Shaft

mines usually have a mill nearby to grind the tons of raw ore surfaced and convert it to ingot gold bars ready for the refiner. Mills are quite expensive and are usually located at or near the top of a shaft.

Open-pit mining has flourished in the past decade. It enables treatment of lower grades of ore in huge volume, and it eliminates the costly sinking of shafts and driving of adits. Bulldozers break out the ore, and it is trucked to a nearby storage area. New mining technology has favored open-pit mining. A bleaching process has eliminated the need to build a mill. In this process ore is gathered, crushed, and piled up on a solid paved surface. Then it is treated with a cyanide solution, which seeps through the crushed ore, extracting the gold from it and depositing the metal on the floor, where it is recovered. This bleaching can convert ore assaying as low as .06 ounces to the ton into commercial gold.

These leaching plants are low-cost compared with shaft mines, but they are tough on the environment. Pit mines leave huge, ugly scars on the earth's surface.

Recycling

A second major source of the annual gold supply is recycled gold. When jewelers fabricate rings, necklaces, brooches, and other items for the rich and fashionable, or redesign or update heirloom jewelry, they generate an amount of scrap metal, or sweepings, which they save and sell. This recycled metal contributes substantially to the gold supply. The volume soars in times of peak gold prices. In 1980, old gold trinkets were dug out of attics and sold at exciting prices. Other recycled gold comes from scrap resulting from production of electronic devices.

Recycling occurs in most countries, but especially in Italy, the world's leading maker of jewelry. In 1980, the peak year, recycling produced about 400 metric tons worldwide.

Reserves

In addition, gold becomes available when a portion of the reserves of gold (held mainly by central banks) changes hands. While all major nations hold stores of gold, a nation may decide to sell some of it, either because the price is attractive or to meet national needs. For example, the Soviet Union usually sells at least 300 tons a year to pay for the imported wheat it needs, or to make up for a shortfall in sales of crude oil. Some countries, including Peru and Brazil, have had to sell gold to make payments on their international debts.

Gold exchanged between central banks seldom reaches the market, but transfer is arranged by physically moving the gold from one vault to another. For example, the Federal Reserve Bank of New York has a maze of vaults below ground, many of which are rented out to various nations so they can store their gold conveniently.

TABLE 7-2

OFFICIAL GOLD RESERVES (1985)

Country	Amount (in Metric Tons)
United States	8,169.3
Canada	625.5
Japan	753.6
United Kingdom	2,545.8
West Germany	2,960.4
Italy	2,073.7
Portugal	628.9
Saudi Arabia	143.1
Libya	112.0
Brazil	96.4
Mexico	73.4
Philippines	46.0
Columbia	57.2
South Africa	150.5
Peru	60.7
Total	18,496.5
Total including Communist countries	29,501.0
International Monetary Fund	3,217.0
European Monetary Fund	2,665.9
Bank for International Settlements	204.3
Total World	35,588.2

Figures for official gold reserves have not been brought up to date, but Table 7-2 shows the totals supplied by the International Monetary Fund for 1985. The table is incomplete, as production figures for the Soviet Union and other Communist nations are not available.

Selling by Individuals

There is also considerable selling by millions of individuals, especially when gold prices are high. At such times, people may sell bracelets, rings, and other jewelry and ornamentation to refiners. There is no accurate tally of gold thus entering the market each year. It must have been 200 tons or more in 1980, when the price of gold hit $850 an ounce.

The Total Gold Supply

It may be assumed that gold coming to the market for use in 1991 will total around 1,950 tons. The most important source, however, is new gold mined.

Most of the refined gold circulated as currency or used for ornamentation or adornment is still above ground and available, even though much of it may have been melted or remelted over the past 6,000 years. A good estimate is that the available world supply of surfaced gold is now on the order of 105,000 metric tons. Gold remains scarce despite higher average gold prices than in any other century, and improved technology for finding and mining gold.

Each year witnesses significant additions to the gold supply by newly mined gold. Gold is never consumed but is stored in one form or another, and the slack is regularly taken up by investors and hoarders. It is the influence of individuals, tempered by worldwide economic conditions, that creates the historic volatility in the price of gold.

THE DEMAND FOR GOLD

Gold has served as, or represented, money for over 2,500 years. Thus, an abiding demand for gold, as the ultimate monetary reserve for central banks, is ever present. This is so much the case that over 40 percent of the stores of gold is held in the vaults of governments or central banks. Much of the new gold surfaced is applied to gold bullion bars, bullion, or gold coins. The bars may remain as inventory for commodity markets, but the coins wind up in the hands of individuals and are thus sequestered from the market for years in the vaults or mattresses of hoarders.

As shown in Table 7-3, the principal industrial demand for gold is for the fabrication of jewelry and in its manufacture through electroplating. The jewelry demand has been increasing worldwide, especially in new lighter-weight earrings, bracelets, and necklaces that use less gold and carry lower retail prices than traditional ornaments. Italy is the leading manufacturer of gold jewelry, accounting for 211 tons in 1987. Next are the United States with 94.4 tons and Turkey with 72.4 tons. Worldwide jewelry demand in 1987 was 1,138.2 tons.

The gold-minting figures are even less up to date and come from the Gold Institute in Washington, D.C. In 1985 Canada minted 1,911,776 ounces in gold coins, South Africa 1,103,418, and Iran 473,108. The world total in troy ounces was 4,228,938 (which converts into 130 tons).

Industrial uses for gold are steadily expanding. Gold is an excellent conductor of electricity, so it has wide application in electronics. Products using gold include microwave tubes, transistors, amplifiers, miniature circuitry, telephone contact points, and computers.

Other uses of gold are in cosmetic and liquor bottles adorned with gold banks, lettering designs, or coatings. In architecture, gold is used for roofing. Threads of gold are used in glass windows for efficient insulation in hot and cold weather. Gold shields are used on space missiles to insulate against heat radiation on re-entry.

Gold also has medical applications. It has long been used in dentistry. Increasingly it is added to medicine in baths, lotions, and pills.

TABLE 7-3

USES OF GOLD IN 1987

Use	Amount (Tons)
Carat jewelry	1,138.0
Electronics	123.7
Dentistry	48.0
Other industrial and decorative	57.0
Medals and imitation coins	15.1
Official coins	206.3
Total	1,587.1

The demand shown in Table 7-3 is for the non-Communist world. Gold use in the Communist countries is difficult to determine accurately, and most of it is accumulated from regional supply, scrap and melted-down gold, and investor hoards. The Soviet Union is the major supplier to these countries. The Communist bloc has enough left over to deliver about 300 tons a year to the free world.

This compact review of the overall demand and supply picture leaves out one major factor: the supplies offered or acquired each year by private investors or hoarders around the world.

Residual stores of gold are particularly important in India (where dowries are customarily gold jewelry), China, and Arabic countries. In the West, France is the nation renowned for its citizens hoarding gold in cellars, mattresses, and other hiding places. Due to 18 currency devaluations in this century, French peasants insist that there is no store of value superior to gold. The French prefer gold coins; in India the savings are mainly in the form of jewelry.

Treasuries and financial institutions buy gold in bars of 400 ounces, usually imprinted with the name of a leading gold bullion house, such as Rothschild, Johnson, or Massey. Bars so identified are usually stored in vaults and are acceptable for delivery anywhere.

If an individual buys gold bars, it's usually in smaller sizes, 1 to 20 ounces, often stored at home or in a bank vault. If this gold is offered for sale at a dealer different from the original seller, it must be assayed (to be sure it hasn't been altered) at a modest charge. Gold coins, however, pass on inspection.

THE TRACK RECORD OF
GOLD AS AN INVESTMENT

Gold has a major and historic place in investment programs. Activity in gold has a great deal to do with its price; thus, a brief review of the gold market may be useful.

Gold has been traded for over 4,000 years and, nearly always, at a great premium to silver. During the 19th century gold was valued generally at 16 times the price of silver. This ratio has greatly changed over the years. For example, at one point in 1990, gold sold at $370 an ounce, and silver at $5.25—a ratio of about 66 to 1. The ratio is not particularly relevant, because gold represents the monetary reserve of last resort, while silver has become an industrial metal with broad usage in photography and electronics.

A major event in the gold price occurred in 1717, when Isaac Newton, then supervisor of the British Mint, set the price of an ounce of gold at £4, 4s, 111/2d. Amazingly, this official price remained unchanged for over 200 years, until England went off the gold standard in 1931.

In dollar terms, gold was officially priced at $20.67 an ounce from 1901 to 1933, then at $35.00 an ounce on January 1, 1934. It soared to an all-time high of $850 an ounce on January 20, 1980. Since then, gold has backed off to a low of $285 in 1985 and at the time of this writing was quoted at $410 an ounce.

This price volatility is significant. In 1980 the high prices prevailing led gold owners to have 400 tons of outmoded jewelry and industrial scrap melted down. Also, the $850 price in 1980 inspired the formation of hundreds of mining companies. Most current producers can surface the metal for $300 an ounce or less, so there is a generous profit in gold mining if you own rich claim acreage.

Complicating this picture, the political upheaval in Eastern Europe has had effects that extended to the gold market. In November and December 1989, East Germany, Poland, Czechoslovakia, and Hungary all renounced the Communist Party, rejected its leaders, and announced plans to create market-oriented economies in place of socialist central planning. The Soviet Union itself, in a meeting of its General Congress, decided to retain one-party Communist control and projected another Five-Year Plan, ignoring any market-based economy or a ruble convertible into gold. This last decision disappointed several economists who had predicted a gold-based ruble and Soviet borrowing by bond issues payable in gold. It was thought that such a program, strengthening the ruble, would cause the Soviet Union to stop selling its gold—and that the gold market would rise in response. In 1990 a division of the Soviet Union threatened to emerge, and there is now no talk about a gold-backed ruble.

Even though the Soviet Union will not take monetary steps, four satellite nations do plan to improve their currencies. To do that, they will need to build gold reserves. Furthermore, with inflation sure to rise in these nations, their citizens will clamor for gold as a safe haven and a store of value. Thus, future demand in Eastern Europe is definitely a bullish omen for gold in the long run.

The future of gold is hard to predict. But considering the $3.2 trillion national debt of the United States and huge annual budget deficits, inflation is likely to return and push gold back above $500 an ounce. That is likely to happen by the end of 1991, which would make gold an excellent investment.

FORMS OF GOLD OWNERSHIP

The ways to own gold are quite diverse. Gold may be held in the form of bars, coins, medallions, jewelry, gold in the ground in the form of mining stocks, and contracts and futures traded on commodities exchanges.

Coins are best acquired from established dealers, then patiently held. Futures are held on margin and are only for the informed, the bold, and the daring. In gold futures you can make a killing or lose your shirt in a day's trading! Jewelry collections are traditional, and investing in mining shares is expanding.

Gold Coins

Individuals shouldn't purchase gold bars (unless they are very wealthy), and speculation in futures on margin is too risky. Collecting gold coins, however, is an attractive and popular way to enter the gold market. Coins are conveniently stored and can be sold readily around the world—in Hong Kong, Zurich, London, Tokyo, New York, and other financial centers.

People of wealth, intelligence, and perception have been collecting gold coins for over 2,000 years. Great fortunes have been made in these, because choice items have constantly appreciated in value, often without reference to the price of gold. Millions of people owe their lives to gold coins, secretly stashed away, which enabled them to survive in times of famine, political upheaval, wars, or natural disasters; to escape persecution or death; or to flee to safer lands by buying off guards or border sentinels. Coins can easily be concealed in clothing.

The Greeks of Plato's day collected gold coins. The Roman popes, the Medicis, the Rothschilds, J. P. Morgan, Enrico Caruso, and

Joseph K. Lilly (former chairman of the drug company) all left coin collections worth many millions.

Gold coins are small enough that you can carry a fortune in coins on your person. Coins are also an invisible form of wealth. They can be acquired without any record of purchase, are not registered in any name (as are stocks and real estate), are instantly negotiable or transferable, and often escape taxation, since there is no record of their acquisition or existence.

Rare coins have increased spectacularly in value. A Panama Pacific $50 gold piece bought in 1915 could fetch $50,000 today. Uncirculated St. Gaudens $20 gold pieces might bring $4,000 or more. An 1862 $2½ gold piece could bring $10,000.

Gold coins are divided into two classes. These are bullion coins and numismatic coins.

Bullion Coins: Bullion issues are coins of very large circulation and selling close to the value of the gold that they contain. The most popular bullion coins are the American eagle, the Canadian maple leaf, the South African Krugerrand, and the Chinese panda. All contain one ounce of gold, and most retail at a premium of 3 to 7 percent over the value of their gold content. The Krugerrand sells at no premium because its resale in the United States has been discontinued. The South African government has issued 50 million of these, however, so there is an active worldwide market in them. Bullion coins are a sensible way to acquire gold, a readily marketable store of value.

Numismatic Coins: The collection of rare gold coins is greatly rewarding if you buy choice items at the right time. The characteristics to stress are the quality and scarcity of the coin. Small mintings can enhance values. Since minting began, over 1,300 different nations, governments, or states have issued gold species, and there are more than 26 billion coins.

Most of these coins have served as media of exchange. That is, they were readily acceptable in payment for goods or service or for settlement of debt.

Numismatic coins are coins valued for their condition, scarcity, or design. They are rated as to quality and condition. From best to worst, the ratings are proof (mirrorlike and shiny); uncirculated, showing no evidence of wear; almost uncirculated, extremely fine, and fine. An acceptable but badly worn coin is worth much less than one in a higher category.

Fineness, or purity, is expressed in karats. A karat equals $\frac{1}{24}$ part of pure gold in an alloy. Therefore, 24 karats is pure gold, or 1.000 fine. Because gold is a soft metal, most gold coins are alloyed with small amounts of copper. Most of the world's coins are .900 fine (about 22 karats).

The most popular coins are the British sovereign, the French napoleon (20 francs), Swiss francs, Mexican centenarios, Russian rubles, Florentine ducats, Dutch guilders, and U.S. $20 and $10 gold pieces.

For researching gold coins, a main source is Friedberg's *Gold Coins of the World*. This book covers many centuries and describes hundreds of coins from the early Persian dinar, Greek drachma, and Roman aureus to the ducat, issued over the years by 23 nations.

Getting Started with Coins: Don't look on your coin collection as a portfolio investment. Make it a pleasant pastime. Get catalogs and magazines on the subject, and by all means locate a respected dealer who can guide you and direct special values to your attention. Some choice coins you come upon may soar. The $3 gold piece of 1875 could fetch $30,000. It's about the size of a penny!

Almost everyone has about the house some gold piece, perhaps an heirloom. That's a good place to start. Get that coin valued, and perhaps buy more like it to start your collection. Some highly reputable coin merchants are Manfra Tordella & Brooks in New York, S. Sloat in Westport, Connecticut, and James Blanchard in New Orleans.

Gold Stocks

An alternative way to invest in gold is to buy it in the ground in the form of stock certificates in gold-mining companies. This is a tricky business. More people have been swindled by sellers of phony gold shares than any other type of equity. Of all the gold-mining companies incorporated, probably only one in two hundred ever becomes an actual producer. The biggest risks are in exploration companies that sell stock to raise capital for drilling acquired claims believed to be "ore-prone." Trouble is, many miners drill in the wrong places, find no ore or poor grades, and run out of money before they run into gold.

After prospecting and exploration comes development and, in due course (hopefully), production. Your best results will be with companies now in production or with a sufficient ore body to assure an ore supply for at least five years.

Gold mines are divided by their stages:

1. Prospecting.
2. Exploration and development.
3. Production.

The great risks occur among the first-stage companies.

Watch out if you're considering early-phase companies. They may be gross promotions run by crooks or they may run out of money long before they ever find a commercial-grade ore body. In general, seek out producing companies soundly financed with long life, high-grade ore bodies, low mining costs (below $225 an ounce), and little or no debt.

Homestake Mining Co.: Homestake Mining Co. (listed as HM on the New York Stock Exchange) is the oldest and best known of U.S. gold-mining companies. It majors in gold but has substantial interests as well in copper, lead, and zinc. Its original gold mine, at Lead, South Dakota, has been producing for 114 years.

In 1989 the South Dakota Homestake Mine surfaced 390,000 ounces of gold at an average cost of $298 per ounce. A newer mine in California, the McLoughlin, produced 284,000 ounces at $218 an ounce. The remaining production came from Round Mountain (25 percent owned by Homestake), El Hueso in Chile, and Homestake and Wood Gulch in Australia.

The major area for growth is in the company's 80 percent interest in Homestake of Australia, which in turn owns 50 percent of the fabulous Kalgoorlie Mines—open-pit and shaft—with annual production of 640,000 ounces (260,000 for Homestake).

Homestake is a traditional stock with 97.8 million shares outstanding. Its original mine is running low on ore, but other properties, particularly in Australia, are attractive. Homestake is market-sensitive and responds swiftly to changes in gold prices.

American Barrick Resources: American Barrick Resources (ABX on the NYSE) has rapidly expanded and now has varying interests in seven producing mines with production of 467,800 ounces in 1989. That year it earned $35.8 million on 128 million outstanding shares. The current dividend is $.15. The company has been shrewd in gold hedging, selling product in advance of production.

Barrick is in contention with Gold Standard Inc. over full ownership rights to the Mercur Mine (115,000-ounce production) in Utah.

The company's brightest prospects are in a mine in the Carlin Trend in Nevada. Reserve estimates here are 18 million ounces, and deeper drilling has revealed higher-grade ore. To finance a major expansion of its Carlin property, American Barrick has taken a 1.05-million-ounce gold loan.

ABX is a lively, leveraged gold exploration.

Echo Bay Mines, Ltd.: Echo Bay Mines (ECO on the American Stock Exchange) ranks among North America's largest producers. The company mined 615,000 ounces in 1989, plus one million ounces of silver.

Mines include Round Mountain (50 percent owned) (159,000 ounces in 1989) and McCoy Cove (214,000 ounces) in Nevada, as well as Borealis Robinson and Sunnyside Mines. Under development is the Kettle Mine in Washington. These produced a total of 717,000 ounces in 1989.

As of this writing, Echo shares were popular and were trading actively on AMEX. There are 98.8 million shares outstanding with an indicated dividend of $.35 a share. Revenues totaled $297 million in 1989, generating a net income of $.16 a share.

This is lively, responsive speculation with an active market following.

Newmont Gold Company: The Newmont Gold Co. (NGC on NYSE) is the "class" of North American producers, with over 1.4 million ounces in 1989 production. It has nine deposit areas in the famous Carlin Trend in Nevada. Some of the ore bodies are very rich, and an interval was reported in August 1989 averaging 0.768 ounces per ton.

Cash production costs for the first half of 1989 were $269 an ounce. Income for 1989 reached $1.13 per share in 1989.

Newmont has become the favorite "core" holding in gold for several mutual funds. It is favored because of its extensive ore bodies (over 17 million reserve ounces in its Carlin Trend properties), rewarding exploration program, and strong balance sheet.

Newmont is also rated high because of its management. Newmont Gold is 90 percent owned by Newmont Mining, a blue-chip company controlled by Consolidated Goldfield of South Africa.

The company's stock is relatively high-priced. Even so, if you were going to buy only one gold stock, Newmont Gold should be that one.

Western Mining Corp. Holdings, Ltd.: I am not particularly partial to Australian mining companies and favor participating there via Australian properties owned by American companies. However, one selection is a standout: Western Mining Corp. Holdings, Ltd. This is one of Australia's major integrated mining companies with a fiscal 1989 gold production of 813,000 ounces. It is also the third-largest nickel producer in the world and has a 44 percent interest in Alcoa of Australia.

The company's main gold mine is Olympic Dam of Roxbury Downs. It has a huge reserve deposit of 450 million tons, averaging 2.5 percent copper in addition to the contained gold.

In 1989 Western Mining grossed $1.2 billion (in Australian dollars, which were worth U.S. $.76) and earned $.53 a share. The stock trades on the London Stock Exchange and in American Depository Receipts in the United States.

FMC Gold: FMC Gold was spun off from Freeport-McMoran Inc. Almost 90 percent of the stock was retained by Freeport-McMoran Inc. In 1987 FMC Gold (FGL on NYSE) sold 11 percent of its shares publicly and also later spun off shares to Freeport-McMoran Inc. shareholders.

FMC Gold mines a rich gold/silver mine at Paradise Peak near Gabbs, Nevada. This is a remarkable deposit, producing in 1988 239,000 ounces of gold, along with 4.3 million ounces of silver. Amazingly, gold surfaced at Paradise Peak in 1989 cost only $92 an ounce. For 1989, net income was $.75 a share, with a $.05 dividend.

Combining Paradise Peak, the interest in Jerritt Canyon, and a third smaller property, FGL Gold, FMC Gold's production was 360,000 ounces in 1989. In addition, FMC Gold has 35 other properties under investigation.

AMAX Gold Inc.: AMAX Gold (AGI on NYSE) is a public company, 87 percent owned by AMAX Inc., a major resource company important in molybdenum, tungsten, aluminum, and gold.

AMAX Gold produced 256,000 ounces of gold in 1989, generating $121 million in total sales and $.55 a share. Properties include the Sleeper Mine and the Wind Mountain property in Nevada, the Hayden Hill joint venture in California, a 28.4 percent interest in the Waihi Gold Mine in New Zealand, and a 49.7 percent interest in Canamex Resources in Canada.

The Sleeper Mine is the major property with reserves—millable and heap leach—of over 2 million ounces of contained gold. Cash production cost at Sleeper in 1989 was about $109 an ounce, an unusually high profit margin.

Wind Mountain, the newest project, is located 75 miles northeast of Reno, Nevada. Here drilling and exploration point to later production at the rate of 40,000 ounces of gold and 300,000 ounces of silver. Sleeper, only 250 miles away, will process the concentrates.

In Canada the company has two operating mines: Bell Creek and Kremzar, both in Ontario.

AMAX Gold is a desirable equity. As of this writing, 60 million shares were outstanding. Strong, capable management and long-life high-grade reserves point to expanding earnings and dividends. This is an attractive, low-priced issue.

Corona Corp.: Corona Corp. has become one of the major low-cost producers of precious metals in North America. It is an amalgamation of five companies: Royex Gold, International Corona Resources, Lacana Mining, Mascot Gold, and Galveston Resources.

In August 1989, the Supreme Court of Canada awarded the very rich Page-William Mine to Corona (after an eight-year legal battle). Corona and its equal partner in the mine, Tech Corp., are obligated to pay about $210 million to Lac Minerals for past development costs. The Williams Mine produced 378,943 ounces of gold in 1988 and about 500,000 in 1989.

Corona also has various interests in nine other producing gold mines and several exploration companies.

Putting all these together, Corona generated production of 625,000 ounces in 1989 at a production cost of around $225 per ounce. The company's capitalization is $210 million in long-term debt, 6.7 million shares of preferred stock (in three series), and 150 million shares of Class A common stock, listed on the Toronto and American stock exchanges. There are also 8.7 million shares of Class B common stock (with 100 votes per share).

This is a rather complicated company but has gathered great reserves and a competent management. Its stock is a lively speculation with an animated market following. The company will no doubt continue making acquisitions. Corona should also be considered because of its Lacana Mining investment. This division is a major producer of silver in Mexico and the United States.

Placer Dome: With indicated output of 1.3 million ounces in 1990, Placer Dome is Canada's largest gold producer. Its gold properties are located in Canada, the United States, the South Pacific, and Chile. Placer Dome is also a significant producer of silver, copper, and molybdenum. Its principal producing mines are Dome, Campbell Mine (with some of the richest ore reserves in Canada), Kiena, Detour Lake, and Sigma in Canada; Bald Mountain and Cortez in Nevada; 51 percent of Kidstown and Big Bell in Australia; and Placer Pacific in New Guinea.

Placer Dome (PDG on NYSE) is outstanding in the amount of 234,685,725 shares and is actively traded not only in New York, but in Toronto and Philadelphia as well. The greatest drawback is the large number of shares, requiring a great volume in trading activity to move the issue.

PDG is a splendid company, capable of dividend increases as production and prices advance.

Agnico-Eagle Mines, Ltd.: A well-managed and growing Canadian company is Agnico-Eagle Mines, Ltd., directed from the start by Paul Penna, one of the ablest gold miners in Canada. Since 1970, Mr. Penna has brought this company along to major production in gold and silver. A recent merger with Dumagami, a nearby property, notably enhanced its stature.

The Agnico gold operations are at the Eagle and the Telbel mines at Joutel, Quebec, with a combined capacity of 90,000 ounces of gold annually. Silver mines, principally in the Cobalt district of Ontario, have a capacity of 1.2 million ounces a year and benefit, in ore treatment, from the company's own Penn Mill, with a capacity of 300 tons a day. Silver operations were shut down in 1990 due to the low price of the metal.

Agnico is an efficient producer and has been reducing its operating costs. At the 1989 year-end, gold reserves at Telbel were sufficient for 10 years' operation.

Recent developments have enlarged the company's horizons. The merger with Dumagami Mines (43 percent owned) was recently completed. Dumagami shareholders received 1.7 shares of Agnico Eagle common for each of their shares, and the combined companies can surface 200,000 ounces of gold per year. Dumagami is a low-cost mine with increasing reserves. Combined management of the companies will achieve notable economies.

There are also plans for a new exploration company, a joint venture with Hecla Mining Co. (a leading U.S. silver producer). The new company, Lucky Eagle Mines, Ltd., will explore attractive mineral properties in the United States and Canada.

Agnico has a strong cash position and no long-term debt, and it owns interests in several affiliated silver and gold properties. In 1989 the company racked up a $7 million capital gain from a real estate holding.

Agnico has 28,500,000 shares outstanding, which are actively traded on the Toronto Exchange and on NASDAQ in the United States (under the symbol AEAGF). Profits should improve in 1991 to $.50 a share.

South African Mines: South Africa generates 60 percent of the annual gold production in the free world. Several South African mines are massive, costing hundreds of millions of dollars before entering production with shafts two miles deep. The shares in the choicest of these companies have been rewarding investments for years. It has been the companies' policy to pay out a high percentage of annual profits in cash dividends. Thus, several issues have regularly returned 10 percent or more each year.

Most of these mines retain their investment quality. Some, however, have been running low on ore reserves and are not suggested for long-term holding.

These issues (in the form of American Depository Receipts, or ADRs) were popular with American investors (primarily because of their high yields) until 1987. Since then, American public opinion has turned against investments in South Africa (because of unfair treatment of the country's black majority). Many institutions and investment companies have sold their South African shares. Congress has eliminated an exemption from the 15 percent dividend withholding tax (levied by South Africa), and Congress in 1988 almost passed a law forbidding American investment in South African companies. As late as November 15, 1989, Merrill Lynch stopped all its trading in South African equities. In view of this rising disfavor, I do not advise commitments in this area.

However, such investments are not illegal, and with the recent political reforms under way at this writing, the admonishment of the world may be mitigated and normal trade relations resumed in the near future. Several issues still yield generous returns. The best are rich, long-life mines that, except for their geography, would get high-quality ratings. Thus, for investors willing to face the risks, including currency losses in the rand, the possibility of strikes by a labor force of 400,000 blacks (paid less than white workers), or sabotage of mines in a political uprising, there are a few dependable performers (still trading without restriction in London and Amsterdam).

The best single way to benefit from the choicest South African equities is found in shares of ASA Limited. This is a closed-end investment company, actively traded on NYSE (symbol ASA). It represents a $600 million portfolio with over 50 percent in diversified gold stocks of South African companies—low-cost producers with long lives, such as Dreifontein Consolidated, Kloof, and Western Deep Levels. ASA also has major holdings in DeBeers (diamonds), Rustenberg Platinum, Anglo-American Coal, and other companies. ·

There are 9.6 million shares of ASA outstanding (with a 25 rand par value). These shares had a book value in American dollars of $70.01 at the 1989 year-end. The dividend for 1989 was $3.50. In 1980 and 1981 (strong gold years), the dividend was $6.

Because of its diversified and quality holdings, ASA represents a prudent way to invest in South African companies. If you don't

mind the uncertainties, you might benefit by owning ASA. If gold
bullion moves up, this issue should respond well.

For investment in individual companies, here are some sug-
gestions:

- Dreifontein Consolidated Gold Mines, Ltd., is the largest South
  African gold-mining company, with annual production of 1.6
  million ounces a year. The cost of production in 1989 was $191
  per ounce. This is a splendid mine with rich reserves with substantial outlays annually to prolong mine life.
- Kloof Gold Mining, Ltd., has production around 900,000 ounces
  annually at costs of $190 per ounce. This is a low-cost, long-life,
  high-quality producer.
- Hartebeestfontein Gold Mining Co., Ltd., is another issue
  of merit.

There are some 35 South African mines to choose from. These
three would rank near the top among steady dividend payers.

There are several to avoid due to rising costs, depleted reserves,
or becoming mined out. Deep Durban and Rand East are very
high-cost producers and have been mined for decades. Avoid!
Libanon's cost is over $360 an ounce, Harmony's $375, and Western
Area's $446.

In concluding, the principal attraction of South African mining
stocks has been high yields. North American mines (in contrast
with African) pay meager dividends and tend to reinvest profits
for the enlargement of mines, or in quest of expanded reserves.
Thus, their major objective is not income but gain, achieved by cost
controls, richer ore bodies, compatible acquisitions, and, of course,
higher prices for gold.

The Future in Gold Stocks: The United States is likely to have
inflation of 6–10 percent by the end of 1991. Inflations have always
increased gold prices (and interest rates). Recessions may also
favor gold investments as stores of value. Between 1932 and 1936,
Homestake Mining shares rose from 65 to over 400!

I have not covered exploration companies because in most cases
they are too small and too risky. If you are a real crapshooter, take
a look at one of these: Goldex, Sudbury Mines, Coronado in Can-

ada, and a very long-shot penny issue in the United States, Stan West (with a $21 million loss carryforward!).

For those who prefer to delegate management custody and buy and sell decisions, there are several excellent gold mutual funds to choose from. These include Dreyfus, Franklin, International Investors, Bull & Bear, and Fidelity. Your broker can get you a prospectus on any of these.

These selections are mine. There are many other good stocks, but these are preferences. (For example, many investors like Pegasus, whereas I think it an erratic performer.) The issues to seek and to own are in low-cost, long-life mines.

The long-term prospects for gold are further brightened by conditions in the Soviet Union and the Soviet bloc countries. As they return to market economies, they will need currencies backed by gold.

SILVER

Silver has always been linked to gold, and for over 3,000 years both have been favored as monetary metals. For every million pounds of rock and soil making up the earth's crust, there are 50,000 pounds of iron, but only about 2 ounces of silver. Silver is 10 times as plentiful as gold in nature.

Silver is found mainly in two kinds of geological formations: in surface shallow deposits, uncombined with other metals, and in "affinity" deposits, where silver is blended in ores bearing other minerals as well (gold, copper, lead, zinc, nickel, or combinations of these). Silver ores are found extensively in Canada, the United States, Mexico, Central America, Peru, and Australia. Table 7-4 (page 180) shows the current supply of silver by country.

Silver was extracted from Asia Minor in the centuries of the pre-Christian era, and from Spain in the days of the Roman Empire. The richest deposits have usually occurred within 300 feet of the earth's surface. The classic American "strike" was the Comstock Lode in Virginia City, Nevada, where ore assaying $3,000 a ton in silver was mined a century ago. Most of these "pure" silver mines have now been worked out.

About 60 percent of all silver is mined and milled as a by-

product of producing other metals, mainly copper, lead, and zinc.
(This accounts for lower silver production during recessions, when
there is slackened demand for base metals.) In general, the farther
below the ground a mine shaft is driven, the scarcer and thinner
are the silver-bearing veins.

TABLE 7-4

WORLD SILVER SUPPLIES, 1988
(Excluding Communist-Dominated Countries)

Source	Amount (Millions of Ounces)
New Production	
Western Hemisphere	
United States	51.5
Canada	48.0
Mexico	70.0
Peru	61.5
Chile	16.0
Other countries	12.5
Total	259.5
Outside the Western Hemisphere	
Australia	33.0
Other countries	64.5
Total	97.5
Total new production	357.0
Secondary Sources of Supply	
From U.S. government	2.8
From stocks of foreign governments	4.7
From demonetized coin	2.0
From Indian stocks	14.5
Net imports (or exports) to Communist countries	6.9
Old scrap and other miscellaneous sources	81.3
Liquidation of (additions to) private bullion stocks	1.8
Total other supplies	104.6
Available for World Consumption	461.6

Courtesy of Handy & Harman.

On the consumption side, the United States is the world's largest consumer of silver. The free world's silver consumption is cataloged in Table 7-5. As the table shows, silver consumption in the free world totaled 461.6 million ounces in 1988.

TABLE 7-5

WORLD SILVER CONSUMPTION, 1988
(Excluding Communist-Dominated Countries)

User	Amount (Millions of Ounces)
Industrial Uses	
United States	120.1
Canada	10.9
Mexico	7.8
United Kingdom	22.3
France	22.5
West Germany	47.2
Italy	18.0
Japan	98.3
India	22.5
Other countries	62.0
Total industrial uses	431.6
Coinage	
United States	7.6
Canada	1.0
Australia	6.5
Mexico	2.0
Other countries	13.0
Total coinage	30.1
Total Consumption	461.7

Courtesy of Handy & Harman

Major industrial demands for silver are for the production of photographs, electronics, jewelry, and silverware.

For centuries silver was the number one monetary metal, and many nations used the same word for money and silver. Silver coins have served throughout the world as the most popular form of currency. Famous silver coins include the drachma of Greece, the denarius of Rome, the rupee of India, the tael of China, the taler of Austria, the shilling of Great Britain, and the dime, quarter, half-dollar, and dollar of the United States.

Since 1964 (when silver was $1.29 an ounce), the metal has soared in price. Minting of silver coins has declined, and coins of 90 percent silver no longer circulate. Silver coins have disappeared from circulation because they are worth many times their face value when melted down into bullion. Peak coin production was in 1965, when 320 million ounces of silver were minted into U.S. silver coins.

THE PRICE OF SILVER

Silver has at times been a fabulous speculation. It rose from an official price of $1.29 an ounce in 1964 to $48.00 an ounce in January 1980 (propelled by the heavy buying of the Hunt brothers in an endeavor to corner the market). The price fell back dramatically to below $5.00, and, as this was written, was $4.20.

Silver has customarily moved in the market parallel to gold. As mentioned earlier, the gold-to-silver ratio for centuries remained 16 to 1. More recently this ratio has spread to 78 to 1, with gold at $418 and silver at $5.30.

The important facts are that gold and silver are both scarce metals. Gold, however, is unique as a monetary metal and the last currency reserve for central banks.

FORMS OF SILVER OWNERSHIP

As in gold, investors or speculators in silver have several choices for silver ownership: bars and coins, silver futures contracts, or silver in the ground (represented by stock certificates of mining companies). I am not enthusiastic about coin collecting or about speculating on margin in silver futures contracts. However, if you know a little about each type of investment you can make a more informed decision.

Bars and Coins

Bars of certified grade come in 1,000, 100, or 10 troy ounces. The weight may be certified by reputable refiners such as Handy & Harman or Englehard. Bars are too cumbersome for convenient investment; they have to be stored in a vault or at home. A better way to hoard silver is in bags of silver coins with $1,000 face value (quarters or halves). These bags were worth $1,000 in 1965 but around $2,100 today. If this type of ownership interests you, get a separate silver broker.

Silver coins are of two groups: common-date coins minted in great quantities and widely circulated, and scarce coins that have numismatic value because of small issue, unique design, or artistic minting. Silver coins of Europe—drachmas, talers, Spanish pesos—are attractive if rare. In the United States the favorite coin is the Morgan silver dollar. These were struck by mints in Denver, Philadelphia, Carson City, New Orleans, and San Francisco. Depending on date, scarcity, and condition, these Morgans can fetch from $40 to $400. A rare year was 1878.

If coin collecting interests you, get a book on the subject, and subscribe to *Coin World* or the *Numismatist*.

Silver Futures
Ask your broker about silver futures. With as little as 10 percent down, you can control quite a large position. However, you can be wiped out in a trice if the market plummets and you get urgent calls for additional margin! Margin trading is for gamblers and plungers! It is not conducive to serene sleeping, although you can make a killing if you are informed and lucky in your timing.

Stock in Silver Companies
The best way to profit from the likely upward trend in silver is through diversified silver stocks. In 1979 Hecla, a leader in silver, topped all stocks on NYSE in profitability, rising over 900 percent from 4⅝ to 45. The following stocks are some that look promising.

Agnico-Eagle: Agnico-Eagle, a Canadian producer, was described among the gold stocks. It also is significant in silver, with properties in Cobalt, Ontario, that can surface 1.3 million ounces yearly. Agnico-Eagle is a good "cross play" in both silver and gold.

Asarco, Inc.: The premier nonferrous metal producer in America is Asarco, which surfaced over 9.3 million ounces of silver in 1988, along with 200,600 tons of copper, 76,700 tons of lead, and 107,000 tons of zinc. These figures exclude associated companies.

Silver is often a by-product of copper production. Copper was in strong demand at rising prices in 1989, so Asarco earned about

$5.50 a share that year. This level of profit is not likely to continue. Accordingly, silver output is likely to fall (as copper demand recedes), with a per-share net income of around $3.30 in 1991.

Asarco has associated interests in several American companies and 34 percent of Mexico Desarrollo Industria Minero, S.A., with 1988 output of silver reported at over 27 million ounces. Asarco has other interests—crushed stone and chemical operations—but remains the outstanding leader in silver.

There are over 42 million shares of common stock trading on NYSE under symbol AR, 25 percent owned by an Australian company, M.I.M. Holdings, Ltd. In 1988 the company bought back 759,000 shares in the open market.

Coeur d'Alene Mines: Coeur d'Alene Mines is a factor in silver and a producer of gold as well. It owns the Rochester Mine in Nevada, believed to be the leading primary silver producer in the United States.

The Rochester silver-and-gold mine, wholly owned since March 1988, is one of the lowest-cost producers. The mine yielded over 4 million ounces of silver in 1989.

Coeur, in a joint venture with Echo Bay Mines, Ltd., owns the Kensington gold property north of Juneau, Alaska. Development began in 1990.

The company's capital consists of over $62 million in long-term debt. (Of that, $50 million is in 6 percent debentures, due 2002, and convertible into common stock at $26.55 a share.) Almost 10 million shares of common stock are outstanding. CDA is a highly leveraged speculation, and it responds sensitively to changes in the silver price.

Callahan Mining Co.: Shares of Callahan Mining Co. trade on NYSE under the symbol CMN. The feature property is the Galena Mine in Idaho, operated under lease by Asarco, which receives 50 percent of the cash flow from mining activities. In 1988 over 3 million ounces of silver were sold. Also, CMN has a 5 percent share of the profits of the Coeur Mine, and an 82 percent interest in the Caladay silver property (now under exploration).

The company also owns the Roper gold mine in Michigan, which sold 43,387 ounces of gold in 1988. However, its ore reserves are running low.

A manufacturing division, Flexaust Co., makes lightweight flexible hose, ducts, and metal tubing for commercial and industrial use. Manufacturing generated 35 percent of revenues and all the company's profits in 1988. (The year showed a deficit of $.82 a share.)

A feature of CMN is its small long-term debt (only $101,000).

CMN is a confusing company, with its odd revenue mix and erratic earnings and dividends. But the shares move with the precious metals. I'm not enthusiastic about CMN, but it should be bought on a weak market and when it lags behind the other silver stocks.

Hecla Mining Co.: One of my favorites is Hecla Mining Co. When the commodity market is strong in silver, Hecla responds instantly. HL (NYSE symbol) has an avid speculative following.

Actually it is a fine call on both silver and gold. Hecla has developed an exceedingly rich gold mine, the Republic in Washington, with 526,700 tons of ore reserve grading 0.9 ounces to the ton.

Hecla's star silver mine is the Lucky Friday in Idaho, which delivered almost 1.8 million ounces in 1988. Its Escalante mine, also in Idaho, surfaced over 1.8 million ounces.

Hecla has, in addition, a 12½ percent interest in the Galena mine, 5 percent of the Coeur mine, and 28 percent of a small gold mine near Juneau, Alaska. There is also a kaolin property acquired from Cyprus Mines.

Unrelated to minerals, Hecla also owns the Kentucky Tennessee Clay mines, which process different kinds of ball clay used in ceramics and abrasives.

The company's long-term debt is in a unique issue: over $62 million of zero-coupon notes, maturing in 2004 at $201 million with a (remote) conversion into common stock. This issue is followed by 27 million shares of common stock, of which 20 percent is held by institutions. Hecla paid a dividend of $.05 in 1989. As with other companies reviewed here, investing in Hecla is essentially a bet on higher gold and silver prices.

Other Possibilities: Noranda, Inc., might be included as a recommended stock, because it is a large Canadian silver miner. But minerals and metals actually contributed only 17 percent to its

1988 revenues. Noranda is a major player in copper, lead, and zinc. Its 173.6 million shares are listed on the Toronto Exchange.

Cominco, Ltd., the huge metal company spun off from the Canadian Pacific Railway, also is a big producer of silver. But that is overshadowed by its vast output of zinc and lead. Cominco, Ltd., is listed on AMEX with 79 million shares outstanding.

United Keno is a seasoned silver-mining company. However, it is less attractive because its ore reserves are dwindling.

Sunshine Mining is a large silver property. I have not stressed it because of its rather uneven management and a long history of labor problems.

Handy & Harman is generally cited when silver shares are discussed. It is not a miner, however, but the leading refiner, processor, and fabricator of silver. The company regularly carries a large inventory in silver. Accordingly, when the silver price moves up, Handy & Harman responds. A renowned investor, Warren Buffett, controls 9.1 percent of the 14 million shares listed on NYSE under the symbol HNH.

Many other silver shares are traded, including some highly speculative ones on the Vancouver Exchange. However, the shares described here are in excellent representative companies. The big propellant in this industry is not so much a particular company as the price of silver. If silver moves back to $40 again, all of them will soar. So this has been a useful shopping list.

CONCLUSION

Gold can explode under conditions of economic uncertainty. It is predictable that gold will hit $800 again in this century!

Silver is propelled by different forces and historically has been an affinity metal. If gold goes up, so does silver. In 1989, silver (at $4.15) appears undervalued.

This chapter's subtitle uses the word *gain*. That is because your objective is price growth, not income. Silver and gold in bullion or coin pay no return, and most mining shares pay meager dividends. Hence, your main hope is a surge in price. If your timing is right, both metals can be fortune builders.

Four principal factors have historically created booms in gold: (1) inflation and currency devaluation, (2) excessive debt, (3) a desire to safeguard value and preserve purchasing power, and (4) wars, revolutions, or disasters, during which everyone searches for the safest financial havens.

Some of these conditions are present now. The U.S. government has the largest debt in its history ($3.2 trillion) and inflation at around 7 percent. Many nations have massive inflations: Poland, 500 percent; Brazil, 240 percent. Furthermore, warfare in Nicaragua, El Salvador, Liberia, Afghanistan, and Ethiopia and political revolutions in Poland, Czechoslovakia, and Hungary drive money into shelter. And that shelter is often gold.

8

... AND ALL THAT JAZZ

AN INTRODUCTION TO
LESS TRADITIONAL
INVESTMENT VEHICLES

Van W. Knox III

SOONER OR LATER, EVERY SERIOUS INVESTOR WILL GIVE AT least passing consideration to one or more of the less traditional investment vehicles available today—rare coins, commodities, fine art, antique furniture, any of a variety of limited partnerships, various derivative forms of life insurance, and collectibles ranging from baseball cards to prints to porcelain figurines.

Sometimes the investor may turn to these vehicles because of a sense of frustration with more conventional stocks and bonds. Or, possibly emboldened by past success in the stock and bond markets, the investor may be seeking out new fields to conquer and a faster-paced level of action. Possibly the interest may have been brought on by the blandishments of a smooth-talking sales representative.

In any case, there are many tempting examples of enormous financial gains achieved by canny or fortunate individuals who have multiplied their investments many times over in each of these fields. It seems as though new records are perpetually being established by the major auction houses here and abroad. A single rare coin has reportedly broken through the "million-dollar barrier," and a recent headline told of a chest of drawers that was sold for well over $10 million! In the area of commodities speculation, stories abound of traders doubling (or losing!) their entire stakes overnight while they slept.

Obviously, whole books have been devoted to each of these highly specialized fields of investing. It would be ludicrous for the same chapter to attempt to discuss the fine points of heating oil futures and the intricacies of the resale market for Erté prints. There is also the danger—although that is certainly not my purpose—of giving the false sense of security that a little superficial knowledge can impart, with potentially disastrous consequences.

Nonetheless, these other investment vehicles do exist, and there are many eager buyers and sellers looking for the opportunity to profit from them. This chapter therefore addresses the basic considerations underlying the most significant of these areas—what drives the prices, what some of the pitfalls are for investors, what to watch out for in general.

The alert reader will notice that if a single thread runs through the treatment of all of these investment vehicles, it is this: In any specialized field such as those we will be looking at, the odds are stacked even more strongly against the unwary individual investor than is the case in the traditional stock and bond markets. Regulation is less stringent than in the market for stocks and bonds, and indeed may not exist at all. To succeed here, the investor must expect to spend much more time and more effort ferreting out information, and needs to become much more of an expert in the specific field of his or her interest. Brokers and salespeople may be less knowledgeable; deception and fraud are not unknown.

These widely diverse areas for investment fall into three general areas—commodities, collectibles, and financial vehicles. Let's take a look at them one at a time.

COMMODITIES

The basic way to invest in commodities is by buying and selling *futures contracts.* A futures contract is an agreement in which the producer of a commodity item guarantees that he or she will deliver a specified quantity of a commodity item, of a standard quality, at a predetermined price, at a specified future time.

USES OF FUTURES CONTRACTS

There are two quite different—but equally legitimate—purposes for using futures contracts. The original purpose is hedging. In addition, investors may buy and sell these contracts as a form of speculation.

Hedging

Hedging is a method of insuring against deterioration in the price of a commodity. The practice of hedging developed in the agricultural arena. Before the advent of commodities futures, farmers could never be sure, when planting, that when the mature crops were ready for market many months later, prices for them would still be high enough that the farmers could recover their costs of farming and earn an adequate profit. The reason is that prices of all commodities, including crops, fluctuate in response to supply and demand. For example, the large supply of wheat resulting from a bountiful harvest would drive down the price of that commodity. Since farmers cannot determine the ultimate supply or demand when they are planting, they had to commit their time and financial resources to producing products they could not be sure they could sell at a reasonable price. Profit margins of commodities are normally quite thin, so even a small deterioration in prices could spell the difference between a successful season for the farmer and financial ruin.

By selling a futures contract on a crop before harvesting it, a farmer can lock in a predetermined selling price, regardless of the price for the product when the farmer actually delivers it. If prices deteriorate, the farmer will make up on the futures contract what is lost on the crop. In return for this security, of course, is the fact that if crop prices improve, the farmer will not be able to benefit from the higher prices. Instead, the farmer will lose on the futures contract whatever he or she gains on the price of the product. Thus, hedging protects the farmer from loss at the cost of limiting the farmer's potential gain.

From their origins in agriculture, commodities futures have spread into livestock, metals, petroleum products, wood, and—since the 1970s—into financial futures covering foreign exchange, interest rates, and stock indexes. Speculators can now even buy and sell *options* on futures contracts! (Options are explained in Chapter 6.)

Speculation

The second use of futures contracts is speculation. This refers to the purchase and sale of futures contracts solely in order to take advantage of changes in the prices of the underlying commodities themselves.

Advantages of Speculation in Commodities: The reason futures contracts are so appropriate as speculative vehicles is that they are traded on margin, and usually on extremely small margin. This gives the trader substantial leverage. For example, a single futures contract covering 50,000 pounds of cotton for delivery next December at 74.28 cents per pound has a nominal value of $37,140. Because this contract may require initial margin of just 10 percent, the speculator pays only $3,714 to "put on" this contract. If the price of cotton goes up just 3 cents, the value of the contract will rise from $37,140 to $38,640—a $1,500 profit, or over 40 percent on the speculator's investment of $3,714. A price movement of this magnitude can easily take place in a week or less, thus yielding the speculator an annualized return on investment of greater than 2,100 percent!

Note that the speculator is interested only in the futures contract itself, and has no intention whatsoever of taking actual delivery of 50,000 pounds of cotton. In fact, well over 90 percent of all futures contracts are closed out ahead of time by offsetting a long position (a contract you have bought) with a short one (a contract you have sold), or vice versa, including many contracts originally purchased or sold as hedging devices.

In addition to the enormous leverage available to the individual speculator in commodities futures, a second advantage lies in the fact that these investments have a very high degree of liquidity. Commodities are traded daily on several major exchanges in New York, Chicago, Kansas City, New Orleans, and Minneapolis. A trader wishing to open or close a position can do so virtually instantaneously.

Drawbacks of Speculation in Commodities: The biggest drawback to speculating in commodities futures lies in the exceedingly uncertain nature of the various commodity businesses themselves. In most cases, the primary forces governing supply and demand for the underlying commodities are totally beyond the control of

the speculator or the producer of the commodity. In the case of
stocks, you can invest in a company based upon your knowledge of
the excellence of its products and your confidence in the management's demonstrable skill in controlling the company's future.
However, no such possibilities exist in the commodities arena. The
direction of the price of wheat will be governed by myriad purely
external factors, including such virtually unknowable elements as
future weather conditions, not only in the growing areas here, but
also in countries that could be potential customers for *our* wheat if
their harvest is poor. Similarly, petroleum prices may reflect political tensions that spring up in the Middle East next month, new
discoveries of oil that have not yet occurred, and legislation regarding air pollution that has not yet been proposed in Congress.
The future value of a lumber contract may depend upon environ-
mentalists' concern over the status of a species of owl.

Because so many of the factors governing the prices of commodities are beyond the control of the owner of the futures contract,
many of the most successful speculators analyze the price action
itself, rather than attempting to understand and follow (and predict) all the fundamental forces that determine the future direction
of prices. The frantic pace of commodities trading and the multi-
plying effect of leverage upon the value of an individual's holdings
virtually mandate that an active commodities speculator remain
able to follow and analyze price movements as they occur, from one
moment to the next. A secondary requirement is that the market
participant establish and maintain a close relationship with a
broker who is in a position to rapidly and accurately execute
orders purchase or to sell the futures contracts.

PROFESSIONAL TRADERS

Given the time, money, and study needed to succeed in commodities speculation, many investors who are turned on by the idea, but
who have neither the time nor the dedication to devote to the game
themselves, may be tempted to participate in a managed futures
program. This involves hiring a professional trader to manage
their futures investments for them. The trader may manage the
investor's futures individually or as part of a pool of capital provided by other like-minded investors.

The SEC restricts participation in such accounts to investors
who can show that they have very substantial net worth, and who

are sophisticated enough to understand the considerable risks that such investments entail.

Normally, the trader's compensation involves not only a fee, but also a significant percentage of all profits generated (20 percent is not uncommon). Even the very best traders have periods in which they lose (their client's) money, sometimes very quickly. When the trader is hot, the investments can realize huge gains.

RISKS AND REWARDS OF COMMODITIES TRADING
Keep in mind that when you are sharing your profits (but not, of course, your losses) with a professional trader, you are reducing the return on your money by a substantial amount. This makes it considerably more difficult to come out ahead in the long run. Look at it this way: If you are playing roulette on a wheel with not one or two zeros (on which the house wins), but *ten* zeros, you may still win money if you are lucky enough. But how long can you fight those odds?

Still, there is no other investment activity that offers the exhilaration and sheer thrill of commodities trading. Fortunes can literally be made (or, regrettably, lost) overnight. Speculation in commodities is an extremely high-risk, high-reward activity best reserved for brave souls with deep pockets.

TYPES OF COMMODITIES TRADED
As of this writing, futures contracts are traded in the United States on the following commodities: gold, silver, platinum, palladium, copper, aluminum, crude oil, heating oil, unleaded gasoline, natural gas, cattle, hogs, frozen pork bellies, lumber, T-bills, 5- and 10-year T-notes, T-bonds, the Municipal Bond Index, 30-day interest rates, the S&P 500 Composite Index, the Major Market Index, the Value Line Index, wheat, corn, oats, soybeans, soybean oil, soybean meal, sugar, coffee, cocoa, cotton, and frozen orange juice. Futures are also traded on the foreign currencies of Britain, Canada, France, Germany, Japan, Switzerland, Australia, and on Eurodollars and European Currency Units.

A CLOSING THOUGHT ON COMMODITIES SPECULATION
According to a saying in the trading pits of the Chicago Board of Trade, there is no such thing as an old, successful commodities trader.

COLLECTIBLES

Since the beginning of recorded history, people have valued the enjoyment of assembling collections of things, as well as the satisfaction of possessing the physical collections themselves. What constitutes a collectible item is limited only by the imagination of the individual doing the collecting. People collect everything from autographs to old master paintings to classical audio recordings and the glass insulators on electric poles. Stamps and coins are probably the most widely collected items today, but hobbyists also continue with undiminished enthusiasm to assemble their collections of butterflies, model railroad cars, Beleek china, heirloom dolls, and antique weaponry.

Besides the purely personal satisfaction, another impetus to pursuing a collecting hobby is the possible profit. Whether describing antique furniture, Beatles memorabilia, or classic automobiles, the news media routinely report astonishing sums of money paid at auction or in private sales for the best examples of these collectibles.

ATTRACTIVENESS OF AN ITEM

Basically, three considerations add to the attractiveness of any specific item in a collection, whether taking the profit motive into consideration or simply reflecting the personal point of view of the collector. These are quality, rarity, and completeness. The first two refer both to the individual items and to the collection itself; the primary focus of the third item is on the collection.

Quality

The concept of the quality of a collectible item is easy to understand but often quite difficult to assess. Therefore, assessing quality represents a potentially dangerous obstacle to the collector in terms of assigning an appropriate value (represented by the selling price). Few will disagree that even the most famous artists produce paintings of differing quality, but it is exceedingly difficult to decide how much more a good Monet is worth than a mediocre one.

Actually, two components make up the quality of a collectible item. These may be called workmanship (for want of a better name) and condition. Workmanship refers to the quality that has gone *into* a particular piece, while condition refers to the current state of a piece since it was first created.

Clearly, both directly affect the quality of the piece, and will thus affect its value. In the case of certain durable collectibles (for example, Chinese porcelain), workmanship is generally a much more important variable. With other kinds of collectibles (coins are a good example), the condition is a much more important factor in determining the quality of the individual example.

The workmanship component of quality is highly subjective, in that it not only refers to the quality of execution of a piece, but also to such virtual intangibles as composition, design, and inherent aesthetic beauty. Expert opinion can and often will differ quite markedly, since questions of personal taste are involved.

Condition, on the other hand, can be determined with considerably more objectivity. In some fields (again, coins offer the best example), standards of condition have been developed and can be applied with some rigidity. However, the collector still must be fully aware of the extent to which so-called standards may be subject to individual interpretation and/or manipulation. Just as one example, in the field of rare coins, there are currently three different independent grading organizations, one of which is recognized and acknowledged to assign ratings one or two categories higher than do the other two. For the uninitiated collector, what may appear to be an excellent price for a certified MS-65 coin may in fact prove to be a rip-off of the first magnitude, if the "wrong" organization has graded the coin.

Rarity

Another consideration affecting the value of a collectible is its rarity. Stamps proved an excellent example of how the rarity of a particular item can markedly affect its value; there may be little else to distinguish one particular issue from another.

Sources of Rarity: Rarity may result from either of two situations: a small number of the items originally created in the first place or a limited number of examples known to exist currently. Oil paintings, obviously, are individually created and are thus rare by definition. There will only ever be one of Van Gogh's *Irises*. The

Fabergé jeweled eggs so prized by the late collector Malcolm Forbes were individual masterpieces as well, with no two alike.

Stamps, coins, political campaign buttons, and baseball cards are examples of collectibles where the original number of pieces issued may have been considerable, but so few specimens are currently known to exist that a significant part of their value stems from that rarity. These cases have been known to backfire, however, when a previously unknown supply of the item in question comes unexpectedly to light. This has occurred in recent years with certain mintages of coins that have been "rediscovered" in federal bank vaults and returned to circulation among collectors, thus destroying their rarity and sharply reducing their value virtually overnight.

A special note is in order regarding art prints, sculptures, medallions, and other forms of collectible art that are issued (and heavily advertised) in "limited-edition" form. A print, which is a lithographic reproduction of an original artwork, is basically reproducible in *un*limited form. "Limited editions" of the same work may be made from time to time by unscrupulous promoters using the same plates, generating what is in reality a supply of the product that is limited only by the demand their marketing can create. True limited editions are those for which the plates are destroyed at the conclusion of a single production run of a specified number of impressions. This is also true of medallions, figurines, or any other piece that is cast, struck, molded, or otherwise designed to be produced in more than one copy.

Also, keep in mind that *limited* is a relative term. A print edition that is limited to 200 copies is clearly more limited than a limited edition of 5,000. On the other hand, the effect of rarity on the value of a collectible is also relative to the demand for it. Even though a print from an edition of 200 is clearly rarer than another print from a larger edition, other factors may have created greater demand for the second item, so that it is less widely available. In that case, it would be more valuable; it will command a higher price.

Enhancing Rarity Value: Marketers may attempt, especially in the issuance of limited-edition art prints, to increase the desirability of individual copies by making them in some way unique. Generally, there are two ways of accomplishing this. First, specimens may be individually hand-signed by the original artist. This is always undertaken in pencil, in order to prove that a work has been individually signed. Note, however, that there is no real guarantee that the signature is actually that of the artist. While this is not likely to be a problem when a work is purchased from the original issuer, there is no way to be sure when purchasing a particular piece in the secondary market.

The second method of enhancing a print's rarity value is through the use of an artist's "remarque," which is a small sketch, in pencil, added individually by the artist in the margin of the print, usually of a subject related to the theme of the print itself. Normally, an artist will remarque only a small portion of the prints he or she is individually signing. These remarqued specimens normally command a considerably higher price, reflecting their uniqueness. Again, remember that there are no guarantees as to the actual authorship of the remarque, especially if the print is purchased from other than the original issuer.

Completeness

The final consideration that affects the value of a collectible is completeness. Many collectible items are originally created as part of a series, and the value of a complete series may be considerably greater than the sum of the prices of the individual items. More to the point, the price of a particular item may be greatly enhanced if that item represents the completion of a series to a collector.

Perhaps the most popular examples of this tendency are commemorative plates such as the Royal Copenhagen Christmas plates, which have been produced with a distinct design each year for many years. Collectors who are attempting to create a complete set will assign much greater value to the one or two plates they are missing.

Coin collectors, early in their hobbies, frequently focus their attention on series of pennies. They can attest to the mounting sense of frustration they feel as the completion of the series increasingly focuses on the one or two missing coins, with a corresponding increase in the price they will willingly pay for the desired items.

General Investment Guidelines

Five general guidelines apply to all collectibles, but are particularly appropriate when looking at this as a potentially profitable investment of time and money. Following these five will not ensure that you make money with collectibles. At the very least, however, it will maximize your pleasure and minimize your financial exposure.

1. *Choose a subject for collection because you love it,* not because you think it will be the most profitable. In the first place, collectibles are notoriously subject to fad and fashion, and what is the hottest item in the collecting world this year may be completely out of fashion next year. Since it takes time, patience, and considerable effort to build up the necessary knowledge of a specific field, it is almost impossible to determine far enough ahead of time which will be the particular area with the best prices at any given point.

An even more important reason is that if you don't really enjoy what you are collecting, it is highly unlikely that you will stay with it long enough to build up the necessary expertise or to build a large or complete enough collection to provide any economic incentive.

Finally, there are enough economic risks in collecting that you may never achieve great economic reward in any case. You are far better off concentrating your efforts on something you enjoy purely for the satisfaction of seeking, acquiring, and having it.

2. *Get help, early on,* from books, from experts, from dealers, and most of all from other collectors. Inevitably, the biggest and most costly mistakes you will make in establishing your collection will be in the initial stages, before your enthusiasm and eagerness have been tempered enough by knowledge and experience. For almost all collectibles, there are established amateur societies, whose members regularly meet and exchange ideas, thoughts, tips on sources, good and bad experiences, and a wealth of useful information. In the fine arts, consultants are available. While they are expensive, they may save you considerable sums in the long run. To succeed, and especially to succeed financially, you must first invest time and effort to develop your own level of expertise.

3. *Develop a network of trusted suppliers*, keeping in mind that most dealers will keep their very best offerings for their long-time customers. This means that you will need to invest a great deal of time up front, first finding out who the best and most reputable dealers are, then establishing yourself as a serious, knowledgeable client who respects the fact that the dealer is in business and requires a fair profit in order to provide the service you want.

4. *Specialize.* The most successful collectors are the ones who maintain their area of interest in direct proportion to the amount of time that they can devote to pursuing excellence in that field. It is far better (certainly from the economic perspective) to be a greater expert, in a smaller and more specialized field, than to attain a lower level of knowledge in a broader field.

5. *Caveat emptor!* This traditional Roman warning ("Let the buyer beware!") is particularly apt in the field of collectibles, where there is virtually no regulation, where prices may often be determined in the emotionally volatile environment of an auction, and where exaggeration in presentation and marketing claims is most often the norm. Above all else, when tempted by the notion of probable appreciation in the future value of whatever it is you are thinking of acquiring, consider first how, where, and to whom you plan to sell the piece. Whether you sell through a dealer or by auction, the intermediary must generate a profit as well, and the spreads are often quite significant.

FINANCIAL VEHICLES

Another major category of less traditional investment vehicles consists of financial vehicles. Most of these fall into either of two groups—annuity contracts and limited partnerships. In both cases, several different products are offered, adapted to different investor needs.

Both categories have advantages; both have potential drawbacks. Annuity contracts, while less often advertised or otherwise promoted, are probably more often appropriate for more investors. Limited partnerships generally offer far higher potential returns, but with considerably greater risks. Either, or both, may have a role to play in your total investment program.

ANNUITY CONTRACTS

Annuity contracts are investment vehicles in the form of guaranteed contracts offered by insurance companies, sometimes with one or more insurance features, and providing for the accumulation of earnings on a tax-deferred basis. In other words, the investor pays no taxes on the earnings until he or she withdraws funds from the account. Annuity contracts are available in many different forms, virtually all of which are variations on one of three main themes: universal life insurance, single-premium deferred annuities, and variable annuities.

Universal (or Variable) Life Insurance

Universal life insurance—also called variable life insurance—is a combination product offering a blend of term life insurance (which provides a death benefit to the beneficiary, and nothing else) and a tax-deferred money-market type of investment called an annuity contract. Generally, the investor is able to tailor the desired blend of insurance and investment components, not only initially but as his or her financial situation changes. The major advantage of this product is that while it offers two distinctly different elements, it is conveniently packaged into a single form.

Interest rates offered are generally the same as those available on money-market accounts, but they accumulate on a tax-deferred basis. This advantage is somewhat mitigated by the fact that front-end charges on this product—as on all insurance-type products—involve substantial commissions to sales agents. Thus, the amount of the purchase price actually available for investment may be significantly reduced.

A second advantage is that most of these policies also contain loan provisions. These allow the investor to borrow against the built-up cash in the account without disturbing the tax-sheltered nature of that cash.

In addition, these policies usually offer a variety of withdrawal options when the investor wishes to terminate the investment. These options range from a single lump-sum payout to a guaranteed stream of payments to the investor, the investor's spouse, or some combination of the two, either for a fixed term or for life.

Note that universal life policies, like other insurance derivatives, are individually developed by their sponsoring companies. Consequently, they may vary widely in the features they provide and in the guaranteed returns they offer. If you are considering such an investment, a detailed, point-by-point comparison of different universal life policies will often show remarkably different values for your investment dollar.

Request a copy of the Best's rating report on any company from which you are seriously considering buying any type of insurance product. These independent analyses of underwriting competence, expense control, financial reserves, and investment soundness have been made by *Best's Insurance Reports* since 1899. *Best's* rates each insurance company on a scale of A+, A, B+, B, C+, and C on each of six quality ratings. Generally speaking, investors should only consider purchasing products from companies with Best ratings of A+ or A.

Single-Premium Deferred Annuities

Often called simply an "annuity contract," a single-premium deferred annuity is quite similar to a certificate of deposit guaranteeing to pay the investor a certain minimum investment rate, with two exceptions. First, these contracts are sold by an insurance company rather than by a bank or other financial institution. Second, earnings from these annuities that are not withdrawn from the account accumulate on a tax-deferred basis. Although these deferred annuities contain no specific death benefit, the proceeds in an account in the event of the death of the insured are paid directly to a named beneficiary and are not required to pass through probate.

An additional advantage of the single-premium deferred annuity is that the sponsoring insurance company offers it directly to investors without any sales charges or other front-end fees. While there are penalties for early withdrawal (again, as in the case of certificates of deposit), these penalties typically do not exceed 5 percent and may decline during each of the contract's first years, rarely being charged at all after five years. Partial withdrawals are normally acceptable, and the investor pays taxes only on the part of the withdrawal considered earned interest. The remainder of the withdrawal is considered a nontaxable return of principal. Note, however, that the IRS has traditionally taxed withdrawals from annuity contracts on the last-earned, first-taxed principle. This means that *all* earnings are taxed before any additional withdrawal may be considered a nontaxable return of principal.

Minimum contract purchases are generally no greater than $5,000. Applications for investments greater than $100,000 may require a physical exam. Withdrawals can be in the form of lump-sum distributions or guaranteed monthly payments for specified time periods. For investors with a long time horizon, who can take full advantage of the compounding effects upon the tax-deferred accumulated earnings, these are very attractive investment vehicles.

Variable Annuities

A variable annuity is a special hybrid form of life insurance policy that is primarily designed as an investment vehicle. While it contains a modest degree of life insurance, its primary attractiveness comes from the fact that the investor is offered—on a tax-deferred basis—several different investment portfolio options. The individual investor can use these to whatever degree he or she considers most suitable. That is, the underwriting insurance company sponsors several different professionally managed funds into which the investor can allocate portions of the total investment in the variable annuity. Typically, these include a growth stock fund, a U.S. government bond fund, a balanced fund, a guaranteed investment contract option, a money-market fund, and perhaps others as well. Usually, the investor has maximum flexibility periodically to reallocate some or all of the investment dollars among the various fund options.

Variable annuities are normally offered to investors with no sales commissions or other front-end charges. However, relatively modest management fees are levied against the funds annually.

Usually the investor may make partial withdrawals from variable annuity agreements. These withdrawals are subject to income taxation only to the extent that they represent earned income rather than return of principal. Some fees are usually assessed for early withdrawal, although the penalty normally declines each year and ends altogether at five years. As noted earlier, the IRS requires that all earned income be taxed before any part of a withdrawal may be considered a nontaxable return of principal. Withdrawal options are similar to those discussed for other annuity contracts, offering maximum flexibility to fit each investor's tax situation.

LIMITED PARTNERSHIPS

The second major type of financial vehicle is the limited partnership. This offers a unique structure for pooling capital resources from individual investors (who become limited partners) to invest under the guidance of a professional manager or management company (the general partner) in the particular field of endeavor contemplated by the partnership. The objectives of pooling resources are to attain far greater diversification than each individual could otherwise achieve and to procure the services of a competent professional to manage the investments of the partnership. Professional management ideally should maximize the return of the partnership (whether that return be in the form of tax-free cash flow, capital gains, tax deductions, or other financial benefits). Traditionally, the two areas that most easily lend themselves to investment via limited partnerships are oil exploration projects and real estate.

Oil Exploration Limited Partnerships

Very few investments available to individual investors offer the chance to earn very high returns and at the same time take advantage of extremely favorable tax treatment. Oil exploration limited partnerships can do this, however. When a drilling project succeeds in tapping into recoverable reserves of oil and/or gas, the investor's original stake may be repaid several times over during the course of the well's useful life. At the same time, the drilling expenses, depreciation expense for equipment, any investment tax credits available to the partnership, and considerable tax sheltering of revenue produced by operating wells via the depletion allowance (a tax break recognizing that oil is a nonrenewable asset) are all passed along to the limited partners.

On the other hand, a very high degree of risk is inherent in the drilling of any exploratory wells. This limits the appropriateness of these limited partnerships to investors for whom the early, significant tax write-offs are particularly important and for whom the low probability of drilling success is not critical.

A second problem, found in virtually all limited partnerships, lies in the allocation of contributions by the limited partners (typically 99 percent of capital) versus the allocation of return (only 80 percent of the gain on sale of assets or 80 percent of net income). Considerable additional sums are paid to the general partner under the guise of organizational expenses, accounting and legal fees, sales commissions, and management fees. All these are paid from the capital contributed by the limited partners *before* the assets are put to work. Because these fees differ significantly from one limited partnership to another, make side-by-side comparisons before deciding which, if any, you should buy.

Real Estate Limited Partnerships
Some limited partnerships formed for the purpose of investing in real estate may be geared to the production of income. In that case the properties are generally owned outright. Other real estate limited partnerships may be seeking maximum capital appreciation. In that case the partnership may use considerable borrowing leverage. Still other limited partnerships may follow a balanced approach in an attempt to generate both current income and capital gains.

The partnership normally will provide the complete range of purchasing and managing expertise required, via the general partner. Thus, the individual investor need not have experience or special knowledge in order to participate in the commercial real estate market. Furthermore, the pooling of funds into a partnership makes possible a level of diversification that is far beyond what is possible to most investors in any other way.

A primary weakness of real estate limited partnerships is the complete lack of any managerial control by the limited partners. A further disadvantage is the decided lack of liquidity of the partnerships, once formed. While some partnerships may make provisions to buy out a limited partner seeking to cash in his or her investment, the investor can normally do this only at a substantial financial penalty. Most such partnerships are designed to be self-liquidating, and even then, the timing of liquidation is at the discretion of the general partner. In other words, the investor is not expected to sell his or her interest in the partnership. Rather, the investment (including profits and losses) will be paid out to the investor as the individual properties are sold. Also, the front-end charges and management fees in real estate limited partnerships tend to be quite significant.

Finally, a specialized form of pooling arrangement through which individual investors may own or finance real estate development is the real estate investment trust (REIT). These trusts may participate in the lending of funds for development of commercial, residential, or industrial properties, or they may purchase these properties and manage them directly. By following special tax rules, they can escape taxation at the level of the business trust. Thus, they can pass along substantial dividends to shareholders of the trust.

In many ways, a REIT is similar to a mutual fund that invests in real estate projects rather than in common stocks. Like a mutual fund (and unlike most real estate limited partnerships), it is a highly liquid form of investment. In fact, shares of most REITs are listed for trading on the New York or American stock exchanges.

REITs were very popular in the early 1970s, but many investors in REITs suffered extraordinary losses when the economy peaked in 1974, followed by a significant recession. Review the portfolio and past dividend record of REITs as part of the selection of one as an investment vehicle. In doing so, it is important to keep in mind that an REIT will frequently declare a special, nonrecurring payment to shareholders that is *not* a dividend. This payment rather represents a return of capital upon the sale of an individual property that was formerly in the portfolio but is no longer available to a new investor.

CONCLUSION

This review of the most significant kinds of "other" investment possibilities is intended to indicate the wide variety and individual flavor of the many ways investors can make (and lose) money beyond the traditional stock and bond markets. Perhaps the most important lesson to learn is that while there are many special vehicles that you can adapt and put to good use in your individual situation, there is still no such thing as a free lunch. Rather, hard work and continuing vigilance are still fundamental requirements in the business of making money through investing.

9

THINKING OF USING A PROFESSIONAL?

THE SELECTION, CARE, AND FEEDING OF AN INVESTMENT ADVISER

―――――――――――――――――――― Van W. Knox III

PROBABLY THE MOST OFTEN QUOTED PASSAGES FROM SUPER mutual fund manager Peter Lynch's bestseller *One Up on Wall Street* deal with Lynch's conviction that the individual investor not only *can* compete successfully in the stock market with the big funds and institutional portfolios, but that the individual has a built-in *advantage*. According to Lynch, this should enable "any normal person using the customary three percent of the brain" to achieve results superior to those of the majority of mutual funds and large financial institutions, and to the overall market itself as measured by the S&P 500 or other such broad measures of market activity.

This is so, the argument runs, because the individual is not constrained by many of the cultural, legal, and social rules—formal and informal—that govern the conduct of professional fund managers. These rules include the following:

• The unfortunate but undeniable emphasis on short-term performance. Fund results are calculated, published, compared, exalted, or condemned every three months, year in and year out.

- The limitations that size can impose upon a fund's ability to move into and out of positions in smaller companies without unduly disrupting the market. This is further compounded by a herd effect, which may lead to a mass exodus from a given position as fund managers stampede out the door based only on the fact that *other* fund managers are doing so. Unhappily, the price of everybody's holding in that stock, whether institutional or individual, is equally affected.
- The proscription at most institutions against investing in any company not already covered (and presumably lauded) by a wide following of analysts and other institutions. Thus, the major funds and institutions are rarely able to see or to take early advantage of technological, marketing, distribution, manufacturing, or other breakthroughs that can result in truly significant gains in stock prices.
- Procedural rules in place at many funds (or enforced by the Securities and Exchange Commission) precluding a fund from investing more than a small percentage of its total assets in any single company, or acquiring more than a given percentage of a single company's outstanding equity. The net effect of these rules, originally designed to ensure diversification, has been to curtail the number of companies in which a large fund can effectively make any investment whatsoever.
- The need for an ironbound excuse in the event of failure. Institutional managers must not only face the ire of clients, but also the wrath of their own bosses, the contempt of their colleagues, and even the potential loss of their jobs, if their stock selections should falter even temporarily. Such multifaceted accountability, with its attendant risks, carries with it an unwavering bias toward mediocrity in performance, and a potential obsession with avoiding failure.

An additional element that reduces the ability of a mutual fund or other institution to generate superior results from the point of view of the individual holder is the institution's own overhead and profit requirement. Much has been written about "load" vs. "no-load" funds, "front-end" vs. "back-end" loads,* and so-called '12b-1" charges,** but the indisputable fact is that these all repre-

sent deductions from the total value of your investment. Consequently, they make it more difficult for a fund manager to show
growth in net asset value relative to an investment that does not
have to suffer these deductions, fees, and charges.

These arguments are quite compelling, and there is a great deal
of statistical data to demonstrate the difficulty that most mutual
funds and other institutional money managers encounter in trying
to outpace the common market averages, especially over a period
of time. According to Lipper Analytical Services, Inc., the average
mutual fund, with dividends reinvested, underperformed *by a
significant percentage* the unmanaged S&P 500 Index, with dividends similarly reinvested, for periods of one, five, ten, and fifteen
years, ending December 31, 1989.

SELLING POINTS FOR MUTUAL FUNDS

Why is it, then, that there are so many mutual funds with so much
money entrusted to them? The February 12, 1990, issue of *Barron's* carried the *Lipper Gauge* performance report covering 2,250
separate funds. The same issue reported assets approaching $240
billion in equity funds alone.

The answer lies in the fact that mutual funds do provide two
essential ingredients that might otherwise be unavailable to the
individual investor, and that intuitively should improve the performance of the individual's portfolio. Those ingredients are the protection afforded by diversification and the benefit of constant
attention from a professional manager whose sole activity is fo-
cused upon enhancing the portfolio's net asset value.

DIVERSIFICATION

There is little argument that diversification is a good—even necessary—way to lower the risk of unexpected unfavorable develop-

---

*"Front-end loads" constitute a percentage of the investment charged against
your account when you first buy in. This charge reduces the net amount of
money actually invested and working for you. "Back-end loads"—also called
redemption fees—are a percentage of your investment charged against the net
asset value of your holding when you get out. An excellent discussion of mutual
fund expenses is found in *The Individual Investor's Guide to No-Load Mutual
Funds*, published by the American Association of Individual Investors.

ments in the operations of any single investment by spreading the total investment across a number of different issues in different industry groups. Furthermore, for the small portfolio, the use of a mutual fund provides excellent diversification of risk at transaction costs that would be prohibitively expensive for an individual. For an individual to diversify this much would require buying very small amounts of a great many different stocks to replicate the mutual fund in an individual portfolio.

The question, however, is how much diversification is really required to minimize this risk? The late Arnold Bernhard, founder of Value Line, called diversification "the First Imperative" but suggested that, for most individual investors, a practical rule is to hold about 15 or more stocks in approximately equal dollar amounts and in at least eight different industries.

In *Secrets for Profiting in Bull and Bear Markets*, Stan Weinstein, called by Louis Rukeyser "one of the best market technicians operating today," states that despite the fundamental need to diversify in order to spread risk, it is also essential to keep portfolio size at a level that makes it possible to stay on top of all the issues held. Weinstein concludes that even for the largest portfolios, "10 or 20 stocks is the most I'd invest in at any one time."

In his excellent and eminently readable *Winning on Wall Street*, Dr. Martin Zweig goes into somewhat more detail. He offers as rough guidelines that for a portfolio of up to $20,000, the investor should hold four to five stocks; at $50,000, eight or nine stocks; at $100,000 up to a dozen; and for the $250,000 portfolio, twenty or more individual issues is enough. In his own model portfolio, Zweig will hold anywhere from 25 to 33 stocks when he is fully invested (thus providing maximum positions of 3–4 percent). He also notes that academic studies have shown that someone who diversifies across several different industry groups can achieve

---

**These are annual expenses charged against the assets of the fund and may include payment for distribution costs, advertising, printing and distribution of prospectuses and annual reports, and sales commissions to brokers. These charges do *not* constitute any incentive for the fund manager to achieve better results. While not "loads" in that they do not reduce the amount of capital put to work for you originally or deducted when you redeem your fund shares, they are annual charges that nonetheless represent a drag on the fund's performance.

nearly 90 percent of the total benefits of diversification just by spreading investments across eight individual stocks.

By contrast, most mutual funds are invested in many times these numbers, and many of them hold *hundreds* of individual issues. Strictly from the point of view of diversification, mutual funds go way beyond what is necessary for all but the very smallest investors who can achieve even reasonable diversification no other way.*

PROFESSIONAL MANAGEMENT

A mutual fund also provides a full-time, professional portfolio manager, backed by a research department of presumably competent people all working as hard as they can to uncover investment vehicles to make your investment grow. This point is absolutely valid, as far as it goes. The individual investor, whether a doctor, lawyer, homemaker, or whatever, *shouldn't* be able to produce results superior to those of investment professionals, simply because he or she is too busy being a doctor, lawyer, homemaker, or whatever! Even Peter Lynch, whose subtitle for his book is "How to Use What You Already Know to Make Money in the Market," later states flatly, "Investing without research is like playing stud poker and never looking at the cards."

In other words, success in investing—like success in any other endeavor in this life—requires work, and that in turn requires *time* to put toward that work. And that most precious commodity is what most individuals lack. Ironically, the ones who are most successful in what they do for a living are generally the ones who spend the most time doing it, and who therefore have the least time available to spend protecting and nurturing the private wealth that their success has made possible.

---

*The valid concept of diversification has been overemphasized and exploited to such an extreme that there is even a lively industry supporting the notion that diversification *between and across* different mutual funds provides even more benefits to the individual than that already contained in a single fund. The logic of this is difficult to comprehend when you realize that the majority of most funds' holdings is concentrated in the 250 or so largest corporations. The difference between funds is primarily the difference in relative weight given to each company by the fund manager. Thus, what is effectively accomplished by diversifying across several funds is simply the canceling out of each manager's judgment—which is presumably what you are paying for in the first place.

The Alternative to Mutual Funds

If mutual funds and institutions can only rarely beat an unmanaged index, and if the individual investor is too busy doing whatever he or she does for a living to spend an appropriate amount of time caring for an investment portfolio, what then is the answer? In many cases, it may be the use of a registered investment adviser—a full-time professional portfolio manager who has available many of the resources of the mutual fund manager but is free of most of the hindrances that have kept mutual funds from delivering on their theoretical promise.

The remainder of this chapter considers the advantages (and the disadvantages) of this kind of approach, the kind of investor who should consider the use of an investment adviser, the best way to select the right adviser, the questions to ask, the ground rules to establish for what is reasonable to expect from the client and the adviser, and the basis for compensation. In short, this chapter is a guide to the selection, utilization, care, and feeding of your investment adviser.

What Is an Investment Adviser?

What does it mean to say that many investors should consider the use of a registered investment adviser? Let's start with what this does *not* mean.

Not Just an Advice-Giver

By "registered investment adviser," I do not, first of all, really mean an adviser at all. I mean a professional portfolio manager to whom you turn over the day-to-day management of your portfolio, giving him or her the discretion to make purchase and/or sale decisions in your name.

While it is certainly possible to hire a registered investment adviser to provide just that—advice—I have never known of a satisfactory long-term relationship with an investment adviser that has not ultimately resulted in the client's authorizing discretionary powers for the investment adviser. For one thing, it is certainly inconvenient and frequently even impossible to determine how good or bad a job the adviser is doing unless the client translates the adviser's advice into immediate action in every situation. And in that case, the adviser already has effective jurisdiction over the account. Secondly, since the use of a registered investment adviser involves a high level of trust in the individual and faith in his or her capabilities, the relationship fairly quickly progresses to the full-faith level of complete discretion over the account. If the trust and faith do not translate into concrete results that the client considers satisfactory, the relationship deteriorates to the point of dissolution.

As discussed later, the basic premise is that you hire an investment adviser to do for you what you would do for yourself if you had the time and the inclination to do it. If you do not feel comfortable allowing the adviser to do just that, you should either find another adviser or accept the fact that you probably will have to be satisfied with whatever results you can achieve managing your own portfolio in your spare time.

NOT A "FINANCIAL PLANNER"

Secondly, by "registered investment adviser" I do not mean a financial planner. Although there are financial planners who are also registered investment advisers, and there are registered investment advisers who may also undertake financial planning, the two terms reflect distinctly different activities. A financial planner should be trying to help you get your financial life in order, and often will help you decide how much you should be routinely saving and investing in order to reach future goals such as financial security in retirement. In contrast, a registered investment adviser is strictly concerned with the investments themselves—what to buy, at what price, when to sell it, and how to reinvest the proceeds. The investment adviser, in other words, is a private portfolio manager whose task is to maximize the value of the investments you have placed under his or her charge, in a manner consistent with risk levels appropriate to your age, economic situation, and comfort level. Whereas a financial planner can be extremely helpful, there is potential danger in confusing the two kinds of activities, or of assuming that a good planner will also make a good investment adviser (or vice versa).

At the current time, the financial planning profession is virtually unregulated as to educational or other accreditation requirements necessary to be in business. On the other hand, to become a registered investment adviser, the applicant must register not only with the Securities and Exchange Commission at the federal level, but also with the local state equivalent. *As part of their registration, investment advisers must also pass a broad-based proficiency examination* (National Association of Securities Dealers General Securities Examination, Series 2) and must maintain a current filing of their original comprehensive registration statement with the SEC by filing amendments every year.

While there are many fine, reputable financial planners in active practice, there are also many insurance and securities salespeople thinly disguised as financial planners. These salespeople may use the come-on of helping you to build a financial plan purely as a vehicle for selling you an investment product or insurance policy. The safest defense—as true for registered investment advisers as for financial planners—is to determine *any and all* ways that the planner (or the investment adviser) can benefit from your association with him or her that will *not* also benefit you. If a planner receives a commission for selling you a product, regardless of whether it is appropriate for you (or regardless of whether the product goes up or down in value), then a real potential exists for a conflict of interest.

The only way I (and most other registered investment advisers) deal with my clients, and the only way I would ever deal with an investment adviser as a client myself, is on the basis of compensation tied exclusively to a percentage of assets under management. That way, the investment adviser's best interests are locked inextricably into the client's best interests, and there is no way the adviser can benefit unless the client benefits as well. This is an important consideration, which I will discuss in a little more detail later on.

NOT A BROKER

Finally, by an investment adviser, I do not mean a broker. Again, there are many fine brokers in the securities industry, and they frequently work for firms with excellent research departments. But you should never, ever forget that a broker makes a living from commissions generated by purchases and sales of stocks and bonds—*any* stocks and *any* bonds! Whereas a good broker can be a wonderful source of information, it simply defies common sense to believe that even the best and most honest broker in the world can completely divorce his or her judgment ("I think you should buy this stock . . .") from his or her pocketbook ("I will earn a nice commission if you buy this stock").

This is not to say you should not listen to your broker. On the contrary, you should definitely listen to your broker—before *you* (or your investment adviser) make the decision to buy or not to buy the stock. Look at it another way: would you ever ask a salesperson in the automobile showroom to decide for you whether or not you should buy the new car the salesperson is showing you?

REASONS FOR USING A REGISTERED INVESTMENT ADVISER

In light of this definition of what the investment adviser is and is not, why should the individual investor consider using one? The crux of the entire argument comes down to a single issue: time. The other benefits are closely related to it.

TIME

The one indispensable ingredient for successful investment in the capital markets remains, as it has always been, a commitment to hard work. The investor must take the time and put forth the effort to review and apply dispassionate judgment to the enormous amounts of readily available published data on a wide range of companies and industries, in order to identify corporations whose future earnings potential has not yet been fully recognized by the investment community. It is clearly of only slightly less importance for the investor to enhance his or her ability to *keep* the profits by minimizing the downside risk through diversification, vigilance, flexibility, and timing.

This concept is deceptively simple but nevertheless points to the single element most frequently and most conspicuously absent from otherwise-successful individuals' management of their personal assets. Such investors quite legitimately are too busy to devote anything like the appropriate time to their own investment portfolios. Their other activities keep them out of touch with the financial markets and often unaware of developments affecting their investments, until prices may already have reacted to a considerable degree. The entire case for using professional portfolio management rests on the fact that a professional investment manager will devote his entire professional time and effort to selecting, monitoring, and reselecting your investment portfolio. This is in contrast to the occasional nights and weekends of "leftover" time that the individual amateur client typically devotes to the task.

It is somewhat surprising that this logic, which is almost too obvious to be taken seriously, does not carry more weight in most investors' minds. Most investors are otherwise perfectly rational in their thinking and decision making; they would never dream of committing money to a project *in their jobs* without conducting as thorough and exhaustive a review as time and money would allow. Yet these same people will time and time again, instantly and with complete aplomb, toss their hard-earned personal assets into the shakiest and most farfetched investment vehicles conceivable, on the basis of the flimsiest of evidence, often presented to them by perfect strangers! Probably this is because we *want* so badly to believe that the hot tip we have gotten, or the telephone pitch from a broker we have never met, somehow really does represent a true opportunity that nobody else knows about yet.

Unfortunately for all of us, the truth is that in investing, as in much of life, what you get out of something depends to a great extent on what you put into it. If you are spending the majority of your working hours and working effort in *working*, then you may well want to consider taking advantage of the time and effort that a professional investment adviser is putting into *investing*. Thus, you can turn the results of the adviser's work to your advantage. The cost for this is quite modest relative to the benefits that can be provided—not only in terms of financial results, but also in terms of psychological and emotional well-being, knowing that your nest egg is being watched over.

INCLINATION

Not only does a registered investment adviser devote much more time (especially "prime" time) to your investment portfolio than you can or will put in, the professional also gives you the advantage of inclination. Registered investment advisers are in that business

because they *want* to spend their full time building and managing
your portfolio. Without putting too fine a point on it, I would
certainly rather take my car to a mechanic who loved working on
cars than to one who did not, or have surgery performed by a
doctor who enjoyed his or her work rather than by a doctor who
really would prefer to be a lawyer or a business executive.

ACCESSIBILITY

Still a third advantage, which is often of great importance to some
clients, is that of accessibility. When you are working with a registered investment adviser, you are entitled to a reasonable amount
of consultation time. You can use this time to discuss the market
outlook, the rationale for any given purchase or sale decision
reached by the adviser, the progress being made by the portfolio
in general, or any other question or topic having to do with your
investments. If you have ever tried to get in touch with (or even
find out the name of) a mutual fund portfolio manager, you can
readily appreciate the difference.

TECHNOLOGY AND SOPHISTICATED ANALYSIS

Another fairly obvious correlate to the time advantage is the technological and analytical resources that the professional adviser can
bring to bear. These are often beyond the means—and almost
certainly beyond the available time—of the individual investor.

Computerized screening programs and the data bases upon
which to use them have greatly lessened the gap between the
individual investor working alone and the institutional investor
backed by a stable of research analysts. But the simple truth is
that even when the individual client is willing to invest the financial resources needed to gain access to the tremendous amount of
information available, and is prepared to install the hardware
necessary to manipulate the data, he or she will still be hampered
by a lack of time to analyze new information and translate the
results of this analysis into tactical management decisions in the
portfolio itself.

RATIONALITY

Finally, using a registered investment adviser can remove a potentially dangerous element from the management of your portfolio:
you! As individuals, we are all capable of falling prey to our

emotions, with potentially disastrous results to the portfolio. We all hate to be wrong—and even more to admit it.

Realizing a loss (that is, actually selling out of a losing position) is probably one of the most painful bruises you can inflict on your ego . . . and it is *so* much easier to rationalize holding on! But holding on to a loser can be even more painful in the long run. It can cost real money as well as forcing us, finally, to admit we were wrong.

Professional portfolio managers live or die by the results they achieve—not the reasons they can conjure up for doing or not doing something. A good one will have learned how to squeeze personal feelings out of his or her professional decisions.

DISADVANTAGES OF USING AN INVESTMENT ADVISER

Despite all the reasons why a registered investment adviser can be of tremendous help, there are also potential disadvantages. The notable drawbacks are loss of control, failure to match your tolerance for risk, and the lack of any guarantee of success.

LOSS OF CONTROL

The most important disadvantage is the loss of control over one's money. This gives some investors a lot more trouble than they realized it would. Few things in the world are more personal than one's own money, and it is not always easy to allow someone else to manage it, no matter how well you understand the benefits, and no matter how you really do accept—at least intellectually—that it is a good thing.

For an investment adviser to do his or her job, however, you really must let that person *do* the job. That means not second-guessing every decision, and not overriding his or her choices. If you really cannot stand aside and let the investment adviser manage the portfolio, then the chances are very good that this kind of arrangement is simply not for you. To the extent that you can anticipate this problem, it is better to decide ahead of time.

FAILURE TO MATCH YOUR RISK TOLERANCE

Another potentially serious disadvantage is that the investment adviser you select may not structure and manage the portfolio consistently with your risk tolerance or your "comfort level." (More on this concept later.) Unfortunately, much of the advertising material published by registered investment advisers stresses the fact that the adviser in question will spend a good deal of effort to devise an investment strategy tailored specifically to your own investment situation and your own investment goals. While this sounds great, my own experience suggests that an investment adviser probably cannot be all things to all people, and in fact is not going to be equally successful in managing all different kinds of portfolios with different risk levels.

The fact is that each adviser has a particular style and is most comfortable investing in a certain way. The best adviser for a retired widow will have great difficulty also being the best adviser for a young, high-salaried gunslinger. Getting a "good" investment adviser really isn't enough. You have to find the right investment adviser for you, or it probably won't work out.

No Guarantees

Finally, it is worth noting that a registered investment adviser, while he or she should provide all the advantages discussed, will *not* provide what we all secretly want most of all: a guarantee that our investment portfolio will always go up, will always beat the benchmark market averages, and will consistently make us the envy of friends, neighbors, and business colleagues. The fundamental basis of investing is the balance between risk and reward, and an investment adviser should be able to *improve* the performance of your portfolio, over time, well beyond the incremental cost of hiring that adviser. Nonetheless, there will inevitably be periods in which the benefits are less obvious and the disadvantages more apparent, when the investments in the portfolio fail to perform as expected (at least as soon as they *should* have), and when an unexpected disaster strikes a company the adviser has just purchased.

At such times, it is tempting to punish. If a close working relationship has developed between adviser and client, such a situation may be far more difficult than the wholly impersonal tie between a client and the faceless manager of a mutual fund.

Selecting a Registered Investment Adviser

If you can avoid the pitfalls, the potential advantages of using a professional portfolio manager to oversee your portfolio can be considerable. How then do you find the right investment adviser for you? This section details several steps to take.

Develop a List of Candidates

The first question, of course, is where to find investment advisers. To develop a list of candidates, you need to collect basic information about a number of them. While it is by no means necessary to use an adviser who is located near you, you should nonetheless plan to sit down and talk face to face with your final group of candidates. Therefore, unless your portfolio is potentially quite large, it probably makes sense to limit your research, at least initially, to an area within fairly easy driving distance.

Yellow Pages
The easiest place to begin, logically enough, is in your yellow pages. There, registered investment advisers are listed under "Investment Advisory Service." (At least that's where we are in New Jersey.)

The Money Market Directory
In your public library is a second source: an annual publication called the *Money Market Directory*. In Part II of this directory, you will find a section called "Investment Managers."

This particular source is more helpful than the yellow pages in that it provides a thumbnail sketch of each adviser listed, giving basic information as to minimum account size, areas of particular specialty, and so forth. Keep in mind, though, that the advisers you find in the yellow pages should be only too pleased to respond to a phone call by sending you complete information regarding the services they provide, costs, track record, and more.

Advertisements
A third possibility is the advertisements you may run across in your local newspapers and regional or special-interest magazines

(such as a college alumni magazine). In the case of larger advisory
firms, advertisements may appear in the national financial press
as well.

Recommendations from Professionals
As a somewhat more personal approach, you can obtain recommendations from a CPA, from the trust department of your bank,
or from a lawyer. Keep in mind, though, that often these professionals are also interested in managing your money themselves.
Based on some of the shortcomings previously mentioned, that may
or may not be the way you want to go.

Recommendations from Friends or Colleagues
Finally, one of the best sources of information is the recommendations of friends or colleagues who are themselves using the services
of a registered investment adviser. These people can provide opinions to you based upon their actual experience, both positive and
negative. An added advantage is that, knowing these people yourself, you can better evaluate the quality of the recommendations
they provide.

NARROW DOWN THE LIST
When you have compiled a list of potential candidates, conduct the
process of narrowing them down as objectively and rationally as
possible. A good first step is to solicit from each candidate the
promotional and informational literature that candidate has prepared—in other words, to hear what the candidates *want* you to
hear. Not only will this give them a fair shot at bringing out the
points they consider the most important, it may also give you
insight into what they feel is *not* important, or even what they do
not particularly want you to dwell upon. Although not all the
candidates will provide all the information you need in this first
phase, the material they provide should give you some good input
in each of the following areas.

Investment Philosophy
The investment adviser will probably furnish a statement of investment philosophy—how he or she approaches the investment of
clients' money. This statement will undoubtedly also contain many
references to the fact that the adviser plans to work with you to

develop investment goals that are particularly appropriate for *you*. However, there is only one legitimate investment goal, and that is to make money!

The real differences between investors have to do with risk tolerance, not with investment goals. You have the right to know, and should insist upon knowing, the risk levels the adviser feels most comfortable with, even granting that he or she should be able—within limits—to structure and manage a portfolio consistent with somewhat different risk factors, based upon the individual client's needs.

The most important aspect of the adviser's investment philosophy is that you should be easily able to understand exactly what the adviser is talking about, and to feel very comfortable that it is a philosophy you would be happy to apply. There are many sophisticated and complicated bells and whistles that can legitimately be applied to portfolio management. But if, for example, such things as hedging with options and/or futures, arbitrage, use of margin, covered-call writing, and other techniques don't make sense to you, they probably don't belong in your portfolio.

Logistics of Handling the Account
Before you reach an agreement, be sure you clearly understand the answers to questions of custody and safekeeping of certificates; record keeping and reports to be provided by the adviser; insurance, dividend, and/or interest accumulations and reinvestment; selection of brokerage firms to be used and brokerage commissions to be paid; the mechanism for withdrawing funds from your account; and the basis and means of canceling your agreement with the investment adviser. These answers can be useful for comparing the services offered by potential candidates to manage your portfolio.

Background, Experience, and Track Record
It is tricky to evaluate background, experience, and track record. Unless that information pertains to the specific individual who will be managing your portfolio, it doesn't really matter very much. Just as a mutual fund's past performance doesn't mean much if the fund has just changed portfolio managers, the background, experience, and track record of a *company* don't really tell you what you need to know.

Furthermore, the interpretation of a manager's track record is fraught with peril, since there is no generally accepted format or procedure for calculating or presenting it. There are many ways of "improving" a track record, of which the most frequent are omitting the portfolios of all clients no longer using the firm (!), omitting the "cash" portion of portfolios in the calculation, comparing portfolio results including reinvested dividends against unadjusted market averages, and using different benchmark portfolios for different periods of time. While there are many different (perfectly honest and fair) ways of calculating and presenting a track record, candidate advisers should be able, and willing, to explain simply and quickly exactly how theirs was derived.

I must confess to another personal prejudice regarding investment advisers: age. While there is no denying that very young managers may be absolutely superb, and while there is certainly no logic in the argument that older managers are good just because they have been at it longer, I am still convinced that experience is a great teacher, and furthermore that there are some things that cannot be learned any other way than by experience. One of these is the fear and psychological damage resulting from a major bear market—which, arguably, we have not seen in this country since the last big surge upward began in 1982 (notwithstanding the '87 crash). I would feel a lot more comfortable with an investment adviser who can show me some battle scars than with someone who has only known and experienced the prosperity we have had in the financial markets in recent years.

Compensation

A fee schedule, and an explanation of how and when fees will be calculated and paid, should be part of the initial package of information you receive. Make sure to check for minimum fees or minimum account size (which amounts to the same thing, since very few advisers will refuse an account only on the basis of failing to meet a minimum size).

The most appropriate basis for compensation of your investment adviser is a fee based exclusively upon a percentage of assets under management. Most advisers use a sliding scale, with an annual fee of 1 to 1.5 percent of the first x thousand dollars in assets, and a gradually decreasing percentage of the next y thousand, the next z thousand, and so on. The reason this is the best compensation scheme is that it ties the investment adviser's interests completely to the best interests of the client, while at the same time giving the adviser a real incentive to generate superior performance. If the adviser does the job well, the client's portfolio will grow, and the adviser's compensation will grow with it; if not, the adviser will suffer in proportion to the client.

A basis for compensation that most investors should avoid except under very special circumstances is one that attempts to provide too great an incentive to the manager by tying the size of the fee exclusively to portfolio growth, rather than to asset size. Typically, such a fee might consist of 20 to 25 percent of *gains* earned in a portfolio over a fixed period of time. Initially, this may appear to be quite attractive from the client's point of view. Growth is, after all, what we all want to see. The problem with this kind of arrangement is that it can quickly place the adviser and the client at odds with each other, for reasons that may have nothing to do with the adviser's performance.

A simple example should demonstrate how this kind of arrangement can lead to trouble. Few people would disapprove of an adviser who had kept his client's portfolio to a loss of 2 percent in a year when the Dow Jones Industrials or the S&P 500 had dropped by 11 percent. At the same time, not many investors would get very excited about an adviser whose management of a portfolio yielded growth of 13 percent in a year when the benchmark average was 25 percent. Compensation based only upon a percentage of *growth*, however, would severely penalize the adviser in the first example and could handsomely reward the adviser in the second.

Much worse, it jeopardizes the alignment of the adviser's interests with those of the client—and severely tempts the adviser in the first situation to increase the level of risk in a bad market, in the hopes of achieving at least *some* return for his or her efforts. Conversely, the adviser in the second situation may be tempted to *reduce* risk, despite a strong upward market, in order to protect the substantial compensation he or she has "earned." Even though this may be happening subconsciously, it is clearly very much against the best interests of the client and can, in extreme situations, be a prescription for disaster.

The only time when it may make sense to pay a manager based purely upon portfolio performance (that is, growth) rather than upon the size of assets managed is when the fully informed investor consciously wishes to place part of his or her assets into a highly speculative, heavily growth-oriented portfolio, recognizing that the risks of loss in such a venture are considerable. In such a case, performance-based premiums for the adviser are more appropriate. Remember, though, that increased reward requires increased risk—and *you* are bearing all the risk, while the adviser is penalized only if he or she does not seek the *greater* risk in the search of greater rewards. The adviser's risk is only that of failure to earn anything; your risk of actual loss is very real.

In short, remember the basic philosophy: the compensation arrangement should precisely tie your adviser's best interests to your own. Anything else jeopardizes you and the well-being of your assets.

CONDUCT PERSONAL INTERVIEWS

Based on a review of the initial information packages gathered from candidate investment advisers, you should be able to decide which of the candidates you want to go ahead and talk with. This step—the personal interview—cannot be emphasized too strongly. One of the most important advantages of using a registered investment adviser is the fact that you will be dealing with a human being, rather than the totally impersonal relationship between a client and a mutual fund. This being the case, it is essential that you feel good about the individual adviser, not just his or her qualifications on paper.

In this regard, your intuition, or gut feel, should play a large part. After all, many of the most important characteristics you look for in an investment adviser—honesty, integrity, intelligence, understanding of your situation and your needs—are hard to quantify. In any case, you will be trusting the investment adviser with the management of your personal asset base. You have the right (and even the obligation to yourself and your family) to be completely satisfied that the investment adviser you choose will add not only to your net worth, but also to your peace of mind.

This aspect, which I call comfort level, does not mean that you should pay attention *only* to your instincts when selecting the investment adviser. Rather, in addition to your satisfaction with his or her credentials and qualifications on paper, you should feel comfortable discussing the details of your financial life and working with that individual.

The personal interview is also an excellent time to establish the feedback mechanism you can expect in the subsequent relationship. That is, how frequently does the adviser expect to communicate with you (orally or in writing), on a routine and an ad hoc basis? What reports will you receive? Will you receive copies of confirmation slips directly from the broker after each trade? What, if any, reports will the adviser receive from the broker that you will *not* receive?

You should also request a copy from each of the candidate advisers of what is called Part II of Form ADV. This is the second section of the Uniform Application for Investment Adviser Registration, which the adviser has originally filed with the Securities and Exchange Commission and is required to keep current through annual amendments. Part II of Form ADV contains material that is specifically designed for clients (and potential clients), giving information regarding the adviser's educational background, types of services and fees charged, and involvement with any other industry activities or affiliations. Each investment adviser is required to provide (or offer in writing to provide, without charge) Part II of Form ADV or equivalent information in a brochure, to all clients on an annual basis. This information is handy for comparing candidates you are considering.

GET REFERENCES

Assuming that at this point you have narrowed your search to the final two or three candidates, request client references. They may provide helpful information in several ways. While presumably only satisfied clients will be offered as potential references, they may be willing to discuss perceived shortcomings as well as strong points. In addition, satisfied clients often may themselves be interesting reflections of the adviser. Talking with them may give you additional insight into the kind of relationship you can expect with that adviser.

REQUEST A PROPOSAL

As a final means of selecting among the remaining candidates, it is reasonable to request a formal proposal, including an indication of recommended investments to be included in the portfolio. While it may be argued that you are thus requesting something for nothing, the service the investment adviser is hoping to sell you includes far more than just the original portfolio recommendations. In any case the adviser would probably be wise to discuss the initial selections with you before they are implemented. At the very least, the adviser should be willing to outline and explain the recommended asset allocation percentages and the selection criteria to be used in building the initial portfolio.

Even if you have settled on a final choice of investment adviser, it makes good sense to request a formal proposal without necessarily indicating that you have basically decided upon the leading single candidate. On the other hand, it would, of course, be unfair to request such a proposal from the entire list of initial candidates. Not only does considerable work go into preparing such a proposal, but also a good adviser will want to talk with you and get a better understanding of your situation *before* putting together a proposed portfolio for you.

LIVING WITH YOUR
REGISTERED INVESTMENT ADVISER

Having reached your final decision, you sign the papers giving the investment adviser the authority to manage your portfolio. What can you now expect? Based upon my own experiences, I'd say that clients' anticipations vary widely. While your adviser should be flexible enough to satisfy many of these expectations, it is sometimes surprising how different the definition of what is "reasonable" can be when you ask the client compared to when you ask the adviser.

Once you have turned over the day-to-day management of your investment portfolio to a professional adviser, probably the most important thing to keep in mind (and maybe the most difficult, too) is that the reason you hired him or her was precisely that you felt you were not in a position to do as good a job yourself as you expected the adviser to do. That being the case, it is a good idea to review in your own mind what should be a reasonable amount of ongoing communication between client and adviser above and beyond the reports you have already agreed will be furnished to you.

A lot of this depends upon the personality of the client, and there is no fixed answer as to what is the "right" amount of interplay between client and adviser. In my own practice, clients run the entire gamut. I have one client with whom I sit down once a year, and we speak on the telephone perhaps two or three times during the year beyond that. At the other end of the spectrum, I have clients who call me several times in the space of a single week. All these clients receive monthly statements showing exactly what is in their accounts, at what price, and they also receive copies directly from the broker of every transaction made in their account. Nonetheless—especially in the beginning of a relationship—clients often feel the need to stay close to exactly what is going on.

In general, make sure your expectations are reasonable, then give the adviser the time needed for you to fairly appraise his or her progress and performance. Otherwise, you may prematurely conclude that the adviser is either a bum or a hero and be wrong either way.

SET REASONABLE EXPECTATIONS

Consider exactly what it is you are hoping the adviser will do. To do the job properly, he or she is spending a lot of time reading, a lot of time talking to informed sources such as company officials, and a lot of time analyzing financial data. This, after all, is what you would presumably be doing in order to find the best investments, too, if you only had the time. What you hope your advisor is *not* doing is spending a lot of time talking to clients on the telephone about *their* portfolios (even if they are the same as yours). It may be tempting to stay continuously abreast of what's going on, but it is well worth remembering that time spent chatting about "the market" with your investment adviser is time when he or she is not doing anything more for your portfolio than you are—and the adviser is getting paid for it!

ALLOW TIME

A second cardinal rule in the proper care and feeding of your relationship with your investment adviser concerns the need for *time* to produce the results that both of you want to see. Unless you have agreed with the adviser that you are interested in extremely aggressive management of the portfolio, with its attendant high risks, you cannot expect to see dramatic results the moment you turn over the portfolio. In fact, immediate results that are dramatically higher than the benchmarks you have agreed upon are either the result of luck (and, as such, temporary) or of risk levels that are probably higher than they should be.

In the unhappy event that your experience in the first six months is substantially less favorable than that of the performance benchmarks, it probably makes sense to meet with your investment adviser to go over the rationale for purchases made and the subsequent failure of that rationale to work out. Barring a complete loss of confidence in the adviser, however, make some allowance for the fluctuations that *will* occur in the adviser's performance vis-à-vis the standard benchmarks.

In addition, remember that the best investment gains are almost always made over time, as the market finally recognizes the inherent worth in a situation. When your adviser selects a stock, it is by definition with the expectation that the rest of the investing public will at some point see the company's future prospects in the same light. No one, however, can successfully guess *at what point* the true value of a company will become obvious to other investors. Nor can anyone choose only undervalued stocks that are *just about to* become discovered by the market.

The need for considerable actual experience in working with an investment adviser before drawing conclusions about his or her performance underscores the need to take time in selecting the right adviser in the first place. The relationship between client and adviser will normally improve over time as greater understanding and greater confidence flow out of the working relationship. In the beginning, however, you should plan to give the adviser at least one year, if not more, before reaching a definite conclusion if it is to be based only upon the actual results achieved over that time.

Obviously, there are many reasons why such a relationship may not work out, and many of these may be apparent in a much shorter time. If, however, you plan to use results as a hard decision criterion, you really should enter the agreement prepared to give the adviser the time to show what he or she is truly capable of doing for you. Needless to say, you should still monitor the investment adviser's activities, even in the first year. Immediately bring up any irregularities or questions you have, and see that they are resolved to your satisfaction.

COMMUNICATE ABOUT THE POSSIBILITIES

It is just as important to keep open the lines of communication between you and your investment adviser—particularly insofar as your situation may change over time, or as items of special concern to you may arise. There are many paths to reach every goal, and the amount of flexibility and control you and your investment adviser can exercise over your investments, while still carrying out a fundamental strategy, may surprise you.

Volatility

For example, volatility in a portfolio is sometimes disquieting to an investor. The investor may find that significant swings that are observable over a relatively short time horizon are harmful to peace of mind. Appropriate diversification will lessen the impact of volatility, as price changes in one issue tend to offset opposite changes in others. Also, the investor or adviser can impose a considerable degree of control over a portfolio's volatility by using a stock's *beta* as one of the selection criteria.

Beta is a commonly accepted, mathematically derived measure of the volatility of a company's stock relative to the observed volatility of the market as a whole. Every stock has a published beta, and a portfolio can be constructed entirely of low-beta stocks, if volatility is a particular concern. Normally, in a rising market, higher-beta stocks will benefit more than lower-beta stocks; in a down market, these stocks may lead the market down.

If this is a concern, share it with your adviser. You are paying for peace of mind, and if volatility is an issue, the adviser can help reduce it. Remember, though, that volatility in and of itself is neither good nor bad in a portfolio. In the long run, lowering volatility should neither raise nor lower your total return. It is, rather, a variable that can be adjusted to your comfort level.

Risk

Another variable that is to a great extent controllable is risk. However, as discussed earlier, risk is tied inextricably to reward. This simply means that an investor who minimizes risk must anticipate a lower rate of overall return. This, in turn, may well also mean that a portfolio will not perform as well as the benchmark averages such as the S&P 500, during periods when the market itself is operating under conditions of higher risk (for example, economic uncertainty, potentially high inflationary pressures, or in the face of a possible recession such as, for example, the later part of 1989, when many portfolios did not match the surprising growth in the market).

The important point here is that you and your investment adviser should share a common perception of the risk levels that are acceptable to you. Many investors go into a relationship professing a very low tolerance for risk but are then disappointed when the portfolio generates less than stellar returns.

Your investment adviser's job is to maximize the total return (income plus capital gains) of your portfolio *consistent with acceptable risk levels*. In other words, the risk levels must be determined first, and the acceptability of the return gauged according to these parameters of risk. To the extent that you are uncomfortable with the risk in your portfolio (either because it is intolerably high for your peace of mind or because you are interested in seeking a higher total return and are prepared to accept a somewhat higher level of risk), communication between you and the adviser is essential.

Current Income

A third variable over which your investment adviser may exert considerable control is that of current income. As a general rule, current income is inversely proportional to a portfolio's growth potential. Smaller, rapidly growing companies typically are plowing back most or all of their earnings into the company's growth, while larger, mature companies will have fewer demands upon cash flow and will consequently pay out a larger portion of earnings as dividends.

Within these general guidelines, however, there are many exceptions and many degrees of difference. Also, the situation with many companies may change over time. International Business Machines, the classic growth stock, traditionally paid an extremely low dividend rate. In 1989, however, with the stock price languishing, the dividend actually rose to a level substantially above that of the median dividend rate for all stocks in the Value Line universe. In any case, your investment adviser can control levels of current income to a large extent, so communicate your changing needs in this regard.

Keep in mind, too, that at certain times stocks that are generally considered low-growth, high-income investments will for a period of time exhibit characteristics that result in rapid stock appreciation. A good example is the electric utility stocks in late 1989. With interest rates declining, these stocks acted very much like bond substitutes. Their prices rose considerably to reflect the value of their high dividend income stream. Part of your investment adviser's job is to recognize these situations and to take advantage of them for you.

Tax Considerations

A final example of variables your investment adviser can help control—if you make sure to let the adviser know—is tax considerations. These can have a major impact on your portfolio's after-tax performance. In the absence of other information, the investment adviser should manage your portfolio with an eye to tax implications, but not necessarily timing purchase and sale decisions exclusively to the tax consequences. Too often, when an investor postpones selling a stock whose situation has changed simply to postpone recognizing capital gains that have accrued in the stock, the decision not only removes the tax liability for the current year, it removes the tax liability altogether—by letting the gains slip away entirely!

On the other hand, changes in the client's situation with regard to *other* taxable income (or losses) outside the portfolio being managed can be extremely important for the investment adviser to know. With this information, the adviser can make tax-wise decisions to maximize the after-tax benefits of, for example, recognizing taxable gains in years during which the client may have suffered a one-time casualty loss. The point is to make sure that your investment adviser is up to date on your entire personal financial situation, so that you can take full advantage of the variables under the adviser's control.

CONCLUSION

That, in a nutshell, is what clients and potential clients should know about registered investment advisers—how to pick them and how to deal with them. Using an investment adviser can be a true "win-win" situation in which clients work with a professional to improve the already positive situation of dealing with an accumulation of net worth. It does involve a careful selection process and requires a certain amount of faith and a willingness to let the adviser know more about your financial situation than may make you comfortable initially. Also, it requires time to produce really convincing results. Developing a strong relationship with the right investment adviser, however, can provide great dividends in psychological as well as financial terms to the busy individual who cannot pay as much attention to a portfolio as it deserves.

10

FADS

Navigating Perilous Waters

by Richard L. Evans

ARE FADS OPPORTUNITIES OR PERILS? THE SIMPLE ANSWER IS they are both. The same fads that are opportunities for exceptional profits also expose the investor to extraordinary peril. Fads can lead informed investors to superior investment returns, yet at the same time be a disaster to the investor who blindly accepts them at their face value.

Stating that a fad can be both an opportunity and a peril may at first appear contradictory. But fads are just trends. It is how we approach them, and when, that determines whether a fad will turn out to be an opportunity or a peril. Probably most investors think of fads with mixed feelings at best. The basic definition of a fad is that it involves exaggerated zeal, which implies all kinds of negative associations: a craze, a frenzy, a mania, a binge, a speculation, a bubble. Fads imply an eventual collapse. To suggest that investors chase fads has a bad connotation in itself. That the investor lacks the discipline to refrain from joining the crowd is mildly insulting, suggesting that the investor is not able to think independently.

The investor's suspicion of fads is usually exacerbated by the various books on the stock market, which invariably cover fads as part of the market history. Most fads result in excesses that make great reading. One of the classic investment books, Charles Mackay's *Memoirs of Extraordinary Popular Illusions*, chronicles some of the most amazing fads on record, from tulip mania in Holland in the 1600s to the South Sea bubble, one of the most fascinating promotional schemes in history. Mackay's classic, and the variety of books that appear periodically on the market that describe past fads, do not leave the best of impressions.

And, of course, there are the recurring bad experiences of investors who get caught up in a fad and are left holding the bag. At the top of every bull market, there is always a group of stocks that will plummet the most, and more often than not that group includes the issues that are the most popular at the time. Usually individual investors are the last to buy these stocks and the ones who get caught in the inevitable collapse. The reason that fads leave a bad taste in the mouth of many investors is that most investors at some point have lost money by being caught when the bubble bursts. No question, all investors have been burned at one time or another. Yet there is that age-old expression—the trend is your friend—and it is all common sense that you have to be on the right side of the trend to make money.

INVESTING WITH THE TREND

To some degree every successful investor benefits from the popularity of the stocks he or she is buying and selling. Stocks do not rise, obviously, if they have no attraction. Investors who are only buying among the issues that are out of favor on Wall Street, those shunned by the institutional money managers, will find their own portfolios sorely lacking in overall performance. Many of the issues out of touch with the market remain out of sync for several years. To some extent, to be successful investors have to keep in tune with the stock issues that are in demand. Thus, they invariably touch upon fads to some degree or another.

In 1989, the stock market's total return was 32 percent. Heading up the advance were issues such as oil and gas, health care, insurance, telecommunications, pollution control, tobacco, and soft drinks. Investors who held issues in these popular sectors did well. Obviously, investors who held only out-of-favor issues such as computers, autos, steel, aerospace, and financials wound up trailing the market.

Indeed, the value investors, who pride themselves on forsaking fads, did not do very well. In 1989, while the market was up 32%, the renowned value players fell short: Lindner Fund was up only 21.2 percent; Mutual Shares was up 14.9 percent, and Vanguard's Windsor Fund showed a 15.0 percent advance. Just as the underlying stocks themselves are subject to fads, the popularity of a basic style of investing will also determine the success of an investment service. For the value player to succeed, the value strategy has to attain some degree of fad in order to achieve superior results. Performance does not occur in a vacuum.

This chapter discusses the different aspects of fads and how they might affect investment performance. Fads vary in time, degree, extent, intensity, and duration. Fads pass through different stages, with some phases providing better opportunities for gains and others being more vulnerable to peril. Fads have beginnings and, of course, endings. Investors cannot lump fads into one category. Fads are not black and white as to their opportunities and perils.

Fads lend themselves to risk-reward measurements. Many investors know firsthand the rewards of fads—they have led to some excellent gains. However, in the risk area most investors lack guidance. Some fads are just too risky, with very limited odds of achieving gains. Other fads should be avoided entirely.

It is possible to identify fads that are conducive to gains without excessive risk, and to spotlight the stages at which investors can buy most safely. Aspects of fundamental analysis described in Chapter 1 can help you buy in anticipation of a full-fledged fad developing. Methods of technical analysis described in Chapter 2 will help you reduce your risk in buying and set exact price limits on where to bail out. Since fads are fickle and trends can change at any time, you need to be ready for them. Thus, with a little understanding, you can increase your chances for gains and avoid some of the perils of fads.

The Nature of Fads

To understand the opportunities fads create and to avoid some of the perils, you need a working definition of what constitutes a fad itself. How you perceive fads is what will allow you to position yourself for profits and to sidestep some of the pitfalls.

The most common definition of a fad is that it is a high degree of zest for something at an exact point in time. Fads tend to be considered what is the most popular, what is in the highest demand, what is in vogue, what is in fashion, all at a specific time. People tend to view fads as a snapshot, what is in at the moment, a still photo. Fads tend to receive their greatest publicity when the public is already most excited about them, as the news media seek to create an exciting product for viewers and readers. Thus, people tend to remember what fads were like at their zenith.

However, fads are also trends. Fads represent what is popular at any one point in time, to be sure, but being trends, fads also have intensity and direction. Fads can be either increasing in popularity or losing ground. They can be on their way in or moving through the exit door. Fads may be just developing, or they may be unraveling. They may be growing, peaking, or waning, becoming a spent force. Fads can be either short- or long-lived. Fads, being trends, are always reversed at some point.

To have a strategy and to develop tactics that take full advantage of the opportunities that fads offer and to avoid their perils, you must think of fads not as something that is random, static, discrete, but as something that is a continuity, part of a trend. By considering that fads have the same attributes as any trend, you can try to define where you are in the trend of any fad, identify opportunities and perils, and weigh the risk/return ratio. Looking at fads as trends will show you when it is best to buy and when to be ready to sell. If you know where you stand in a trend, you will never need to buy in at the top of a fad; instead, maybe you will be among those selling at the top.

Phases of a Trend

Trends have three phases. The phases of a trend are among its most important characteristics. Since most stocks do not operate independently of the overall market but parallel to some degree, let's first consider the three phases of a major market trend. These are illustrated in Figure 10-1.

FIGURE 10-1

THREE PHASES OF A BULL TREND

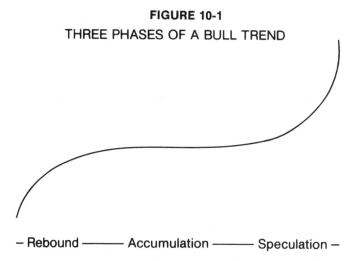

– Rebound ———— Accumulation ———— Speculation –

    The first phase of a bullish trend occurs when stocks are rising from depressed levels—in other words, when stocks are in the midst of a rebound from a previous sell-off. For the major market trend, the first stage is a recovery from the previous bear market. Individual stocks are recovering from sentiment that might be described as panic, if not despair. The second phase is when stocks are being bought in view of higher earnings, when advancing profits and dividends have become a reality, and the momentum for improved future earnings is strong. The fundamentals are linked to performance most closely in this second phase. The third phase is the speculative phase, when investors are purchasing stocks solely on the basis of further capital gains—that is, based on price speculation rather than on the investment merit or for investment purposes. During the third phase, investors are buying stocks that have already demonstrated they can advance sharply. Thus, in the third phase, price momentum, not earnings momentum, is the dominant factor.

Rebound
Generally the first phase of a bullish trend is not associated with many fads. Interest in stocks in general is very low, and any advances in stock prices are not due to the popularity of stocks but

instead are a rebound from very depressed levels. Nonetheless, many stocks in this phase are issues that during the previous bull market had ridden high on the crest of a fad and had fallen hard. These issues, being the most overvalued at the previous cycle, have moved to a position of probably being among the most under-valued. Stocks that were a fad once are highly likely to achieve a similar fad status again. Later, we'll highlight a couple of stock groups to show how this tendency works to the investor's advantage.

Accumulation
The second phase is when most stock fads begin. The majority of stocks that end up attaining fad status generally do so at the end of a long rise in earnings as well as capital gains. It is earnings momentum that first flings stocks toward fad status. However, there are exceptions, such as the takeover fads and the new-issue fads, where there is an absence of a first and second stage alto-gether.

Stocks that are deemed fads at some point may become popular based solely on the upward momentum in their price. This happens during the speculative phase. Capital gains appear to be earned instantly. Generally the popularity of these stocks origi-nates in improving fundamentals. The investor has the opportu-nity to identify them in the second phase, which represents the best risk/reward ratio.

Speculation
The third phase represents the sharpest price gains and poses the greatest risks for investors. Price momentum replaces earnings momentum. The third phase is the riskiest to develop and the quickest to vanish. Whereas the second phase tends to be a period of gradual appreciation, the third phase is of very high intensity, with stocks jumping sharply and making the news. What might have taken several years to achieve in terms of capital gains may be duplicated in a matter of months. You can see this in the charts, as stock prices appear to be rising nearly vertically.

In the third phase of the stock market as well as individual stocks, most people will begin to consider fads. That is the phase when many individuals will begin to buy stocks for the first time, when speculative interest in stocks reaches its peak. It is the phase when the most risky fads, such as new issues, first appear. However, while some of the best gains can come from participating in stocks during the third phase, it is also the most dangerous time. Indeed, investors should be in stocks when they are entering the third phase and should look for profit-taking opportunities at the time stocks are in a high fad status. You want to be the one selling, passing on the higher risk to those who fear they are missing out.

Thus, you primarily should be buying stocks that have the potential to develop into fads. That means buying them in the first or second phase of the trend. It does not guarantee locking into a fad, but since earnings momentum leads price momentum, it is by far the best approach.

TRACKING THE PHASE

There are any number of sources of information for tracking stocks where momentum is building and earnings are on the rise. The Value Line system (Value Line Publishing, Inc., 711 Third Avenue, New York, NY 10017, $525 for 1 year) weights earnings momentum to a fairly high degree. Stocks moving up in Value Line's ranking system do so primarily because they have better than expected earnings; those moving lower reflect earnings disappointments. Value Line also ranks the industry groups based on their momentum. Figure 10-2 shows examples of Value Line rankings. At year-end 1989, Value Line's top groups contained many of the most popular issues—toys, drugs, shoes, household products, oil field services, medical supplies—all showing good earning momentum. The system does not get you out at the very top, but it can help you get in during the first or second phase.

Ford Value Report (Ford Investor Services, Inc., 11722 Sorrento Valley Road, Suite I, San Diego, CA 92121, $120 for 12 monthly reports) is one of the lesser advertised services, but it is one of the best sources for determining earnings momentum. Figure 10-3 shows a sample page from one of these reports. Earnings increasing by a consistent 10 percent each quarter have basically zero momentum. Their trend is a flat 10 percent. However, the stocks that have the best potential for attaining fad status are those where earnings are increasing at an increasing rate. For example, if the last four quarters show earnings improvement of 9 percent,

FIGURE 10-2

INDUSTRIES, IN ORDER OF TIMELINESS*

Arrow (▲▼) before name indicates that a **significant change** in Rank has occurred since the preceding week.

1	Toys & School Supplies	25	Chemical (Specialty)	49	Steel (Integrated)
2	Shoe	26	Telecom. Equipment	50	Canadian Energy
3	Drug	27	Grocery	51	Metal Fabricating
4	Investment Co.(Foreign)	28	Investment Co. (Income)	52	Securities Brokerage
5	Financial Services	29	Japanese Electronics	53 ▼	Broadcasting/Cable TV
6	Beverage	30	Toiletries/Cosmetics	54	Homebuilding
7	Medical Supplies	31	Precious Metals	55	Food Wholesalers
8	Household Products	32	Electrical Equipment	56 ▲	Petroleum (Integrated)
9	Oilfield Services/Equip.	33	Electronics	57	Drugstore
10	Coal/Alternate Energy	34	Insurance (Life)	58	Office Equip & Supplies
11	Medical Services	35	Machinery (Const&Mining)	59	Home Appliance
12	Computer Software & Svcs	36	Retail (Special Lines)	60	Recreation
13	Industrial Services	37 ▲	Telecom. Services	61	Electric Utility (East)
14	Copper	38	Aluminum	62	Machine Tool
15	Tire & Rubber	39	Apparel	63	Metals & Mining (Gen'l)
16	Investment Co.(Domestic)	40 ▲	Bank (Midwest)	64	Semiconductor
17	Insurance(Prop/Casualty)	41	Packaging & Container	65	Retail Building Supply
18	Advertising	42	Tobacco	66	Bank
19	Restaurant	43 ▲	Furn./Home Furnishings	67	Hotel/Gaming
20	European Diversified	44	Metals & Mining (Ind'l)	68	Multiform
21	Petroleum (Producing)	45	Machinery	69	Steel (Specialty)
22	Insurance (Diversified)	46	Natural Gas(Diversified)	70	Electric Utility (West)
23	Chemical (Basic)	47	Paper & Forest Products	71	Building Materials
24	Food Processing	48	Railroad	72	Steel (General)

73	Natural Gas (Distrib.)				
74	Newspaper				
75	R.E.I.T.				
76	Electric Util. (Central)				
77	Precision Instrument				
78	Retail Store				
79 ▼	Real Estate				
80	Air Transport				
81	Maritime				
82	Auto & Truck (Foreign)				
83	Aerospace/Defense				
84	Auto Parts (Replacement)				
85	Textile				
86	Chemical (Diversified)				
87	Manuf. Housing/Rec Veh				
88	Bank (Canadian)				
89	Computer & Peripherals				
90	Thrift				
91	Cement				
92	Publishing				
93	Trucking/Transp. Leasing				
94	Auto & Truck				
95	Auto Parts (OEM)				

*Based on the Timeliness ranks of the stocks in the industry

Noteworthy Rank Changes

Listed below are some of the stocks whose Timeliness ranks have changed this week. We include mostly rank changes caused by fundamentals such as new earnings reports. Even when a significant change in earnings momentum has been forecast, the stock's rank will not be affected until the actual results, confirming that forecast, are reported. In most cases, we omit stocks that have been bumped up or down in rank by the dynamism of the ranking system.

STOCKS MOVING UP IN RANK

Stock Name	Old Rank	New Rank	Reason for Change	Earnings Est. 12 months to 6-30-90
Delchamps Inc.	3	2	Higher than expected earnings. Dec. quarter 39¢ vs. year ago d1¢. Our estimate was 15¢.	Under Review
Family Dollar Stores	4	3	Earnings turnaround. Nov. quarter 22¢ vs. year ago 20¢. Our estimate was 20¢.	$.83
Fuller (H.B.)	5	4	Surprise factor, earnings turnaround. Nov. quarter 53¢ vs. year ago 51¢. Our estimate was 44¢.	Under Review
Kentucky Utilities	4	3	Surprise factor, greater than average gain. Dec. quarter 57¢ vs. year ago 30¢. Our estimate was 35¢.	(A)
Star Banc Corp.	4	3	Greater than average gain, as forecast. Dec. quarter 57¢ vs. year ago 49¢. Our estimate was 56¢.	2.10
Town & Country	5	4	Earnings turnaround. Nov. quarter 53¢ vs. year ago 47¢. Our estimate was 60¢.	Under Review

STOCKS MOVING DOWN IN RANK

Stock Name	Old Rank	New Rank	Reason for Change	Earnings Est. 12 months to 6-30-90
Ames Dept. Stores (B)	4	5	Lower than expected earnings. Management forecasts a loss for the year vs. year ago $1.20. Our estimate was 30¢.	Under Review
BayBanks	4	5	Lower than expected earnings. Dec. quarter 43¢ vs. year ago $1.44. Our estimate was 98¢.	Under Review
GenRad (B)	4	5	Lower than expected earnings. Management forecasts d11¢-d17¢ for the Dec. period vs. year ago 11¢. Our estimate was d3¢.	Under Review
Hannaford Brothers	1	2	Dynamism of the ranking system.	
Hovnanian Enterprises (B)	3	4	Surprise factor, earnings reversal. Nov. quarter 2¢ vs. year ago 34¢. Our estimate was 40¢.	Under Review
Knogo Corp. (B)	3	4	Lower than expected earnings. Nov. quarter 19¢ vs. year ago 25¢. Our estimate was 32¢.	
McCormick & Co. (B)	1	2	Decreasing profit growth. Nov. quarter 83¢ vs. year ago 75¢. Our estimate was 86¢.	$.43
Outboard Marine (B)	4	5	Lower than expected earnings. Management forecasts d75-d95¢ for the Dec. quarter vs. year ago 6¢. Our estimate was d20¢.	2.59
Teledyne, Inc.	3	4	Surprise factor, earnings reversal. Dec. quarter $5.68 vs. year ago $8.70. Our estimate was $8.85.	.60
United Stationers	4	5	Lower than expected earnings. Nov. quarter 24¢ vs. year ago 47¢. Our estimate was 40¢.	Under Review

(A) New full-page report in this week's Ratings & Reports.
(B) Supplementary report in this week's Ratings & Reports.

Factual material is obtained from sources believed to be reliable, but the publisher is not responsible for any errors or omissions contained herein.

241

FIGURE 10-3

FORD VALUE REPORT

Financial Data for 2000 Common Stocks
Intrinsic Value Analysis • Earnings Trend Analysis

Feb. 28, 1990

COMMON STOCK	QUALITY RATING	CURRENT PRICE	12-MONTH EARNINGS	GROWTH RATE NORMAL EARNINGS	DIVIDEND YIELD	NORMAL P/E RATIO	PRICE/VALUE RATIO	EARNINGS TREND
A + W BRANDS	B-	29	1.14	1.14	17	0.0	25.4	1.92	24
3 AAR	B	31	1.67	1.67	14	1.5	18.6	1.33	4
AARON RENTS	B-	9	0.78	1.00	12	2.1	9.4	1.04	94
ABBOTT LABS	A	64	3.85	3.85	15	2.2	16.8	0.81	4
7 ABITIBI-PRICE	B	13Q	0.65	1.25	5	3.3	12.2	1.67	42
ACCEL INTL	B-	8	1.08	1.08	9	0.0	6.9	1.17	-2
ACETO	B+	15	1.28	1.28	10	0.9	11.5	1.29	2
ACME-CLEVELAND	C+	10	0.71	1.10	7	4.0	9.2	1.27	-108
ACME ELECTRIC	C+	10	0.78	0.78	7	3.6	11.4	1.50	-161
ACME STEEL	B-	16	3.00	3.00	10	0.0	5.2	0.79	-113
ACTION IND	C+	3	0.19	0.80	10	0.0	3.6	0.60	171
ACUSON	B-	33	1.60	1.60	25	0.0	20.7	0.70	-6
ADC TELECOM	B	22	1.45	1.45	14	0.0	14.8	1.38	96
ADDINGTON RES	C+	16	0.67	1.20	18	0.0	13.3	1.00	51
3 ADIA SERVICES	B	24	1.63	1.63	19	0.6	14.4	0.76	10
ADOBE RESOURCES	C+	13	-1.07	0.75	11	0.7	17.7	2.66	91
ADOBE SYSTEMS	B-	30	1.55	1.55	22	0.7	19.5	0.81	12
ADVANCED MICRO	C+	8	0.44	1.00	13	0.0	8.3	1.02	167
2 ADVANTA	C	10	0.91	0.91	12	1.0	10.7	1.38	231
ADVEST GROUP	C+	6	0.74	1.00	11	2.5	6.4	0.79	-119
3 AETNA LIFE	A-	50	5.54	6.00	7	5.5	8.3	0.81	3
7 AFFIL PUBLICATNS	B+	11	0.63	0.65	13	2.2	16.5	1.12	-172
AGENCY RENT-CAR	B	14	0.68	0.68	18	0.0	20.0	1.25	-61
AHMANSON, H F	B	19	1.95	2.50	8	4.6	7.6	0.86	59
7 AIFS	C+	5	-0.24	0.60	13	0.0	8.5	1.05	-244
AILEEN	C+	2	-1.07	0.50	7	0.0	4.3	0.95	-334
AIR EXPRESS INTL	C+	16	1.46	2.00	12	0.0	7.8	1.06	-43
AIR PRODUCTS	B+	45	3.74	3.74	11	2.9	12.1	1.08	-10
2 AIR WIS SERVICES	B-	9	0.36	1.25	11	0.0	7.3	1.00	-24
2 AIRBORNE FREIGHT	B-	42	2.67	2.67	10	1.4	15.7	1.03	53

COMMON STOCK	QUALITY RATING	CURRENT PRICE	12-MONTH EARNINGS	GROWTH RATE NORMAL EARNINGS	DIVIDEND YIELD	NORMAL P/E RATIO	PRICE/VALUE RATIO	EARNINGS TREND
7 AMER BARRICK RES	B-	19U	0.40	0.40	18	0.4	46.6	2.68	51
AMER BRANDS	A-	63	6.51	6.51	10	4.3	9.7	0.76	10
AMER BLDG MAINT	B+	37	2.21	2.21	11	2.5	16.7	1.38	-21
AMER BUSINESS	B+	22	1.90	1.90	10	3.9	11.8	0.96	32
AMER COLLOID	C+	11	0.95	1.00	10	3.9	11.3	1.14	-7
AMER CYANAMID	A-	50	3.35	3.35	10	2.7	15.0	1.19	-10
AMER ELEC POWER	B+	31	3.25	3.25	9	7.9	9.4	1.05	25
AMER EXPRESS	B+	29	2.70	2.70	12	3.2	10.7	0.74	-3
3 AMER FAMILY	B+	15	1.00	1.40	14	2.1	10.7	0.74	16
AMER FILTRONA	B+	24	2.08	2.08	7	3.5	11.7	1.26	26
3 AMER GENERAL	A-	30	3.34	3.40	10	5.3	8.7	0.66	-1
AMER GREETINGS	B	31	2.11	2.11	9	2.1	14.8	1.60	39
AMER HEALTH PROP	B	21	1.65	2.00	4	10.9	10.4	0.88	0
3 AMER HERITAGE	A-	24	2.02	2.02	7	4.2	12.0	1.12	-37
AMER HOME PROD	A	100	7.16	7.16	10	4.3	13.9	0.90	21
AMERITECH	A	58	4.59	4.59	6	5.5	12.6	1.04	4
AMER INTL GROUP	A	97	7.83	7.83	14	0.5	12.4	0.82	-8
7 AMER MAIZE A	C+	17	1.91	2.00	16	3.2	8.3	1.39	-102
AMER MGMT SYSTEM	B	12	0.56	0.75	19	0.0	16.2	0.91	198
AMER NATL INSUR	B+	34	3.59	3.59	6	4.8	9.3	1.06	22
7 AMER PETROFINA	B-	77	6.31	7.50	8	4.1	10.3	1.16	10
AMER PRECISION	B-	21	0.77	0.90	11	1.0	22.8	2.43	-3
AMER PRESIDENT	C+	25	-0.04	0.50	25	2.4	7.0	0.85	-80
AMER SHIP BLDG	C	19	-0.60	0.60	5	0.0	4.4	1.31	469
AMER SOFTWARE	B	19	1.13	1.13	18	1.7	16.5	0.82	0
AMER STORES CO	B	54	1.79	4.00	14	1.8	13.6	1.00	122
AMER TEL + TEL	A	40	2.50	2.50	9	3.0	15.9	1.20	-5
3 AMER TV/COMMUN A	B-	33	0.84	2.00	18	0.0	16.4	1.12	14
3 AMER WATER WORKS	A-	17	1.56	1.56	8	4.7	11.0	1.02	-67
AMERITRUST	B-	21	3.11	3.11	8	6.1	6.8	0.68	-62

#	Name	Rating								
	AIRGAS	C+	17	1.09	1.09	14	0.0	15.4	1.71	-103
	ALASKA AIR GROUP	B-	22	2.41	2.41	10	0.9	9.3	1.27	-38
	ALATENN RESOURCE	B-	11	0.51	1.75	3	9.9	6.4	0.86	4
	ALBANT INTL A	B-	18	1.75	1.75	12	2.0	10.1	1.01	22
	ALBERTO-CULVER	B+	22	1.17	1.17	17	0.9	18.6	1.02	-6
	ALBERTSONS	A-	52	2.81	2.81	15	1.6	18.3	1.02	-5
	ALCAN ALUMINIUM	B-	20U	3.29	2.75	6	5.5	7.4	0.99	-75
3	ALCO STANDARD	B+	29	2.68	2.68	10	2.9	10.9	1.00	-4
3	ALDUS	B-	21	1.21	1.21	22	0.0	17.4	0.79	13
3	ALEXANDER + ALEX	B-	27	1.34	1.75	9	3.8	15.1	1.40	-42
3	ALEXANDER + BALD	B+	30	4.38	2.50	13	2.7	12.0	0.85	91
	ALEXANDERS	B-	49	-0.92	1.75	14	0.0	28.0	2.85	-50
	A L LABS A	B-	20	0.97	0.97	20	0.8	20.9	1.02	21
3	ALLEGHANY CORP	B	84	8.59	8.59	11	0.0	9.8	1.23	56
	ALLEGHENY LUDLOW	B-	39	5.94	3.75	10	3.1	10.4	1.10	-11
3	ALLEGHENY POWER	A-	40	3.72	3.72	3	7.7	10.8	1.06	-13
	ALLEN GROUP	C+	12	0.75	1.25	10	1.4	14.3	1.22	13
	ALLERGAN	B	15	1.04	1.04	12	2.0	14.3	1.22	-178
	ALLIED PRODUCTS	C+	6	0.21	2.50	8	0.0	2.5	0.52	-204
	ALLIED-SIGNAL	B-	35	3.39	3.39	8	5.1	10.4	1.00	-19
	ALLTEL	B+	31	2.26	2.26	11	4.1	13.8	0.96	7
	ALLMASTE	B-	9	0.39	0.39	19	0.0	22.1	1.37	-41
4	ALPHA INDUST	C+	3	-0.02	0.40	11	0.0	6.6	0.99	-51
	ALTOS COMPUTER	B-	5	-0.74	0.65	11	0.0	8.1	1.11	411
4	ALUM CO OF AMER	B	64	10.67	7.50	8	4.7	8.6	0.93	-93
	ALZA	B-	38	0.55	0.70	25	0.0	53.6	1.82	56
2	AM INTL	C+	4	0.27	0.50	9	3.4	7.5	1.38	-274
2	AMAX	C+	24	4.20	3.75	7	3.4	7.1	1.04	-119
	AMBASE	B-	9	2.63	2.63	9	2.2	3.4	0.52	-39
3	AMCA INTL	C+	3U	0.11	0.50	8	4.6	6.5	0.89	23
	AMCAST INDUST	C+	10	0.84	1.40	9	4.9	7.1	0.85	59
	AMDAHL	B	14	1.39	1.39	13	0.7	10.1	0.96	3
7	AMDURA	C		-4.53	0.85	9	0.0	4.4	0.96	-707
	AMERADA HESS	B-	50	6.24	3.00	8	1.2	16.8	2.39	-602
2	AMER BANKERS INS	B-	11	1.40	1.75	8	4.7	6.1	0.79	168
	AMEREN	B-	46	3.54	3.54	8	2.8	13.1	1.57	0
6	AMES DEPT STORES	B-	7	-0.09	1.10	16	1.5	6.0	0.46	285
3	AMETEK	A-	12	0.87	1.00	10	5.4	11.9	0.80	-7
4	AMGEN	C+	58	0.18	1.00	25	0.0	57.5	2.11	507
	AMOCO	A-	55	3.12	3.12	6	3.7	17.6	1.59	-23
	AMP	A-	49	2.63	2.63	12	2.7	18.6	1.16	-11
3	AMPCO-PITTSBURGH	C+	9	0.86	1.00	9	3.3	9.1	1.15	53
	AMR	B	60	7.16	7.00	9	0.0	8.6	1.32	-123
	AMREP	C+	7	1.00	1.00	11	0.0	7.3	1.09	-39
	AMSOUTH BANCORP	A-	23	2.60	3.30	8	6.0	7.1	0.65	-5
3	ANACOMP	C	4	0.12	0.75	12	0.0	4.7	0.69	107
	ANADARKO	C+	32	0.74	1.50	13	0.9	21.2	2.09	-17
	ANALOG DEVICES	B	8	0.40	0.70	15	0.0	11.6	0.98	-69
	ANALOGIC	B-	10	0.73	0.60	13	0.0	16.5	1.85	-221
2	ANDREW	B	22	1.72	1.72	11	0.0	12.8	1.61	3
	ANGELICA	B+	29	1.96	1.96	9	2.8	14.7	1.35	26
	ANHEUSER-BUSCH	A	35	2.68	2.68	14	2.5	13.1	0.71	-20
	ANTEM ELECTRON	B	23	1.39	1.39	14	0.0	16.8	1.56	44
	ANTHONY INDUST	C+	15	1.57	1.57	10	3.0	9.5	1.12	-3
	AON CORP	A-	37	3.54	3.54	10	3.7	10.6	0.84	3
	APACHE	C+	16	0.64	0.75	7	1.8	20.7	2.83	12
	APOGEE	B	15	1.03	1.20	13	1.3	12.6	1.09	15
5	APPLE COMPUTER	A-	34	3.02	3.02	15	1.3	11.3	0.70	20
	APPLIED BIOSCI	B-	32	1.47	1.47	19	0.0	21.8	1.35	9
4	APPLIED BIOSYST	B	14	1.01	1.01	22	0.0	13.6	0.57	-152
2	APPLIED MAGNET	B-	9	-1.28	1.30	17	0.0	6.8	0.52	169
	APPLIED MATLS	C+	26	2.92	2.92	15	0.5	8.9	0.82	-24
	APPLIED POWER	C+	23	1.48	1.48	18	0.5	15.7	1.09	-5
3	ARBOR DRUGS	B	18	1.09	1.09	18	0.9	16.7	0.93	-27
	ARCHER-DANIELS	B+	21	1.71	1.71	11	0.5	12.3	1.32	-20
	ARCHIVE CORP	B-	8	1.16	1.16	14	0.0	6.5	0.66	-55
7	ARCO CHEMICAL	B+	35	4.22	3.50	8	7.1	10.1	0.60	-72
	ARDEN GROUP	C	51	6.98	6.98	11	0.0	7.3	1.01	-22
	ARISTECH CHEM	B-	27	2.36	2.36	11	3.7	11.3	0.94	14
	ARKLA	B	24	0.90	1.50	9	4.5	15.8	1.23	67

Copyright, 1990, by Ford Investor Services, Inc., 11722 Sorrento Valley Road-Suite I, San Diego, Calif. 92121, (619) 755-1327. Published monthly and furnished to clients for their private use. Information and opinions are based on sources believed to be reliable, but accuracy and completeness can not be guaranteed. All security analyses are based on a limited analysis of statistical data and should not be interpreted as recommendations based on a complete investment evaluation. Principals or employees of Ford Investor Services, Inc. may from time to time hold interests in securities mentioned.

12 percent, 16 percent, and 20 percent respectively, then the momentum is positive. Fads develop from these types of performances. The Ford Value Report can often spotlight the first phase, that is, when an issue is depressed, selling under the line of value, but in the midst of an earnings rebound.

The *Wall Street Journal* publishes a table in the "Digest of Earnings" section entitled "Quarterly Earnings Surprises." The table lists the reported quarterly profit figures that are substantially different from the average of analysts' earnings as supplied by Zacks Investment Research. There is some evidence that a stock's price will not immediately fully reflect a change in earnings trend. Therefore, by keying in on the issues showing improving earnings momentum and taking a hard look at those showing disappointments, investors may well get a jump on developing fads and be alerted to some fad issues that are beginning to wane.

When looking at fads, consider the role of fundamental analysis as covered in Chapter 1. Fads, at least the most profitable ones, rarely just drop out of the sky. Some do, to be sure, but these are usually the most short-lived of the group. The majority of fads are simply an extension of a trend, a trend that more often than not has been built on a string of powerful earnings. That is the time when the average investor is on an equal footing with the professional trader. The speculative phase of a fad is quick and dangerous. The earnings momentum phase, however, can last several years, providing an investor with ample time to take a position and lock in an attractive cost basis (purchase price) well before the issue takes off.

CASE STUDY: HOME SHOPPING NETWORK

A typical example of the opportunities as well as the perils of fads is one of the most spectacular of the fads, Home Shopping Network. You can follow its stock performance in Figure 10-4.

Home Shopping Network had all the earmarks of a fad. It created the innovative marketing concept of selling products over cable television. On live sales programs, salespeople showed "club members" quality merchandise, giving the full retail price and a discounted price available to members. Viewers at home could buy on the spot by dialing a toll-free number and putting the charges on plastic.

FIGURE 10-4

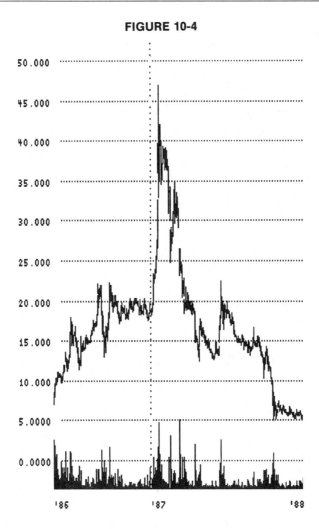

Around the time of Home Shopping Network's initial public offering, several hundred thousand households were members, and the number was growing dramatically. By the end of 1986, sales jumped from $11 million to $160 million and earnings were accelerating sharply. Home Shopping Network had about as much sizzle as the underwriters could have hoped for.

Home Shopping Network went public on May 14, 1986. This issue was to be offered in the range of $14-$16 per share. But given the level of demand, the price was raised to $18, and the number of shares offered was increased from 1.2 million to 2 million. Insiders, no doubt pleased as well by the prospects of heavy demand, upped the number of shares they were selling by over 50 percent. However, the underwriters would find that the issue was apparently still underpriced.

On May 14, the stock opened with the first trade at $42 per share, up 133 percent from the offering price! With the feeding frenzy in full force, trading on the first day was volatile. Over 7 million shares traded hands, and the issue traded as high as 50 before closing at 47¾. Would a prudent investor have bought at 47¾? Probably not. But on the crest of a fad, Home Shopping Network within two months would be trading at over $100 per share. Some of the country's leading business publications were making references to the greater-fool theory at the time, but the fools who bought Home Shopping Network on the first day of trade saw their capital double in about seven weeks.

There would be still more. After the issue hit a high of 108 on June 25, 1986, profit taking sent the issue down 30 percent in just a few weeks. But the buyers were ready to step in, pushing the stock higher once again, past 100 to nearly 130 by Labor Day. In light of the tremendous advance in the stock, Home Shopping Network declared a 3-for-1 stock split in September. A prudent investor at that point could have taken profits at over 40 on the "when issued" shares, but there was still more.

In the weakness that often follows stock splits, Home Shopping Network traded under 30. However, the strength of the fad was still great. Speculators stepped in and pushed the stock back over 30, then over 40, in about two weeks. The stock traded around 40 for the next several months. At the time, the market was undergoing a secondary reaction, so the zest in Home Shopping Network was being tempered. It would not last for long.

When the stock was trading at around $40 per share, the insiders apparently thought it was due for another split. Management declared a 2-for-1 split, and the stock began trading on a when-issued basis at 18½ on December 26. What a Christmas present the split was going to provide!

On the first Monday of the new year, when the Dow Jones Industrial Average first moved above the 1986 high, it was apparent that the bull market was alive and well. On January 8, 1987, when the Dow closed above 2000 for the first time ever, the mood was electrifying, and the implications for a hot fad such as Home Shopping Network were predictable.

In just 11 trading days, Home Shopping Network doubled, moving from a close of 18⅞ on January 2, 1987, to a close of over 38 on January 20. A 100 percent move in just two weeks would be quite a reward for the investor who ignored all the rules of fundamental analysis and had bought this vastly overpriced issue at any time. The same week that the issue doubled, it traded as high as 47, and closed at an all-time high of 40. When it closed at 40 on January 23, Home Shopping Network had moved up 112 percent since the first of the year. For the favored few (the big institutional investors, not the public at large) who were able to buy the stock at the offering price at a split-adjusted price of $3.00, the gain was now over 1,000 percent.

With the potential of a 1,000 percent gain in just a little over half a year of committing one's capital, it is no wonder that fads such as Home Shopping Network generate so much of a frenzy. The profit potential can be enormous, and anyone who says that fads are always a disaster for investors obviously is not considering the potential rewards from playing the fad. Fads have been, and will continue to be, great sources of profits. As explained later in this chapter, it all comes down to timing. Right now, though, consider how this fad collapsed.

On January 26, Home Shopping Network would trade at 40 for the last time. In the several weeks following its January 26 close of 40⅛, Home Shopping Network would trade in the upper 30s, but the balance between buyers and sellers was changing. On Friday of the week ending February 13, the stock had broken to the low 30s. A month later, by the week ending March 13, the issue had broken into the 20s. Two weeks later, on March 23, the stock was trading at under $20 per share, a 50 percent loss in just two months.

The stock took a few weeks longer to come down than it did to rise, but a 50 percent drop in eight weeks is rather startling. Exactly one year from the date of the new issue, by May 15, 1987, Home Shopping Network had lost 80 percent of its gains. Thus,

Home Shopping Network had dropped nearly as fast as it had risen.

There was some attempt to rally the stock during the Dow Jones Industrial Average's final push to the August 1987 high. Home Shopping Network rallied briefly during the summer to above 20 for a few weeks. But the back of the Home Shopping Network fad had been broken, and the October 1987 crash saw Home Shopping Network driven down to under $10 per share. By the end of the year, Home Shopping Network was trading at 5¼. After taking into account the splits, Home Shopping Network was trading at a loss of about 37½ percent compared to when the issue first traded on May 14, 1986. It is probably fair to assume that most investors who had come in contact with the Home Shopping Network fad wish they had losses of *only* that amount.

Not all fads are as dramatic as that of Home Shopping Network, but the lessons are about the same. The potential for gain is offset by equal potential for loss. There are ways to play the fads, to try to position oneself for some of the gains, to buffer oneself against some of the perils. But these only work if investors in hot pursuit of a fad keep the big picture in perspective.

PATTERN OF STOCK PRICES

Since a picture is worth a thousand words, think of the Home Shopping Network fad in the following terms. After all the hoopla of a new issue, after the splits, after all the days when Home Shopping Network was leading the list of new highs, after all the factors that seemed to create the illusion that Home Shopping Network's stock price would keep curving upward at an even faster clip, the eventual pattern looks a lot like the standard bell-shaped curve so beloved by statisticians. As shown in Figure 10-5, the bell-shaped curve shows the price accelerating at an ever-faster clip, followed by a process of topping out, followed by a rate of descent that mirrors the rate of the prior ascent. Thus, although there is nothing normal about fads at all, they are most predictable in their eventual chart pattern. The steeper the rise, the steeper the fall, which is nearly always inevitable.

FIGURE 10-5

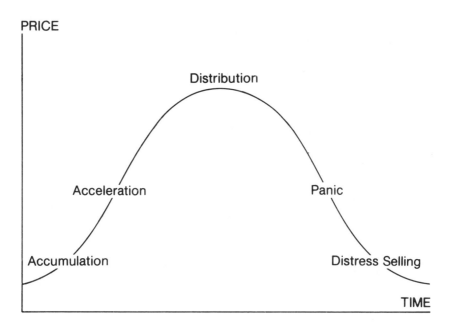

Perhaps you remember Minnetonka, the original manufacturer of liquid soap. As a new issue in 1972, Minnetonka's stock assumed the bell-shaped curve distribution, as you can see in Figure 10-6 (page 250). When liquid soap was all the rage at the beginning of the 1980s, the typical bell-shaped pattern emerged again. For every fad that continues to live up to promises, there are probably a hundred that look like Minnetonka.

Figures 10-7 through 10-10 (pages 250–252) are four charts of issues that were reflecting not so much fads in themselves as the frothy markets that had developed in the over-the-counter issues fad in 1983. These stocks are in Douglas & Lomason, a steel fabricator; Food Lion, a retail supermarket chain; Nike, which started the shoe fad; and Quotron Systems, a distributor of financial information. All had the familiar characteristics of a fad—the meteoric rise followed by the meteoric fall. The bell-shaped curve is the rule, not the exception.

FIGURE 10-6

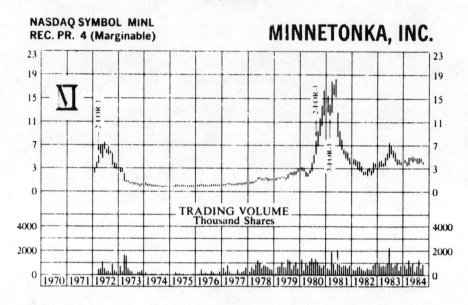

NASDAQ SYMBOL MINL
REC. PR. 4 (Marginable)

MINNETONKA, INC.

FIGURE 10-7

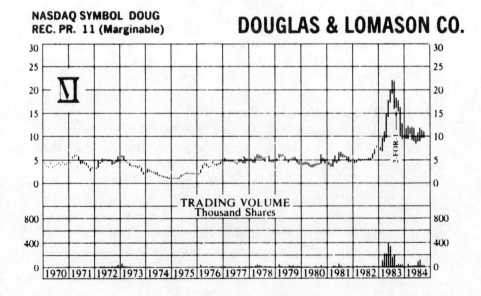

NASDAQ SYMBOL DOUG
REC. PR. 11 (Marginable)

DOUGLAS & LOMASON CO.

FIGURE 10-8

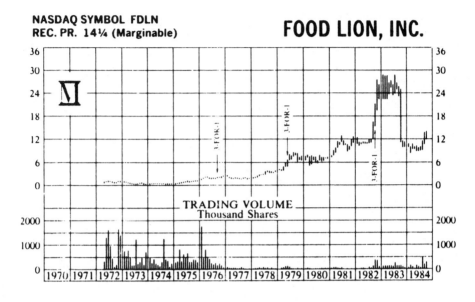

FIGURE 10-9

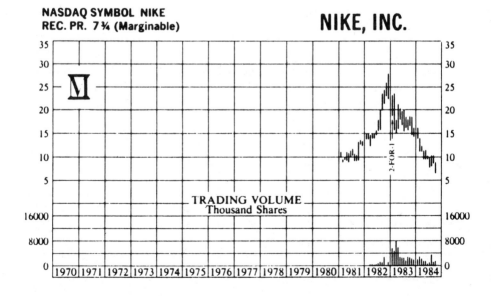

FIGURE 10-10

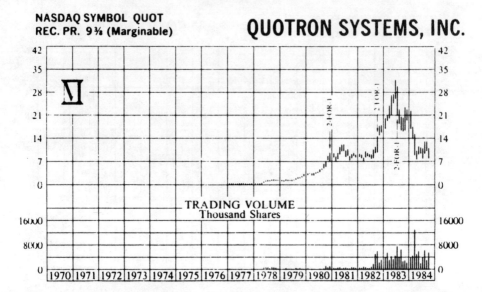

NASDAQ SYMBOL QUOT
REC. PR. 9¾ (Marginable)

QUOTRON SYSTEMS, INC.

CASE STUDY: THE NIFTY 50

One of the all-time greatest fads on record, the epitome of how earnings momentum can develop into fad status, was the Nifty 50, which developed in the later stages of the 1970–1972 bull market. The Nifty 50, a neat descriptive term for the top-rated institutional glamour issues, was first coined by Kidder, Peabody and was later to become almost generic. The original Nifty 50 is most often highlighted today as an example of the perils of participating in a fad. In the end, the passing of the Nifty 50 fad was devastating. However, the Nifty 50 would not have come about at all without earnings momentum, and that it turned into a fad by itself underscores the importance that earnings play in the evolution of any fad.

The Nifty 50 had several attributes that made those stocks top investment choices to begin with. For one, they included only the most stable of the companies in the country, with names such as Anheuser-Busch, Coca-Cola, Eastman Kodak, Hewlett-Packard, IBM, Johnson & Johnson, McDonald's, Polaroid, and Xerox. These issues were not speculative stocks in any sense, but the bluest of the blue chips. The Nifty 50 contained the most respectable and the safest stocks an institutional investor could own.

The Nifty 50 were primarily issues with a proven earnings record and proven earnings gains, and that implied multiple advantages. For one, they were considered one-decision issues. That is, just by investing in the proven earnings gainers, an investor could sit back and take it easy. The issues represented the ultimate of a buy-and-hold strategy, since their growth was considered locked up. Timing the purchase of the stocks became a nonfactor, because the earnings growth would eventually bail out the money manager. Even if the market valuations on the stocks began to rise to fairly lofty levels, the earnings advances would turn out to justify the large premiums. The future growth would vindicate paying the large premiums.

What is probably the most important lesson is that, in the later stages of this premier growth stock fad, these issues were riding purely on price momentum and speculation. They were being purchased not because their earnings were rising, but because their price momentum was so strong. In mid-1972, many stocks had already entered a bear market. A two-tiered market concept came into being, with the proven growth issues moving forward while the lesser-grade issues began to fall by the wayside. The Nifty 50 seemed immune to the bear market that was taking other issues lower. While the Nifty 50 issues were investment grade, their purchase had turned totally speculative.

Table 10-1 (page 254) lists some of the most popular of the Nifty 50 during that time period. The price-earnings ratios on the stocks rose to some fairly lofty levels at that time. For these stocks as a group, the average price-earnings ratio was 52, with one of the most proven of the stocks, Polaroid, commanding a price-earnings ratio of over 100. The price-earnings ratio of the Dow Jones Industrial Average was around 15, so the investment community was willing to pay over three times more for this group.

Eventually, as with any fad, all stocks revert to a price that is average for that stock and for the market as a whole, and may even decline below that price. When the Nifty 50 issues corrected, the losses were absolutely devastating. Some of the companies did stumble in terms of slower earnings growth. The fundamentals did shift for some stocks. However, the most damage was incurred just as the realities of the bear market caught up with them, and the majority of the price declines came as a result of the shrinking

TABLE 10-1

REPRESENTATIVE NIFTY 50 ISSUES

Stock	P-E Multiple	1972–1974 Stock Price		Loss (High to Low)
		High	Low	
American Hospital Supply	55	55	18	−67.3%
Anheuser-Busch	40	69	20	−71.0
Automatic Data Processing	86	97	20	−79.4
Avon Products	64	140	18	−87.1
Bausch & Lomb	74	97	17	−82.5
Baxter International	72	61	24	−60.7
Black & Decker	48	41	20	−51.2
Chesebrough-Pond's	37	46	13	−71.7
Coca-Cola	41	150	44	−70.7
Digital Equipment	55	122	45	−63.1
Walt Disney Productions	81	115	16	−86.1
Dr Pepper	58	30	7	−76.7
Eastman Kodak	37	151	57	−62.3
Emerson Electric	34	53	20	−62.3
Emery Air Freight	56	75	25	−66.7
Heublein	34	45	17	−62.2
Hewlett-Packard	52	100	52	−48.0
Holiday Inns	39	55	4	−92.7
Honeywell	38	170	17	−90.0
IBM	33	365	150	−58.9
International Flavors & Fragrances	65	49	19	−61.2
Johnson & Johnson	61	133	72	−45.9
Eli Lilly & Co.	40	92	47	−48.9
Marriott	56	37	6	−83.8
McDonald's	81	77	21	−72.7
Merck	41	101	46	−54.5
Minnesota Mining & Manufacturing	35	91	44	−51.6
Polaroid	114	149	14	−90.6
Schering-Plough	44	87	41	−52.9
Schlumberger	54	92	48	−47.8
Texas Oil & Gas	53	35	7	−80.0
Upjohn	44	104	41	−60.6
Xerox	7	171	49	−71.3
Average	52			−67.6%

price-earnings ratios. When the price-earnings ratio on the overall market declined from the midteens to less than 7 by the time the 1973–1974 bear market had run its course, the price-earnings ratio on the Nifty 50 had lost even more ground.

As a group, the issues that had ridden the crest of the proven-earnings-performer fad had average losses of 67 percent. Losses ranged up to over 90 percent in many cases. Not one of the group had a loss that was less than the loss on the overall market. This was not so much a price decline due to a decline in fundamentals, as it was the waning of a fad, a shift from high confidence, as presented by sky-high multiples, to a period of sobriety, as represented by price-earnings ratios that were now down in the single-digit range.

The Nifty 50 fad will go down as one of the ultimate fads, one that was due to buying, not by the often-maligned individual investors, but by the best and the brightest of the Ivy League MBAs, running the biggest of the institutional funds. The Nifty 50 fad is simply the best example of the natural development of a trend, a trend that starts with rising earnings being translated into higher stock prices, then moves into the fad stage, where the principal driving force is buying on the basis of rising prices.

Earnings momentum to some degree has always carried the seeds of most of the stock market fads and will continue to do so. Fads just don't appear out of the blue; they develop, and they do so after a period of rising earnings creates the potential for fad conditions. And due to the nature of the evolution of a fad, it is very practical for the individual investor to buy during the developing phase. Indeed, given the risks of buying at the very top, investors should probably buy only during this part of the phase or not at all. There is, of course, no guarantee that the speculative fad phase of the trend will develop. But as the Nifty 50 shows, when it does, there is no telling to what dizzying heights the fad will push stock prices.

PAYING A PREMIUM

The case of the Nifty 50 shows the excesses that can enter the stock market even concerning issues with proven track records. With the Nifty 50, investors thought they needed to make only one decision: buy the issues with the best growth rates. But as stated earlier, the premiums paid for stocks inevitably regress to the mean. Long-term investors generally draw a line on what price they are willing to pony up in light of current earnings. If the price-earnings ratio of the market is 14, then common sense dictates that relatively higher risk comes into play for every dollar a stock is priced at higher premiums. In the case of the Nifty 50, a group priced at a 200 percent premium to the market, the inevitable regression to the mean resulted in a 67 percent loss.

It is a truism that history repeats itself. As the Nifty 50 abounded in the early 1970s, the New Wave Nifties were in the forefront in the 1980s to the present. Today, the "Brand Name" stocks hold forth to the exclusion of most of the market. Investors would be wise to exercise caution in paying up for such labels.

If investing in the proven growth stocks carries a risk, then what can be said about the issues trading at speculative price levels when there are no current earnings, where the price is solely based on the prospects of future earnings potential? In this type of fad, the old adage that a bird in the hand is equal to two in the bush commands little respect. But as is usually the case, the investor who disregards it can live to regret it. Today the ultimate risk—investing in issues lacking any track record of earnings—is represented by one of the most faddish sectors of the market: the cellulars (telecommunications) and biotechnology issues. Investors should be giving these groups a wide berth. They too will regress to the mean.

THE NEW-ISSUE FAD

By far, the most risky fad that an investor can participate in is the new-issue market. No other fad that investors might play seems to take them in at the very top quite the way the new-issue market tends to do time and time again. The painful results for the average investor participating in the new-issue market not only add up to some major losses on the whole, but unfortunately tend to sour investors on the entire market.

The concept of new issues by itself can be appealing from any number of angles that shape the attractiveness of this fad. For one, a new issue is a chance for an investor to get in on the ground floor. A new issue is generally stock of a company that is emerging in some form or another—that is growing rapidly, has outstanding revenue and earnings figures, has an innovative technology, or offers some bright market concept. The new issue holds the promise of getting in at the beginning and, by definition, implies future gains. But as investors find out, the gains can be extremely short-lived; new issues give way to future losses more often than not. Getting in on the ground floor is not generally the end result—most investors find they have gotten in at the top.

A new issue seems to appeal to the investor's ability to buy something that is not dominated by Wall Street institutions. Trading in Dow Chemical or General Motors is perceived to be controlled by very few. Whether insiders, the pension funds, or the specialists, it is always some group seen as conspiring against the individual investor. The new-issue market, however, is often perceived as fair game.

Unfortunately, the institutional investor is usually at the head of the line with the new issues, and the individual investor is more often than not the last in line. The most promising of the new issues is first offered to selected institutional investors. The individual investor usually receives the trickle-down effect.

The pricing of new issues seems to be right where most individual investors can buy them. The price of a security, as most investors know, is relative—relative to earnings, sales, book value, and so on. However, for new issues what counts is the absolute price. When the average new issue is brought to market at under $20 per share, the price seems right and appears low enough for the individual investor who balks at paying $70, $80, $90 per share for blue chips.

As it usually turns out, this apparent affordability is just another illusion. Given the risks involved with investing in firms offering new stock, the stocks at the time of issue are generally vastly overpriced. Ultimately, the inevitable decline in price of most new issues is due to their basic overvaluation at the start.

What may be the most important reason why new issues seem to be one of the riskiest fads to play is their timing. New issues tend to be most popular when the market is in its most speculative phase. Naturally, Wall Street is going to package the product when the demand is highest. In the third stage of a bull market, prices have already moved into the speculative phase. They are being advanced no longer on expectations of future earnings, but simply on capital gains. Here the new-issue market tends to be the most active and poses the greatest risk for investors.

THE TRACK RECORD FOR NEW ISSUES

Some of the most speculative bull markets in the past have been followed by busts in the new-issue market. The drastic decline in the 1962 market was precipitated by a runaway market in new issues. Electronics was the name of the game in that market, with Texas Instruments setting the pace at over 80 times earnings. However, while the individual investor no doubt saw some profits quickly develop, the profits evaporated even more quickly. Texas Instruments declined 76 percent in the bust. Most investors wished their new issues had held up as well. Many investors never did get back into the market after that debacle in the new-issue market.

New issues were back in force in the 1969 market. During the 1968–1969 bull market, the Dow Jones Industrial Average did not move substantially higher than the levels it had attained back in 1966, undoubtedly, one reason the name "blue gyps" was coined. But, the premiums paid for concept stocks such as Four Seasons Nursing Centers and National Student Marketing resulted in price-earnings multiples of over 100. In such a climate, the new-issue market boomed once again, as shown in Figure 10-11. Predictably, it was short-lived, and in the subsequent bear market, issues such as Four Seasons Nursing Centers and National Student Marketing were trading under $1 per share, reflecting nearly a 100 percent loss. The losses to investors who had jumped into the new-issue market were horrendous.

The next bubble occurred during 1983. The new-issue market had a stirring of interest in 1980, with names such as Apple Computer making the scene. But by 1983, the new-issue market was off and running. During this new-issue boom, major investment banking houses flooded the market with new issues as fast as they could find products. The issues brought to market during the 1982–1983 boom were valued at greater than the cumulative total of new issues for the entire previous decade. While the core of the new-issue boom centered around the technology companies, such

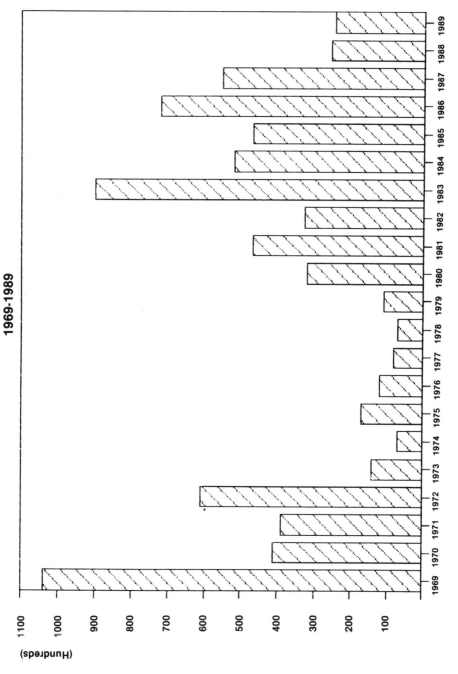

FIGURE 10-11

INITIAL PUBLIC OFFERINGS
1969-1989

as personal computers, software, and disk drives, the feeding
frenzy quickly spread to other issues.

The 1984 decline in the overall market, as measured by the Dow
Jones Industrial Average, was only 15.6 percent. In contrast, the
debacle among the emerging growth stocks and the new-issue
market was devastating and has to this day soured investors'
appetites for new equity issues. The new-issue market, sometimes
thought of as letting the investor get in on the bottom, is in effect
always drawing the investor in at the top. While the investor is
thinking about getting in on the ground floor, the underwriters
have priced the stocks to get top dollar for the issuing company. If
the promoter is charging top dollar for the new issue, can the
investor be getting in at the bottom? Yet that is how new issues are
marketed.

Sure, there will always be success stories. Microsoft is probably
the most successful new issue in recent years. The stock was
brought public on March 13, 1986, at $21 per share by Goldman,
Sachs & Co. and Alex Brown & Sons Inc. At year-end 1989, as
shown in Figure 10-12, the stock was selling at $87 per share, up
64 percent for the year. After factoring in a 2-for-1 stock split in
September 1987, investors who purchased Microsoft for $21 per
share had in 1989 a 728 percent return on their investment, and
the price as of this writing is still going higher. But, as with the
lotteries, there will always be a winner but mostly losers.

For the majority of the new issues, Microsoft is the exception,
not the rule. Over the last 10 years, 60 percent of all new issues
have shown a loss compared to the new-issue price. Worse yet, the
funds invested in the new-issue market showed a loss relative to
the market. In the new issues that were brought to market during
the mid-1980s, only one out of three managed to better the return
of the S&P 500. While there may be a Microsoft in the group, there
are also issues that will end up trading substantially lower. Half of
all new issues during the 1980s were down at least 50 percent
versus the market, and over one out of ten issues were down nearly
a full 100 percent. Picking the next Microsoft is like winning the
lottery, and those who participate in the quest for the next Microsoft among new offerings will wind up taking losses.

FIGURE 10-12 **Microsoft Corp.**

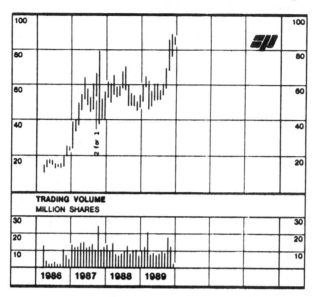

WORST YET: THE CLOSED-END FUND NEW ISSUES

With interest in the traditional new-issue market down in the past few years, Wall Street has revived another new-issue product to promote to the public: the closed-end funds. These new closed-end funds are actually more perilous than the traditional new-issue market. Admittedly, the odds of a 90 percent loss in the prices of closed-end new issues are lower, but the odds of *some* loss in these issues are higher, just by the very nature of the beast.

For starters, shares in closed-end funds trade in the market. They are subject to the forces of supply and demand, just as any other common stock. Unlike the shareholder in an open-end fund, the closed-end fund shareholder doesn't have a safety net to be able to redeem net asset value from the fund in order to bail out of a position. More important, as new issues, the closed-end funds promise almost instant losses to investors. This is because the closed-end fund generally pays a 7 percent commission to the selling broker. This makes them very popular with the brokers, but unfortunately also takes dollars away from the fund's net asset value. Hence, the best you can hope for on an investment in a new-issue closed-end fund is an immediate *negative* 7 percent.

Furthermore, these funds tend to sell at a discount to net asset value anyway, so chances are the loss will be greater still. The 1989 year end average discount for existing closed-end funds is about 19 percent, and the record for new offerings shows that 14 out of the 15 largest were at a loss by year-end. It's tempting to provide detailed examples of recent disasters, but suffice it to say that these funds are the worst of the new issues that the investor can buy!

This type of investing is not to be confused with buying and selling existing closed-end funds. Depending upon their level of discount to net asset value, that can be smart investing.

BUYING STOCKS IN PLAY

When a stock is in the latter stages of its trend—when the price has already jumped sharply in response to increased public awareness, when it has already moved up 50 percent in less than three months, when the price-earnings ratio of the stock is twice the level of a year ago, when the chart of the stock shows the issue breaking through its upper trendlines and rising almost verti-cally—then it is fair to assume that the stock may be in play as a fad. The stock is in the third phase of the trend, the phase that contains the most spectacular run-ups in price, and also the most spectacular declines.

At this point an investor can no longer approach the stock as an investment. Investors have to begin to think like traders. Such a stock can no longer be bought on the basis of earnings momentum. A buy-and-hold approach is the last strategy an investor should use in this case.

At this point an investor has to focus on the short term in timing a purchase as well as in beating a quick exit. While most investors at this stage tend to become mesmerized by the potential of a stock doubling and tripling, the reality of the speculative phase of a fad is such that an investor must become keenly risk-averse. Paradox-ically, preservation of capital becomes the goal, not capital gains.

FINDING THE FAD STOCKS

Finding an issue that is riding on the crest of a fad is least difficult at this time. There will probably be many fads to choose from, a multitude of stocks, and investors have access to a variety of quick references to spotlight them.

The *Value Line Investment Survey* will probably contain many of these stocks in its list of "100 Timely Stocks." Whatever industry group interests you, you are likely to find the hottest representative of that group listed in Value Line's top 100, since the Value Line rankings give considerable weight not only to earnings momentum, but also to recent momentum of stock prices. Just to highlight which groups are the most faddish, Value Line also publishes a table showing those stocks ranked 1 or 2 for "timeliness." These stocks also occur in Value Line's highest-ranked industries, where they are called "timely stocks in timely industries."

Investor's Daily provides excellent coverage of stocks riding high on a fad by the emphasis they provide in "The World's Most Intelligent Stock Tables." Chances are, a stock with an earnings per share ranking of 90 or better and a relative strength ranking of 90 or better is probably enjoying some form of fad status.

Finding a stock in the latter stages of a fad, when public interest is running high, is not difficult at all. The difficulty is buying right during the most speculative phase of a fad, to avoid buying at the top. When an issue is under accumulation in the first or second phases, time is on the side of the investor, who can make the mistake of buying high and still be bailed out. However, when a stock is "in play," then the crucial variable is no longer the stock itself, but timing.

To reduce risk when buying a stock in the latter stage of its cycle the tactic that you must consider involves support levels. This chapter is not intended to be a dissertation on technical analysis, but just as fundamentals play a role in spotlighting a stock that may develop fad status, the form of technical analysis that involves support levels becomes important both for buying and selling.

There is nothing unique about support levels that makes them especially appropriate for fad stocks. Support levels are a basic tool for all stock buying, but especially when a stock is hot. They can provide much-needed discipline at times when an investor is prone to throw caution to the wind. Quite simply, the closer to the support levels that you can buy, the less your downside risk. And limiting the downside risk is the most important consideration; the gains will take care of themselves.

Most investors tend to be lured into buying a stock when the issue is "in the news," drawing attention to itself by perhaps posting a sharp one-day gain, when volume has surged, when the stock perhaps has just made a new high. Of course, it may well be that a stock is indeed breaking out of accumulation, gapping to the upside. However, for every stock that has gone on to post dramatic price advances, these high-volume, sharply advancing stock prices more often than not represent the end of the move for the time being. The stock typically is running up against a resistance level. The more realistic expectation is that there will be a pullback to support; the least risky strategy is to wait to buy these stocks until that occurs.

SUPPORT LEVELS

Support levels are defined as the levels where buyers come into the stock after its price has had some correction, where there is enough demand not only to halt the decline, but possibly to start the stock moving up again. Interestingly, while support can enter into a stock to stem the slide at any time, this tends to occur around a former top. A theoretical support level for any stock that has advanced and is correcting is a former top area of congestion, the price level where considerable stock had earlier changed hands and where buying should enter the picture. For our purposes, the support areas will determine when to buy as well as where to eventually sell a stock.

To see support levels in action, consider the chart of AT&T in Figure 10-13. With a price-earnings ratio of 20, AT&T's stock had become somewhat of a fad in 1989. While the overall picture that year was of a stock that had an excellent move from the mid-20s to the mid-40s, the closer view of the issue shows that following every advance of three to five points, there was some pullback to support. After the advance to 35 in April, the stock had some reaction to 33⅜, just above the tops of late January and early March. After

FIGURE 10-13

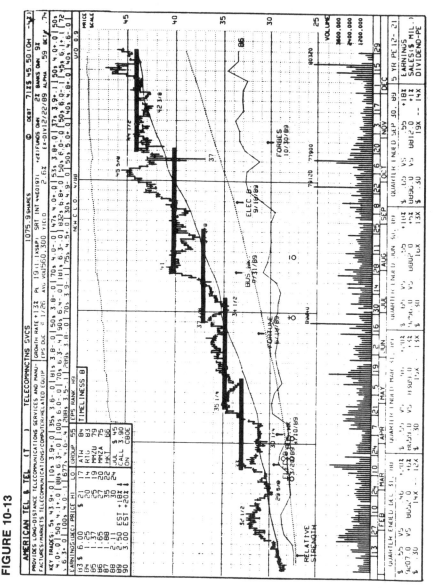

the move to 37⅛ in late June, the issue pulled back to around the April high of 35. After the very sharp advance to 41 in August, the issue had a pullback toward the June highs. After the sharp advance in September to 45⅝, support entered the stock during the mini-October panic at the August highs. After the issue advanced to 47⅜ during December, the pullback was to the top of the congestion that formed at 42–44 following the October panic.

Support levels are among the most interesting and potentially rewarding tools of investing. They are what make up trend development. They are used to construct trendlines. They tend to coincide with important moving averages. The 50-day moving average often intersects minor trend support levels, and the intermediate trend support levels parallel the 200-day moving average.

Above all, support levels help measure risk. The further away a stock has moved from an intermediate support level, in terms of both time and points—in other words, the more space between the stock's current price and the last intermediate support level—the higher the risk. The lack of a close intermediate support level in a "hot" stock should indicate that excessive risks are involved.

For example, Woolworth was a takeover play during the fall of 1989, just as it had been during 1987. When in July the issue had a dramatic breakout through the 55 level, as shown in Figure 10-14, it signaled that buying on minor pullbacks to support would be in order. However, after four minor advance/pullback moves, the issue was trading more than 15 points above its intermediate support level. This indicated that there was room for correction back to the mid-50s once the intermediate move expired. The further away the stock has moved from its last level of intermediate support, its last intermediate consolidation, the greater the downside risk.

The number of times a support level has developed in an intermediate move helps define risk. During an intermediate trend, you can buy after a breakout on the first pullback to support and after the next rally on the second pullback to support, but not any more. After the stock has made three moves in the primary direction, it pays to be on the alert for an important intermediate correction. The more the stock is a fad, the greater will be the correction.

SELLING THE FAD STOCK

When to sell is probably the most frequently asked question by investors. Chapter 11 addresses the subject of when to sell and pin down your profits, so refer to that chapter for a detailed discussion

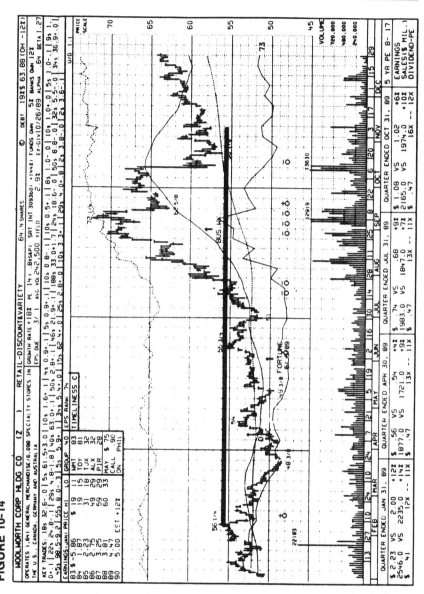

FIGURE 10-14

of timely selling in general. However, with fad stocks, the art of timely selling is even more critical than elsewhere.

THE STOCK SPLIT

The first fail-safe system is based on the role of stock splits in selling out of stocks that are riding the crest of a fad. The common notion is that a stock is split in order to bring the issue into a more popular price range, where it is more affordable to investors. On the surface, this may seem to be the case. A stock that has risen from 50 to 100 and then is split 4-for-1 is apparently more "affordable" at 25. However, this is very much an illusion.

Problems with Stock Splits

On the contrary, stock splits often come at the top of important advances, and sometimes right at the very peak of such a run. Several explanations may account for this.

For one thing, a stock split facilitates profit taking because of the very nature of a split. There is an increase in the supply of shares (in absolute numbers, although not in terms of available equity in the corporation), but there may or may not be an increase in the demand for the new "lower-priced" shares among investors whose interest was formerly dampened by what was seen as a higher price.

Another concern is whether the stock is passing from stronger hands into weaker ones. An issue that has just doubled probably no longer offers the same value, so there is less room for error. The investors who are then buying the issue are doing so based on a higher degree of speculation regarding future price gains. These latest investors do not, as a group, generally have the same staying power as the earlier investors, who have the luxury of a lower cost basis.

Finally, consider what the company is saying by declaring a stock split in the first place. If corporate insiders believe that a stock has moved to such high levels that it is necessary to lower the price artificially through a stock split, then the investor should perhaps also think of other ways the price might be lowered.

For a blue-chip issue that has advanced in line with the market, a stock split may not have quite the same negative significance. If the split reflects an overall bullish stock market, then selling does not have the same urgency.

Case Study: Gambling Stocks

Any number of examples of fads could demonstrate the surprising frequency with which stock splits seem to occur with important tops. One of these was among the greatest fads on record: the gambling stocks in the late 1970s. Before the late seventies, the gambling issues had been an average group. Aside from a few periodic run-ups, nothing happened that could have been considered of semi-fad proportions. However, the legalization of gambling in Atlantic City, New Jersey, in 1978 sent the issues skyrocketing.

FIGURE 10-15

CAESARS WORLD, INC.

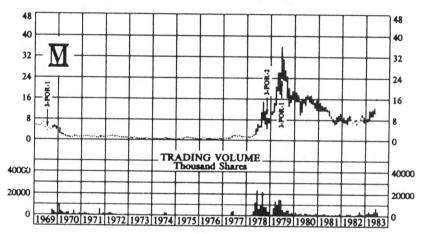

Caesars World had been showing some moderately positive price action before 1978, but when the gambling fad caught Wall Street, the issue soared. As shown in Figure 10-15, the stock price moved from around $7 per share to over $100 per share by June 1979. The stock, which previously had a price-earnings ratio of 7, now carried a ratio that also ran up to over 100. At the time, right when the enthusiasm for the gambling issues was sky-high on Wall Street, investors who took advantage of Caesars' 3-for-1 stock split in June of that year would have had a chance to nail down some timely profits. A month after the stock split, the stock began its descent, quickly declining 50 percent, then gradually eroding in price until it was selling in 1981 at under $10 per share. Investors who sold on the split could have avoided some of the over 80 percent loss.

Bally Manufacturing, which at the time was the major U.S. manufacturer of pinball and slot machines, skyrocketed on the news of its plans to build a hotel/casino in Atlantic City. At the height of the gambling fad in mid-1979, Bally Manufacturing was selling for nearly 100, as shown in Figure 10-16. Investors who took advantage of the 2-for-1 stock split paid in June 1979 were able to avoid a decline that would take Bally back down to under $20 per share less than one year later.

FIGURE 10-16

BALLY MANUFACTURING CORP.

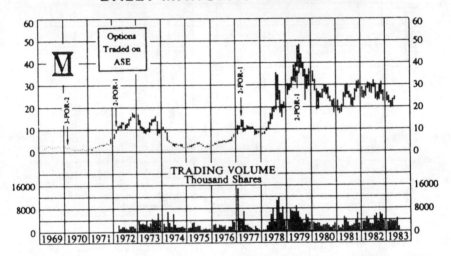

Resorts International was probably the hottest number on the block. The firm was granted the first gambling license in Atlantic City. Envisioning unlimited riches, Wall Street frantically bid up the issue from a price of under $20 per share to a high of over $200 per share. As Figure 10-17 illustrates, in only four months the stock was up 850 percent. Investors who took profits on the 3-for-1 stock split in October did not get out at the very top, but they did avoid much of the pain: the stock by year-end was back to nearly where it was trading before the advance.

In Bally, Caesars, and Resorts International, investors who bought anywhere in the year the gambling stocks were split were going to be left high and dry for a number of years. The one exception proved to be Golden Nugget. Like others in the industry, Golden Nugget had a nice advance in 1978. As shown in Figure 10-18, the stock moved up 350 percent to a high of 45. And in what

FIGURE 10-17

RESORTS INTERNATIONAL, INC.

FIGURE 10-18

GOLDEN NUGGET, INC.

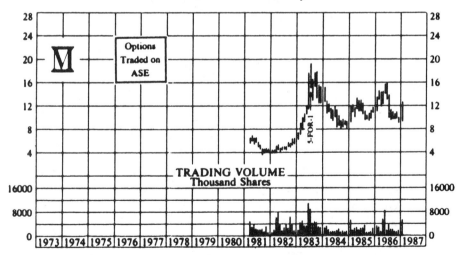

apparently reflected a fad among the companies themselves, Golden Nugget declared a 3-for-1 stock split in July 1978, then proceeded to lose all of its gains of 1978 and then some. It was selling under $7 per share by 1981, an 85 percent loss. However, investors who had failed to bail out on the stock split had another chance in 1983, when Golden Nugget was once again one of the darlings on Wall Street. In mid-1983, Golden Nugget was selling for nearly $100 per share, and in what should be the standard pattern by now, declared a stock split—5-for-1 in July. Investors who had learned their lesson the first time around could have avoided the subsequent 58 percent decline in stock price over the next 12 months.

STOP-LOSS ORDER

Possibly the most important tool of an investor is the use of the stop-loss order, especially for a stock in play. As we've discussed, getting out of a fad stock at the top is a matter of luck. More often than not, there is no fundamental factor that suggests selling, and the technical patterns that signal reversals are sometimes minor. An investor's primary line of defense is the stop loss.

The stop loss, generally considered the last resort, is not always viewed as optimum, since it involves selling after the stock has already declined. But it is often the most practical and only available tactic. By all means, it introduces a discipline that is critical to avoid potential disaster. "Stops" keep a small loss from becoming ruinous. They keep an investor from getting locked into a hopeless situation. Given the catastrophic losses that can develop quickly when a fad wanes, stop-loss points are crucial.

Sometimes an investor sets a stop loss as a percentage of dollar decline that he or she is willing to accept before selling—some percentage retracement of the stock price, perhaps from the high, perhaps from the initial purchase price. Given how steeply a stock can drop and the ruinous losses that can occur, setting a rule to accept only a 10 percent loss of capital is certainly important, if there is no other rule. However, a rule of accepting an arbitrary 10 percent decline from the top price is more than likely going to get an investor out too early, only to see the stock rise to higher levels. The more useful system for setting stops is to use the characteristics of the stock itself.

Progressive Stops

One stop is the progressive stop. The progressive stop is useful in a situation when an investor has good reason to exit a stock. A stock may have already reached a predetermined price objective. More likely, in a fad, the stock is at a point where an investor detects a buying climax. The stock might be at the point of run-away, moving rapidly above a trend channel on heavy volume. Exceptionally high volume typically characterizes the end of moves, and it is the volume indications that call for progressive stops. While this type of formation does not necessarily suggest the final top, but only a minor top, an investor riding a fad stock most definitely will want to protect profits. If so, setting a stop at $\frac{1}{8}$ under the close of an exceptionally high-volume move would be in order.

For example, investors who had been playing AMR as a take-over in the fall of 1989 might have used the progressive stop when the issue rose sharply on August 29, gaining $10\frac{1}{4}$ points on heavy volume of 3.8 million shares. The stock had been in play thanks to takeover speculation in the airline group over the preceding couple of months. The straight-up move on August 29, shown in Figure 10-19 (page 274), could have justified setting the stop at $\frac{1}{8}$ under the close of $91\frac{1}{2}$. On the following day, AMR rose again, and the investor would have raised his or her stop to $97\frac{7}{8}$, $\frac{1}{8}$ under the close of $91\frac{1}{2}$. On the following day, AMR rose again, and the investor would have raised his or her stop to $92\frac{7}{8}$, $\frac{1}{8}$ under the close of 93. As it turned out, the stock gapped down on the very next day, so the stop might well have been taken out at $85\frac{5}{8}$, or $7\frac{3}{8}$ points under the close of 93, on the decline. Subsequently, the issue did spurt to higher ground for a few days, but in the October minicrash, the price plunge of over 30 points ended up well under the price at which the investor had been stopped out. The progressive stop did not result in a sale at the exact top, but it would have nailed down profits in a stock where further gains proved fleeting.

However, progressive stops are very limited in their application. They are designed to trigger an exit after what appears to be the end of a very short-term move. For broader applications, protective stops are preferable.

Protective Stops

A protective stop is used to protect profits or capital, whichever the case may be. It is best used for stocks already riding the strength of a fad. Of course, as previously discussed, getting out at the exact top is more luck than not. A protective stop is designed to (1) take the investor out of the stock whenever there is enough evidence that the intermediate trend has changed, and (2) keep the

FIGURE 10-19

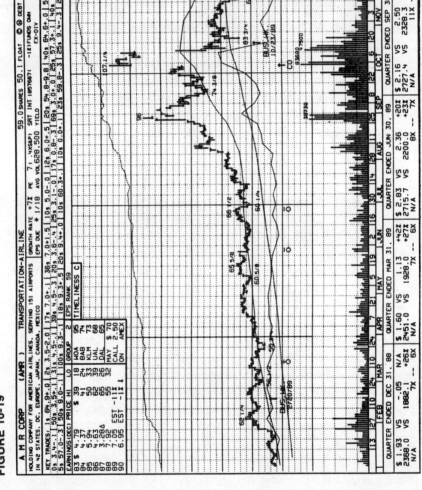

investor in the stock during the bulk of an important move, rather than being taken out by the periodic major corrections along the way.

The protective stop should be set below the last established minor low point. The percentage at which the stock is set below the minor low will vary; a 5 percent stop will probably suffice for the average stock. A stock that is showing greater volatility, or beta, may require somewhat greater percentages, but in general a 10 percent stop below the last minor bottom is the maximum. Your objective is to allow for the issue to have periodic corrections along the way, setbacks in an intermediate uptrend, without your getting taken out of the stocks. On the other hand, when the trend is changing and key support levels are definitely violated, you want to be out of the stock.

As an example, consider another airline—USAir group, which was also riding the crest of the takeover speculation in the airline group in 1989. As shown in Figure 10-20 (page 276), the USAir chart depicts the normal trend development—an alternating series of minor advances followed by minor declines. Through the first seven months of the year, this staircase trend allowed an investor to move up his or her protective stops every time USAir moved to new minor highs, establishing the previous minor lows, and the investor would set the protective stops 5 percent under those lows. Should there be a change in trend, the investor would not be out at the top, but certainly would not be among those riding the stock all the way back down.

In this example, the pattern of increasing protective stops would have resulted in upping the limit many times. The last protective stop was 46½, established after the August 2 advance to 54 set a new minor high as it allowed the investor to set a stop 5 percent under the previous minor low point of 49⅛ on July 25. The previous stop loss of 42 had been set 5 percent under the July 7 intraday low of 44¼ of the previous reaction, and the previous low in turn had been established by USAir rising to a new minor high of 50⅞ on July 21. Every time the stock reaches a new minor high, the investor would advance the stop to 5 percent under the previous minor low.

The length of an intermediate trend is unpredictable, but such a trend cannot go on forever. Note that on USAir's first move over 50, on July 20, volume did increase to its highest level for the year (1.4 million shares). In the subsequent move to over 54 on August 2, the issue rose above its upper channel. In both volume and trend implications, USAir was giving clues that it might be nearing the end of its intermediate move.

FIGURE 10-20

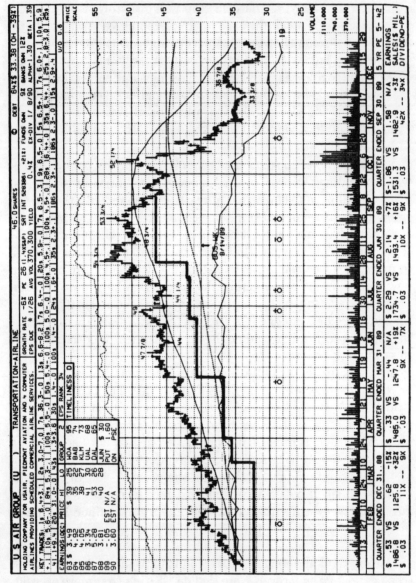

An investor could have sold when the decline from the August 2, high of 54 carried below the previous support low of 49⅛ on July 25, but the reason for setting protective stops 5 percent below the previous lows is to allow for such returns to minor support. Sometimes a return to previous support is a sign that the overall trend is reversing, but sometimes a return to support is necessary to generate enough buying interest to send the issue up for a clear-cut breakout. Note that in June the stock returned to support lows a second time. Nonetheless, when the stop loss of 46½ was taken out on September 15, the trend had most definitely been signaled as being down, so investors should have sold then.

Other Methods

There are other methods for setting stop-loss orders. One method is to set the stop loss under the previous minor high once a new minor high has been established. In the case of USAir, the stop loss would have been set at 48⅜, 5 percent under the July 21 high of 50⅞, given the subsequent move to 54. That would have resulted in getting out of USAir with better profits.

At other times, stocks do not have reactions, but horizontal corrections. The investor can use them for establishing stop-loss points.

Many variations are involved in setting stop-loss points, but the major import is that investors need some predetermined level, to draw some line, when they are going to sell a stock riding the crest of a fad. When the correction becomes obvious to all, the stocks will drop in a tailspin.

When they use stock splits and stop-loss points in dealing with stocks that are riding the crest of a fad, investors risk selling below the top, leaving perhaps substantial sums on the table. However, with fad issues, preservation of capital is more important than selling within ⅛ of a point at the top. When fads stop, they turn on a dime as the airlines did. The greater risk is not getting out in time.

When it comes to fads, investors have to be very careful about being penny wise and pound foolish. An investor may well be able to move out of a stock upon detecting that the stock is not acting well. However, the fail-safe system is to avoid the ruin that can come from hanging on just a little too long.

SELLING FAD STOCKS SHORT

In the day-to-day perception of fads, investors generally think of the opportunities for profits to be made in the rise of a stock propelled higher by fads. The typical investor's psychology is tuned in to the basic strategy of buying stocks long—for example, buying at 30, looking to see the stock rise to 100, split 3-for-1, then repeat the uptrending cycle all over again. During a strong bull market, hundreds of stocks are being pushed higher by some fad or another, and investors typically are repeatedly enticed by the profits to be made through buying long. After all, buying "right" and then seeing a stock move to new highs on heavy volume is one of the most satisfactory experiences an investor can have. Scanning the list of new highs in the morning and seeing your stocks among the honored is a great satisfaction. However, there may be a better and more practical method of profiting from fads—and that is on the short side.

For all practical purposes, by the time the average investor wakes up to a fad in progress, the stock is normally well into the speculative stage. The stock is already hitting new highs; it is in the news, analysts are issuing bullish reasons why to buy, and it just seems that the issue is not going to give investors a break by conveniently letting them in to "buy low." Usually the investor buys into a fad situation near the very top. Once the average investor has caught on, the best gains are usually past. Buying on a minor dip may allow an investor to make a quick 10 points, but most investors are buying late in the move when the volume has expanded, after most of the news is out, and when the early buyers are beginning to take profits. Typically, investors who buy into the fads with a long position do it at exactly the wrong time, and they buy at the top. A far more profitable way to play the fad—and more practical for most investors, given the stage at which they finally discover a fad—is by selling short. "What goes up must come down" is a cliché, but most investors would do well to consider the downside as well as the upside potential for making money in fads.

How to Sell Short

The basics of selling short are quite simple. Instead of buying a stock in the hope it will go up, then selling it when it does, short-selling reverses the process: the investor sells the stock in anticipation that it will go down, then buys it when it does, profiting from the difference between the higher selling price and the lower buying price. To sell the stock without actually owning it, the brokerage house borrows stock from another account and lends it to the short-seller (who is then responsible for paying any dividends declared by the company to the actual owner of the stock from whom it was borrowed).

The only other difference between short-selling and normal investing is that exchange regulations require that a stock may only be sold short when the most recent sale was at a higher price than the prior sale. This so-called "uptick rule" is intended to keep short-sellers from creating a downward cascade in the price of a stock that may be suffering from adverse news developments. In addition, short-selling requires the investor to establish a margin account and post a suitable margin to guarantee the ability eventually to repurchase the stock that has been sold short.

For some reason, buying long is thought of as investing, while selling short is thought of as speculation. For the blue chips, the policy of buying and holding quality common stocks over the long haul is frequently the best policy for most investors. However, buying the fad issues is not investing. Buying the fads is price speculation in its purest form, and if an investor is willing to speculate on the upside, he or she ought to be willing to speculate on the downside. Besides, it may be potentially much more profitable and more practical as well.

Short-Sale Candidates

The stocks that have benefited from fad demand usually have premier qualifications that make them excellent candidates for selling short—big percentage price gains. Because they have achieved some of the most spectacular price gains on the upside, they have the potential to achieve some of the most spectacular price losses on the downside. The greater the distance covered over the shortest period of time on the upside, the more potential for gains from selling short.

In considering stock to sell short, the laws of gravity apply all too well. It takes time and volume and a great deal of effort to push stocks higher, even the fads. However, a stock will fall under its own weight, and sometimes precipitously. Fad issues generally have the furthest to fall, and just as the preceding upswing developed a momentum all its own, so will the ensuing decline. Making money on the downside once the fad issues pass their peak is much quicker than making money on the upside. What may have taken months, if not longer, to achieve by buying and holding can sometimes be achieved in just weeks on the short side.

Simply put, there are profits that can and will be taken in the fad stocks. The fundamentals may still appear bright, but when selling begins to enter the picture, when the emotional sentiment has changed from bullish to bearish, the fad issues typically have the most to lose. Investors should not short the laggards—they should short the leaders, and these include the fads. The potential for profit taking will define the extent of profits on the downside for the short-seller.

Support and Resistance

In a sense, an investor might consider the support and demand zones of stocks. By looking for the stocks that have ridden the crest of popularity, you're apt to find issues that are now trading far above areas of long-term or even intermediate support. Remember, stock prices are a function of supply and demand. When a stock is selling far above its area of support and potential demand, it does not take a great deal of supply to come out to tip the balance toward the selling side.

What you should look for in any stock to short is that there be a long way down to potential support. The fad issues typically paint such a picture. It is not uncommon for some of the stocks that have had the most spectacular advance to have losses of up to 90 percent or more. It is a long way down before a new batch of buyers will be willing to step in. If a fad issue appears to be falling in a vacuum—it is.

Timing Short-Selling

In looking for where to short a fad issue, the first step is to look for stocks that have had some sort of breakdown after a long uptrend in prices. A short-selling candidate reveals itself because it has already suffered a potential reversal. A stock is not sold short because it has tripled, because it has risen from 30 to 120, or because the price-earnings ratio is high. A stock cannot be shorted because investors feel that it is too high. In a bull market, when speculative fervor is running high in the fad issues, they can move up a lot higher than many investors expect. That a stock is high is no reason to short. Not until a high-priced stock has had a reversal—a crack in the armor, so to speak—does it create the potential opportunity to sell short.

In shorting, an investor will rarely be able to get out at the exact top. What you should look for is evidence that a top may have developed. If a stock has just made a new all-time high on a given day, it may or may not be part of a top formation. However, if a stock has had a clear-cut breakdown from some sort of area of congestion, when the stock appears to have been in a consolidation, then an opportunity for shorting may be at hand.

After a stock has consolidated and broken down, chances are that a new group of investors will enter and buy the stock. After all, this fad issue has finally given them a "buying" opportunity. The stock has declined 10 percent, and many investors who have felt left out and have seen the particular fad issue rise and rise will then begin to initiate positions themselves. As a result, the stock will, after the breakdown, be temporarily buoyed from the new investors, and the price will rise. It is on this price rise after a break that investors will be given an opportunity to short.

What the investor is betting on is that the resistance that is now defined as part of the top formation will be too much for the johnny-come-latelies, and that the stock after a rally attempt will fall short of moving to new highs, then begin a serious decline. Selling short a stock after a breakdown or a reversal on the subsequent rally to resistance certainly does not guarantee any success. However, in picking a place to short, it is a logical choice. If the stock continues to rise, then a stop-loss order may be extended. However, if an important reversal formation is at work, the investor will be able to capture 90 percent of the subsequent declines.

Fad stocks can be very rewarding on the long side, especially if an investor is getting in on the ground floor. However, after every run-up, declines are inevitable. Given the rapidity of the decline in fad issues, it pays to consider speculating on the gains to be made on the downside as well as profits to be made by buying long. Shorting definitely requires more attention to positions than does the traditional buy-and-hold approach. However, given the money that can be made on the downside, by selling fad stocks short when they appear to have passed their peak, shorting should be considered by any investor who approaches investing as serious business.

Conclusion

In a very real sense, fads represent extreme examples of the normal forces that operate throughout the equity markets every day. You can generate superior returns on your portfolio by knowing how to recognize fads and by taking advantage of them early on. In that way, you can multiply your gains by buying in and riding them up, then using your knowledge again when they reach a peak, riding them back down again on the short side. Along with the increased potential for gain, however, the savvy investor must never ignore the increased exposure to risk inherent in fads.

11

WHEN TO SELL AND PIN DOWN YOUR PROFITS

THE ART OF TIMELY SELLING AND SUCCESSFUL PROFIT TAKING

Peter J. DeAngelis, CFA

ALL INVESTORS, SMALL AND LARGE, INDIVIDUAL AND INSTI-
tutional, broker and customer, have bought a winning stock,
watched it soar, and then failed to sell when it crested. They have
all moaned for weeks afterward as the stock continued to decline
and profits melted away. Compounding their dismay, these unrealized profit opportunities often develop into "hard losses."

All the advisory services, hundreds of books, and thousands of
articles on investing are designed to guide the investor in three
major areas: (1) what to buy, (2) when to buy, and (3) when to sell.
A review of this literature reveals that many of these stock market
services, books, and articles provide excellent and diverse counsel
in the first two sectors but are deficient in the all-important consideration of when to sell. There are few organized or defined
materials, procedures, or formulas to provide consistent, dependable, and effective decision-making counsel on the subject of profit
taking.

The most recent "crash" of October 1987 and the scary Friday
the 13th, October 1989 near-crash correction gave rise to momentary old-time religion and a flurry of Monday-morning quarter-

backs and 20/20-hindsight pontifications on selling signals. Like the sinner facing a personal tragedy who turns devout for the duration of the crisis and later returns to the error of his or her former ways, investor and broker, with the market recovery, returned to preoccupation with what and when to buy, to the virtual exclusion of sell considerations. At this writing, the stock market had threatened former high ground, during July 1990, signaled excess and then corrected dramatically 600 points down in the few short months following. International concerns aside, the market is again showing signs of weakness, and investors would be wise to be wary. Investors can avoid the distasteful experience of profit erosions and notably improve investment performance by following basic and proven guidelines for strategic selling. These guidelines alert the investor not only to stages of when the whole market is getting too high, but also to the need to sell specific stocks. Perceiving these sell signals enables the investor to liquidate near the crest of each major upward move. Accordingly, this chapter provides useful ratios and indexes that monitor the altitude of stocks and the general market, together with techniques of the most successful traders and investment professionals.

Historically, most individuals have been too reluctant to sell and might benefit from the philosophy of the fabulously wealthy and successful Baron Rothschild, who contended that he "sold too soon"! The decision to sell is an individual one most often reached by a blending of emotion and logic. In general, the individual investor sells stocks for several reasons:

- Funds are needed for a major purpose such as home purchase or children's college.
- The investor senses the market is too high.
- The investor is itchy to cash in on a profit.
- The investor has lost faith in a specific stock or broker.
- The proceeds are needed in order to switch to another stock.
- The broker has issued a margin call.
- The investor is in fright or panic.

To add to these reasons for selling, this chapter's aim is to develop logical reasons for a general liquidation or for exiting from particular stocks.

OVERALL MARKET CLIMATE OR MARKET PANORAMA

In deciding whether or not to sell, a major consideration should be the level and health of the whole market. An investor, large or small, must always be aware of market conditions and elevation. As you look at Figure 11-1 (page 286), which graphs the Dow Jones Industrial Averages (DJIA) for the past 75 years, you will note three standout periods when the market peaked and it was time to sell. These zeniths were in 1929, 1972, and 1987. Also, there were several tops in between where prudence should have called for substantial selling.

Without going into the stock market's history in depth, it is necessary to accent the forces that propelled stocks to historic highs, so you can recognize similar or parallel conditions in the future and sell before a deluge. Look at the historic patterns briefly recounted, and ask yourself whether you see similar currents in the economy and financial markets today.

1929 CRASH

The first classic peak was in autumn 1929, just before the onset of the Great Depression. In the early 1920s, there was a quick depression followed by a period of steadily expanding prosperity. The auto, oil, steel, railroad, utility, investment trust, and communication industries flourished. Among the great companies of that era were Standard Oil of New Jersey, New York Central, Woolworth, U.S. Steel, General Motors, Coca-Cola, National City Bank, Radio Corp., General Electric, and Consolidated Edison.

Warning Signals

In 1926, the stock market moved steadily upward, buoyed by persistent annual gains in corporate profits and dividends, modest inflation, low interest rates, and only 10 percent margins on stock purchases (the percent of the purchase bought with cash, the remainder being borrowed at prevailing rates). Market conditions began to explode in 1927. The first day on which 5 million shares traded on the New York Stock Exchange was June 12, 1928.

"Call money" fueled the market. Call money is the funds loaned to stock exchange firms for reloan to their stock buyers on margin.

FIGURE 11-1

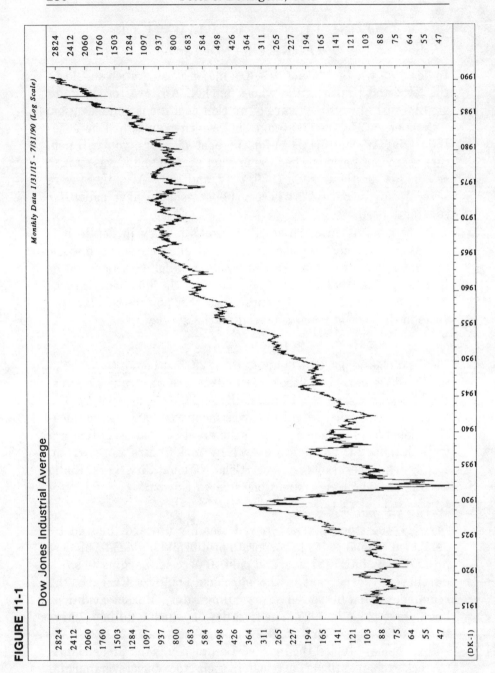

Dow Jones Industrial Average

Monthly Data 1/31/15 - 7/31/90 (Log Scale)

(DK-1)

TABLE 11-1

HISTORIC DATES FOR THE DOW JONES INDUSTRIAL AVERAGE

Date	Event
1896	Dow average first appears in the *Wall Street Journal*.
Jan. 12, 1906	Closes above 100 for the first time, at 100.25.
Sept. 3, 1929	Reaches its closing peak for the bull market of the 1920s, at 381.17, less than two months before the Great Crash.
Oct. 28, 1929	Plummets 38.33 points, the worst drop on record until 1987, cutting nearly 13 percent of the average's value, closing at 260.64.
July 8, 1932	Closes at its Depression low of 41.22, having fallen over 89 percent in less than three years.
Mar. 12, 1956	Closes above 500 for the first time, at 500.24.
Jan. 18, 1966	Reaches 1000 for the first time in midseason, but drops back to close at 994.20.
Nov. 14, 1972	Closes above 1000 for the first time, at 1003.16.
Jan. 11, 1973	Peaks at 1051.70.
Dec. 6, 1974	Closes at a 12-year low of 577.60, ending the worst bear market since the thirties.
April 27, 1981	Closes at an eight-year high of 1024.05.
Aug. 12, 1982	Closes at a two-year low of 776.92, just before the start of a historic rally.
Aug. 17, 1982	Rises 38.81 points, to 831.24, in its then-largest one-day gain as the long rally begins on Wall Street.
Feb. 24, 1983	Soars 24.87 points to close at 1121.81, its first finish above 1100.
April 26, 1983	Breaks the 1200 level for the first time, rising 22.25 points to close at 1209.46.
Jan. 29, 1985	Gains 14.79 points to 1292.62, as NYSE advances outnumber declines for a record 17th straight season.
May 20, 1985	Jumps 19.54 points to finish above 1300 for the first time, closing at 1304.88.
Nov. 6, 1985	Rises 6.77 points to 1403.44, closing above 1400 for the first time.
Dec. 11, 1985	Increases 12.50 points to close at 1511.70, its first finish above 1500.
Feb. 6, 1986	Rises 7.57 points to 1600.69, the first close above 1600.

Feb. 27, 1986	Jumps 17.09 points to 1713.99, closing above 1700 for the first time.
Mar. 20, 1986	Rises 16.29 points to 1804.24, closing above 1800 for the first time.
July 1, 1986	Jumps 10.82 points to 1903.54, the first close above 1900.
Jan. 8, 1987	Breaks the 2000 level for the first time, rising 8.30 to 2002.25.
Jan. 19, 1987	Jumps 25.87 points to 2102.50, closing above 2100 for the first time.
Jan. 20, 1987	Edges up 1.97 points to 2104.47, setting a record of 13 consecutive rises.
Jan. 23, 1987	Plunges to end day down 44.15 points at 2101.52, after rising 64 points at midafternoon; NYSE volume hits a then-record 302.39 million shares.
Feb. 5, 1987	Rises 10.26 points to 2201.49, closing above 2200 for the first time.
Mar. 20, 1987	Jumps 33.95 points to 2333.52, closing above 2300 for the first time.
April 6, 1987	Rises 15.20 points to 2405.54, closing above 2400 for the first time.
July 17, 1987	Climbs 13.07 to 2510.04, closing above 2500 for the first time.
Aug. 10, 1987	Soars 43.84 points to 2635.84, closing above 2600 for the first time.
Aug. 17, 1987	Rises 15.14 points to 2700, closing above 2700 for the first time.
Aug. 25, 1987	Surges 25.35 to a record 2722.42.
Oct. 16, 1987	Plunges 108.36 points to 2246.73, falling more than 100 points for the first time.
Oct. 19, 1987	Nosedives a record 508.00 points to 1738.74, a drop of 22.6 percent, which dwarfs the drop on Oct. 28, 1929, in the market's Great Crash.
Oct. 21, 1987	Soars a record 186.84 to 2027.85, a climb of 10.1 percent in the second day of the rebound from the Oct. 19 collapse. The broader market also rebounds.
Feb. 4, 1988	Falls 5.63 to 2057.86, the same day New York Stock Exchange announces it will experiment with new restraints on computerized stock trading.
Feb. 8, 1988	Falls 14.76 to 1895.72, its low for the year.

Mar. 25, 1988	Closes down 44.92 to 1978.95, triggering a 50-point "collar" at the NYSE for the first time.
April 6, 1988	Jumps 64.16 to 2061.67, triggering the collar on the up side for the first time.
Oct. 18, 1988	Rises 19.38 to 2159.85; federal regulators authorize one-year experiment for coordinated trading halts of one hour in the stock and futures markets when the Dow falls 250 points or more from the previous day's close.
Oct. 21, 1988	Rises 2.31 to 2183.50, its high for the year.
Jan. 24, 1989	Gains 38.04 to 2256.43, regaining its Oct. 16, 1987, level for the first time since the Black Monday crash on Oct. 19, 1987.
Aug. 24, 1989	Gains 56.53 points to close at 2734.64, establishing a new all-time record and marking a symbolic recovery from ground lost in the Black Monday crash.
Oct. 13, 1989	UAL Corp. is unable to complete the financing for the nearly $7 billion takeover of United Air Lines. The Dow falls 190.58 points, the second-biggest one-day drop in history. The Dow closes at 2569.26, a drop of nearly 7 percent from the day before.

Courtesy of the Associated Press.

Not just banks loaned these funds, but large corporations as well. Little was done to control the flow of call money. Call loans were $3.5 billion at the 1927 year-end, $4 billion by June 1928, and $7 billion by August 1929. Today this is a not inconsequential sum, but in the 1920s, it was enormous. A key to the excesses of the era was this rapid expansion of call money. Before the bubble burst, the banks were "cleaning up" on the market's speculative fever. By the fall of 1929, banks were borrowing at 5 percent and lending at 12 percent or higher.

There is an interesting and dangerous twist to the syndrome that develops when call money and margin buying (brokerage loaning to its customers) are combined. To illustrate, a customer puts up $2,000 cash to purchase $20,000 of stock(s) on margin. The customer borrows $18,000 from the brokerage firm. If the stock gains in value, the customer's equity base (the value of the customer's holdings) increases proportionately. As a consequence, the customer, without putting up any more cash, has the ability to borrow additional funds from the broker to purchase more stocks, using the increase in the value of the holdings as collateral. If the stocks rise even further, the scenario continues.

In this way, it is possible to build a very large portfolio of stock value on a pittance of cash investment—provided, of course, that the upward direction of stock prices continues unabated. The customer's margin position (borrowed brokerage money) is, of course, equally large, and the percentage of an individual's total assets represented by margin loans could be very high, with devastating downside leverage. Hence, the potential for gain is great, but greater still is the potential for financial disaster. Imagine a market collapse or merely a sharp correction. Without the cash available to meet a call (the demand by the brokerage firm to put up cash immediately to cover a decline in value), the broker will promptly sell the stocks at their market value. At this point, if you turned a chart of value increases upside down, you'd have a graphic view of the breakage.

By 1929, over 1.5 million Americans were investing—or, more appropriately, speculating—in the stock market, an astounding number at the time. With interim dips (including a heavy sell-off in December 1928), stocks continued to move up until autumn 1929. The percentage swings in 1928 were awesome. Radio Corp. rose from 85 to 420 and would gain 15 or 20 points a day; Montgomery Ward soared from 117 to 440, and Du Pont from 309 to 525. It was a happy time.

There were a multitude of warning signals. Several major frauds and swindles heralded the unbridled greed and excess. In March 1929, there was a major sell-off, but more call money was made available. Too little and too late, in a halfhearted effort to restrain the flood of call money, the Federal Reserve raised the rediscount rate from 5 percent to 6 percent.

The beginning of the end was in September 1929. Heavy selling began—a final warning. On October 24, 1929, a record 12.9 million shares traded, culminating in the infamous crash. Bids (offers to buy stocks) faded at light speed. Thousands of margin calls were sent out as brokers called in their loans to customers. Failing an immediate covering with cash, the stocks were mercilessly sold out, adding further to the crescendo of panic selling. The market plummeted, and on Tuesday, October 29, 1929, doomsday arrived with 16,410,030 shares trading. Tens of thousands more margin calls were issued. The result, more sellouts, added to progressively lower stock prices. This became a self-defeating action, creating further pressure and even greater erosion of stock prices.

Consequences

The saga of panic has been chronicled many times before, and there is no need to prolong it here. Several rallies in the market between 1929 and 1932 carried stock prices back part of the way, but these only obscured, in the long run, the prevailing disaster that set in with a vengeance for years to come. Suffice to say, few held on to their profits. Most investors gave years of gain back in moments during those fateful days in October 1929, and many lost everything beyond their investments and profits.

As time passes, fewer and fewer people remain to recall that time through personal experience. Therefore, to preserve the memory of the pain and the lesson learned, it would behoove us to take a moment to view the wreckage. For example, from 1929 to 1932, the DJIA dipped from a September high of 386 to a low of 41 (July 1932)—a decline of over 89 percent! Just look at the ultimate stock price collapses among the nation's corporate elite. As Table 11-2 shows, the carnage was fantastic!

TABLE 11-2

SOME STOCK PRICES COLLAPSES, 1929–1932*

Stock	1929 High	1932 Low	Decline
Radio Corp.	114¾	2½	97.8%
Montgomery Ward	156⅞	3½	97.8
General Motors	91¾	7⅝	83.4
Goldman, Sachs	121¼	1	99.2
North American Co.	186¾	13¾	92.6
Chrysler	135	5	96.3
U.S. Steel	261	21¼	91.9
New York Central	256½	8¾	96.5

*All stock prices are adjusted for splits and stock dividends.

As if this debacle isn't shocking enough, try this scenario on: Imagine an investor who bought stock on 10 percent margin—say $2,000 to purchase $20,000 of stock (with $18,000 on loan from the broker). Then this person witnessed the stock price collapse 90 percent while being unable to sell. His or her loss was $18,000—the investor's entire $2,000 stake plus $16,000 more. Haven't got it yet? Well, there goes the car, house—whatever. Remember, it was 1929. The dollars back then were very real and large. Of course, the same disaster applies to a larger and more substantial investor. Although the figures are larger, the destruction is just as complete.

Wait! The horror isn't over yet. Enter the Great Depression. By the time the depression spent itself, the investor stood a good chance of being among the 25 percent unemployed to boot.

These examples provide some insight into the magnitude of the 1929 crash. Can't happen again, some will say. That's pure bull——! Maybe not an accompanying depression, but stock price crashes of major proportions have and will continue to occur as long as there are free economies and financial markets.

If there ever had been a need to recognize and heed the warning signs, it was in 1929. The signals were there, as they always have been. With the benefit of 20/20 hindsight, some of the most obvious were:

- A huge percentage increase in call money fueling continued speculation.
- Stocks trading at unrealistically high price-earnings ratios CP/Es). The DJIA reached a P/E of 17.
- A total disdain for income—capital gains were everything.
- The DJIA selling at over two times book value.
- Insane bidding up of prices. Radio Corp. sold above 400, yet never paid a dividend. Technicolor Corp., a new dimension in the motion picture industry, sold as high as 100 before diving to 1 in 1932.

1972: HISTORY REPEATS ITSELF

In many later periods, stocks have moved up to levels where investors should have considered selling. The year 1972 seems best indicated on the charts. The DJIA had crossed the 1000 mark six years before achieving a 1972 high of 1067. After two major corrections, taking the market down to 736 and 627 in 1966 and 1970, respectively, the market staged two unsuccessful recoveries with descending tops of 995 and 958 in 1968 and 1971. A fateful assault on the 1000 level was launched in 1972 and achieved momentary success at 1067.

Aside from the chartist warnings, there were several other key signals of a topping-off phase. The popularity of stocks in general was waning, with excessive valuations in evidence. For example, McDonald's Corp., Avon Products, and Polaroid Corp. all sold at 70 times earnings or higher, indicating market zeal that was out of control. Unsatisfactory conditions were further documented by the departure from the gold standard on August 15, 1971, wage and price controls, a rising level of interest rates, and the 1972 Watergate scandal. Last but not least, the 400 percent rise in the price of oil signaled the crest. The sell-off to the 1974 low of 570 put a damper on the market that was to last for a decade. Investors by the droves deserted the stock market and placed their funds in money instruments, which yielded 14 percent or better.

THE 1987 STOCK MARKET MELTDOWN

Remember that old adage "The bigger they are, the harder they fall"? The higher the market soars, the harder it will fall. To this bit of conventional wisdom, one should add, "What goes up (stock prices) will come down a lot more rapidly."

Monday, October 19, 1987, the stock market paid the price of a nonstop binge and went into cardiac arrest and died. They (whoever they are) called it a meltdown. It was beyond the crash experiences just discussed. Those market declines were pillow fights compared to this baby! This was the first truly global crash. It raced through the world's financial markets, wiping over $500 billion from market values and from investors' portfolios on that Monday alone. Storms raked the financial landscape mercilessly. As they looked into the abyss, the market's participants (brokers and customers, large and small investors, individuals and institutions) experienced despair, panic, disbelief, shock, disgust, and fear.

Rational thought was abandoned as the carnage plunged the market 508 points (DJIA) in heavy volume on October 19. It was the largest one-day loss in history. On the New York Stock Exchange, the Dow Jones Industrial Average lost 13 percent of its value in a week and closed at 1950.76, nearly 800 points behind the heights of the previous August.

History has shown that the 1987 market debacle really began on Wednesday, October 14. The DJIA sank 95 points that day, reacting to the disappointing U.S. trade statistics. Two days later, the DJIA sank another 108 points. Pressure built over the weekend, and the bomb went off on "Black Monday." Early Monday morning in Tokyo, while the New York Stock Exchange was yet to open, the financial storm gathered. The Japanese market sold off right away. London followed Tokyo hours later, opening down an unprecedented 137 points, while New York still slept. So the global stock market rout was at full gallop before the NYSE's opening bell. Foreign investors were shoveling equities into the market, and when the American market opened at 9:30 A.M. EDT, the Europeans continued, joined by the American investors, to dump equities.

Consequences

I'm not going to recount the statistics of the 1987 market collapse. I'll leave that to the many books that have and will continue to be written on that subject alone (notably *Black Monday* by Tim Metz). If you wish to do so, you can immerse yourself in the gruesome statistics to your heart's content. Most of us won't have to read the statistics to recall and understand the event. After all, at this writing, it's only been a few years since that fateful time. My memory is intact, and I can see it vividly without a body count of the damage. In many segments of the economy and certain businesses, the '87 crash lives on, as the shock waves continue to be felt. Some businesses may never fully recover. Others have been permanently transformed. Most affected is the financial community. Continued cutbacks, industry losses, rescue consolidations, and brokerage failures continue to this day as a direct result of the 1987 crash.

Eventually, the panic ebbed. The market recovered. However, this market crash has been the most frightening. In fact, it scared the hell out of me! A colleague offered the opinion that it was because I experienced it personally, whereas the heretofore benchmark of fear, the 1929 crash, was just so much history-book-reading. I dismiss his reasoning. After all, I was every bit in the fray with the 1972 market crash and numerous severe "corrections." No, this one was different.

Sell Signals

It is true that most of the sell signals recounted in the preceding section were present in 1987. For example, overvalued stocks were evident by the extreme P/Es. At the stock market's August peak, common stocks in the broad market were trading at an average of more than 20 times their annual net profit. That is a level reached only twice before, in 1929 and 1965. (While not of crash dimensions, the market, as measured by the DJIA, also experienced a major correction in 1966.) In a healthy market environment, a more normal P/E is about 15. In bear markets, a P/E of 10 or less is typical. A P/E of 20 or more is a warning signal that should not be ignored! At this level, a reasonable investor will at the very least kick out all the highfliers. Other sell signals in the 1987 market were excessively leveraged balance sheets, due in large measure to leveraged buyouts (LBOs), high margin buying (50 percent margin), corporate takeover mania, the growing U.S. deficit, a poor trade balance, and a weak dollar.

But most of all, there was a major difference in 1987. Some new wrinkles had been added. They were designed to give vigor and new market dimension. Instead, what they did was create a casino for thinly disguised gambling vehicles, which in turn brought on the enormous market erosion. Perhaps the biggest of these was program trading.

Program trading refers to the use of computers and the new forms of stock trading that have evolved in tandem with their use. There are two basic concepts: portfolio insurance and index arbitrage. Each involves computer programs that automatically accelerate the buying and selling of equities when certain events occur.

Additionally, there were items like index-futures markets. Rather than trading actual stocks, investors in index futures bet on what stock indexes will be at future dates. These devices serve no economic purpose other than to further the gyrations of the market.

The Near-Meltdown

Another frightening aspect of the '87 crash is that the market came very close to a complete meltdown, or shutdown. Stock, options, and futures trading all but stopped during a crucial interval on the Tuesday following Black Monday. Many blue chips couldn't be traded, and lesser listed stocks and those traded on the over-the-counter market all but disappeared. Investors, large or small, couldn't sell their stocks. There weren't any buyers! Market makers and listed exchange specialists were overwhelmed with unfilled sell orders. Also, capital for their brokerage firms was depleted. Banks were refusing to extend credit to their security dealer customers. Some banks, terrified by the loss in value of stocks used as collateral for loans to securities dealers, called in major loans. The closing of the U.S. financial markets was prevented only by the intervention of the Federal Reserve and by corporations that bought back their stock.

Make no mistake—the market did break down. For a time, there was no liquidity (ability to sell) and no communication (brokers didn't even answer their phones). All the while, the market was in a free-fall.

The critical difference from 1929 was that it didn't last long. The market came back—just barely. For a while, it could have gone either way. It was the most dangerous day for the U.S. in 50 years.

The lesson of the '87 crash is that there are major weaknesses in the U.S. financial system and such a crisis could strike again. Did the crash leave the investment community with a healthy residue of fear and caution? What do you think? Remember the scandals, insider trading, fraud, and flamboyant rampage of greed in the three years that followed. Do you believe that "they" learned anything?

The only one you can count on is yourself. Remember, the second most important decision after what to buy is when to sell. Look for the signals of market crests as a clue to timely selling.

FRIDAY THE 13TH: THE CRASH THAT ALMOST WAS

On Friday, October 13, 1989, two years later than the October 1987 crash, almost to the day, the market took a 190.58-point plunge. At first it appeared that history might repeat itself.

Friday began as a fairly routine day. With a little over an hour of trading left, a news item was released, announcing the collapse of a takeover of UAL Corp. The collapse of the deal murdered the risk arbitragers and set off a stampede of selling in takeover stocks, helping to push the DJIA down to its second-biggest one-day loss.

The slide started at 2:53 P.M. Within an hour the market dropped more than 100 points and ended the day down 190.58 to 2569.26, a 7 percent decline from the day before. Over the ensuing weekend, investors pondered in an atmosphere of melancholy: was history repeating itself? On the surface, the similarities to 1987 were eerie. The 1987 crash also began on a mid-October Friday and cumulated in the infamous "Black Monday."

Indeed, the market's open on Monday, October 16, 1989, didn't inspire much hope. Stocks of the nation's biggest companies couldn't open for trading due to a flood of sell orders. Within half an hour, the market fell 63 points. But then, mercifully, the market turned and ended the day with an 88.12-point gain to 2657.38. Investors had escaped, but just barely. The market had indeed corrected. The premium had been taken out of the market by eliminating the takeover frenzy that had pushed the market to the precipice.

Could trouble with just one stock cause the market to drop? Was it all emotion, fear, and superstition? Hell, no! Signs of excess were again clearly in evidence. Prices of stocks of companies perceived as takeover candidates had been run up to speculative levels. The DJIA had advanced about 30 percent—up 591 points. The market for junk bonds—the high-yielding issues that financed the takeover boom—was faltering. And inflation was on the move as wholesale prices surged. The number of major companies filing for Chapter 11 bankruptcy was increasing. Those companies included giants such as Southmark Corp., American Continental Corp., Eastern Airlines, L. J. Hooker Corp., and Dart Drug Stores. A few months later the huge Campeau Corp. (parent of Federated Department Stores and other retailers) would join the Chapter 11 bankruptcy club.

Yet for all the danger signals, many investors were caught again. The suddenness of the drop at this point in market history, particularly in more recent times, shows just how fragile stock market rallies have become. The problem is multifaceted. The stock market is global, and while world markets may take their lead from the U.S. financial system, U.S. investors are no longer alone or insulated from pressures from abroad. The U.S. system is old, even with all its much-heralded updates; it is inappropriate and can't cope with today's huge and complex financial world. The extent and frequency of nosedives, as shown in Table 11-3, including the "near miss of 1989," are sobering reminders of just how complex the financial markets are and how agile the investor must be to enter and exit the market as a whole.

TABLE 11-3

WORST DAYS OF THE DOW JONES INDUSTRIAL AVERAGE*

Date	Percent Decline	Point Decline	DJIA Close
Oct. 19, 1987	22.60	508.00	1738.74
Oct. 28, 1929	12.80	38.33	260.64
Oct. 29, 1929	11.70	30.57	230.07
Nov. 6, 1929	9.90	25.55	232.13
Aug. 12, 1932	8.40	5.79	63.11
Oct. 26, 1987	8.00	156.83	1793.93
July 21, 1933	7.84	7.55	88.71
Oct. 18, 1937	7.75	10.57	125.74
Oct. 5, 1932	7.15	5.09	66.07
Sept. 24, 1931	7.07	8.20	107.79
July 20, 1933	7.07	7.32	96.26
Oct. 13, 1989	6.91	190.58	2569.26
Jan. 8, 1987	6.85	140.58	1911.31
Nov. 11, 1929	6.82	16.14	220.39
May 14, 1940	6.80	9.36	128.77

*From worst to least, the 15 largest one-day percentage declines for the Dow Jones Industrial Average since October 1, 1928, when the average was increased to 30 stocks. Courtesy of the Associated Press.

BENCHMARKS FOR SELLING

Besides watching for selling signals from the market as a whole, investors must consider when to sell specific stocks. Marketable securities are made to be sold as well as bought. Everyone at some time needs to convert assets into cash. Stocks have proved useful not only for income and gainful investment of surplus funds, but for the cash values they generate, either through borrowing or by partial or total sale.

As mentioned in Chapter 3, there are four main market phases: accumulation, markup, distribution, and markdown. This chapter is concerned with fine-tuning the distribution phase. That is when shrewd and agile investors unload and avoid the markdown phase, when most adroit investors have already exited, and sellers outnumber buyers.

Conspicuous by its absence from this chapter is a discussion of technical analysis for selling. Technical sell signals are very valuable, and that particular subject is left in the capable hands of David Krell in Chapter 2.

Stock price cycles are very important to the price of most individual stocks. Many market models assume that price trends will continue for periods beyond the short-term perspective of most investors. Price trends are usually explained as reactions to the staggered spread of new information entering the market. Superior profits can be achieved by recognizing a trend change early.

Although catching the absolute top is very hard to do, knowing when the signals turn bearish can preserve much of your profit. Of course, none of the following signals are foolproof, and no one technique alone should be used for decision making. For our purposes, we will focus on the nonchartist benchmarks for timely selling. As you will see, they are often interrelated.

PRICE-EARNINGS RATIO

The "old faithful" benchmark is the price-earnings ratio (P/E). Very simply, when P/Es hit absurd heights, you should sell. What's absurd? As already stated, a DJIA selling P/E over 17 is pricey. When a stock trades in excess of that level, it is prudent to consider what justification there is for such lofty levels.

In doing so, there are general and specific guidelines. First, as a general rule, whenever a P/E goes above 40, it is usually an occasion for liquidation. Also, when a P/E surges from, say, 14 to 20 or higher, it strongly indicates that the market may be overstating the value of the stock. And if a reasonable P/E of a stock doubles in a year or less, selling the stock is often the better part of wisdom.

High P/Es (absolute and relative to the DJIA) are nevertheless found within certain market sectors. Sometimes they are legitimate, and in other instances they represent sucker plays.

Dangerously high multiples are often noted in initial public offerings of stocks (IPOs) and early or development-stage companies. This is an immediate warning sign that you are dabbling in stocks with "a broad spectrum of risk" (a euphemism for rank speculation or gambling rather than investing). These stocks are born with inherently excessive P/Es, and are more likely to represent trading vehicles than investment-grade holdings.

On the other hand, growth stocks typically develop relatively high P/Es. Along these lines, two popular benchmarks have developed for evaluating growth stocks. The first and more conservative one holds that a growth stock that doubles its sales and net income within five years can justify a stock price of 50 percent above the DJIA's P/E. For example, if the P/E of the DJIA is 15, then you should not pay over a 22 P/E for a growth stock.

A second respected formula is that a stock is entitled to sell at its growth rate. To illustrate, if a stock is increasing its net operating income at the rate of 30 percent annually, it may properly sell at a P/E of 30 without being regarded as price-inflated.

These two approaches result in widely varying appraisals for the same stock. In practice, the latter formula (a P/E equal to the growth rate) is probably more on the money and will come closer to market reality. However, I believe that, with rare exceptions, when an authentic growth stock trades at 40 times earnings or higher, it is probably overpriced. Such a limit would surely have converted millions of dollars of paper profits into cash in the bulging and phasing out of the market crests recounted in the preceding portion of this chapter.

Another method employed is to target for sale those shares whose P/E has exceeded the historic average for that stock. For the general run of stocks, the DJIA is historically a sale at 18 times earnings. However, individual stocks in different industries have their own historic P/E patterns. Smokestack stocks such as steel and metals have low P/E ratios; utilities, food, and the like are in the middle P/E range; and proprietary technology, communications, and medical care stocks are at the upper levels. (P/Es for the NYSE and AMEX stocks are shown daily in the *Wall Street Journal*.) Therefore, a better barometer for a stock's relative position is to compare its P/E to that of its industry as well as to the DJIA. For example, what constitutes a high P/E for a steel or cement stock may be an abnormally low P/E for a medical care stock.

GROUP ROTATION AND MIGRATION

In programming the sale of stocks to maximize profits, the securities of preference are actively traded issues that are in a rising stage of earnings and situated in popular industries perceived to have impressive growth potential. Such industries and stocks become market favorites, attracting enthusiastic sponsorship. These are stocks where the action is and where perceptive investors capable of making sell decisions can capture handsome capital gains.

All industries and the dominant companies within them have gone through the four classic market stages (accumulation, markup, distribution, and markdown) with strong uptrends along the way. These groups moved in random rotation, propelled invariably by outstanding increases in profits. They gained investor recognition and moved to sometimes dramatic stock market highs. Then the trading pace slackened, quotations for the stock's price faltered, and the spotlight moved on to a new group.

All investors have witnessed this migration, which regularly occurs when a given industry group is driven up to excessive highs and the prospect for future gains is diminished. After all, how high is up? Barring a catastrophe, there are always ample warning signs that a plateau has been reached. The wary investor also has generous amounts of time to liquidate holdings; there are always investors who stubbornly hold on and even buy (for a while) at the peak.

The signs, in addition to the charts, are low volume, major resistance to stock price advances, huge unrealized paper profits at present price levels, high stock price as measured by traditional analytical tools, and a diminished notoriety among the financial community. These are but a few of the clear signals to exit. History is full of examples such as the stocks of the casino industry, electronic games, CB radios, airlines, nursing homes, personal computers, software, and petroleum.

So when the bloom is off the rose, do not tarry. Get out of that stock.

INSIDER SELLING

One of the classic instances of the need to sell when the selling is good, is inside selling. "Insiders" are generally defined as the executives, directors, senior management, and large holders (5 percent or greater) of the company's stock. Federal securities law requires these insiders and other major shareholders of a company to report to the Securities and Exchange Commission (SEC) when they buy or sell their own company's stock. Reports must be filed with the SEC by the 10th day of the month following any transaction. Hence, insiders' actions in the market are readily available.

Insiders (directors, management, and executives) are also restricted as to the amount of shares they may sell in a quarterly period. An insider may sell the greater amount of shares as calculated by 1 percent of the shares outstanding or the average weekly volume during the last four weeks before the sell order.

Stock sales by insiders can often flag some trouble spots in the company's stock. Insiders do know about the fundamentals of their industry and company. Tracking the insider trades can give investors solid clues about the outlook.

To a large degree, insider trading is skewed in favor of selling. However, insider selling isn't always bearish. As with all selling tools, the investor must temper his or her analysis to reflect the nature of the insider's selling activity. Many of these companies were established by entrepreneurs who due to age or estate considerations later find it necessary to cash out or diversify their wealth. This and other valid reasons for selling, such as cash needed to exercise stock options, can account for some insider sales and may, therefore, be discounted.

Nevertheless, there are telling signals to look for in insider transactions:

• *Number of insiders selling*—If a large portion of the senior management is selling, there is cause for concern.

- *Quantity of shares sold by insiders*—If the transactions represent the maximum amount of stock permitted to be sold under securities law, it is likely to be a bailout.
- *Timing*—If the transactions occur consistently early in the month, which defers reporting for the longest time, it is a warning.
- *Market price*—If the insiders are heavy sellers, particularly in the face of a strong stock price, it is a clear signal that they believe the stock price is vulnerable.
- *Net sales*—When net sales by insiders are considerably larger than historic levels, it is a red flag.

Insider trading is sometimes noted in the press, but there are services that maintain a computer data base of insider trades. Some of these services are Invest/Net Group, the Insiders, Consensus of Insiders, and Insiders Chronicle. Perhaps you can review one of these services at your local broker's office, or you may want your own subscription.

In any event, there is a message here. It pays to follow sales made by insiders. For example, in 1989, computer, securities, and retailing stocks all were among the year's troubled industries, and all were actively sold by industry executives and other insiders.

In the computer industry, where stock prices declined almost 20 percent, more than twice as many insiders sold their company's stock as bought it. Similarly, brokerage firm executives and other insiders were active sellers. Brokerage firms' stocks substantially underperformed the market as a whole, while some specific stocks of major firms ran aground in early 1990. A clear example is insider sales in the apparel-retailing industry. Insiders sold into strength for 1989 as a whole. It is now clear that the industry encountered significant problems and that 1990 was a difficult year for the group.

To summarize, the average investor is much better off selling when the insiders are selling.

The 10 Percent Rule

Another approach, called the 10 percent rule, employs a simple discipline: sell any stock that is down 10 percent from its purchase price. This rule is based upon the premise "Let your profits run, and cut your losses." Under this popular Wall Street approach, an investor sells losers, not just winners. The investor is made to face his or her losses.

PRICE OBJECTIVES

A sound sell indicator is to weed out a portfolio when a stock no longer fits the rationale under which it was purchased. Decide how high the stock you have carefully researched might reasonably advance within 24 months, and set a price objective. Keep a vigil for signals along the way that may indicate when the industry and the company may be topping out. If, during the course of holding the stock, the basic fundamental reason for purchasing it has changed for the worse, sell immediately. In any event, upon achieving your price objective, at least lighten up on the holding.

INSTITUTIONAL HOLDINGS

Today institutional investors (mutual funds, insurance companies, investment advisers) account for 75 percent or more of trading on the NYSE. As a result, many of the companies with large share capitalizations trading on the NYSE are substantially owned by institutional investors. The myth is that institutional participation is an endorsement of a stock's quality and its potential.

What do you think? Chew on this for a moment, if you will. Remember the Friday the 13th stock market plunge in 1989? Do you also remember the flood of explanation from all those professional analysts and money managers, speaking with authority as to what had caused it and why it was inevitable? Doesn't it strike you as strange that not one had actually predicted that it was about to happen?

In keeping with this behavior of the "professionals," it follows that large institutional holders are mostly a sensitive and sheeplike lot. If one decides to sell, several others may quickly follow suit. Often in a matter of weeks or even days, a given stock may shed 20 percent or more of its market value by this progressive selling pressure. Institutional liquidations are motivated by any number of factors, such as a less than expected quarter's performance, international exchange loss, increase in debt, misguided mergers, and management fights.

You don't want to own a stock excessively owned by institutions. When institutions acquire a large percentage of a company's stock, there may be little additional demand for the stock to push its price higher.

If you hold shares in an institutional stock, it is important to watch the extent of sales by these wholesale investors in the daily financial press or in quarterly institutional summaries in *Barron's*. Also look at trades of 10,000 shares or more. These trades tell the direction of institutional decisions. If three or more institutions start to sell a stock you own, their selling may become contagious and swiftly depress the price. In any event, it is obvious that if they are selling, the stock is most unlikely to advance in price.

It is important to buy before a stock is institutionalized and to sell before the institutional investors get a leg up on you!

EARNINGS

You don't have to be a rocket scientist to realize that revenue and earnings growth ultimately fuel the rise in a stock's price. When an earnings disappointment is evident, selling is advised. A Wall Street adage worth remembering is "The first earnings disappointment is rarely the last."

The real trick is to spot the early red-flagging. Simple rules will give insight and lead time in a selling program. The simplest is to sell when 12-month earnings decline. Some will undoubtedly criticize this rule as being overly concerned with the short term. But remember, you are in this for profit, not tenure.

There are other more sophisticated guidelines for earnings sell rules. For example, debt is a burden that during a slowdown or recession could be the final nail in the coffin. If long-term debt exceeds 50 percent of equity (a company's assets less liabilities), the situation could be headed for trouble. If long-term debt exceeds equity percent, the stock is a sale candidate. If debt exceeds equity, the stock is an out-and-out sale. If you have any doubts, look at all the failed junk bond offerings used to finance the leveraged buyouts in the recent few years. And this is just the beginning of the Chapter 11 bankruptcies to result from the ill-conceived leveraged balance sheets of the 1980s LBO era.

INVENTORY OVERLOAD

A company's inventory that over time is becoming higher and higher in relation to its sales can mean trouble lies ahead. Why? Among other things, it can point to several less than pleasant developments under way. For one, it may be a signal that sales are weakening. It also may be a sign that the company is stocking obsolete goods.

A company's inventories are investments. They tie up capital. They can be carried only until generally accepted accounting principles require they be written off. Inventory adjustments can kill earnings.

The nature of inventory glitches is that they sneak up on management. This is especially true when, after a period of prosperity, growth is interrupted or stops. Managers are caught by surprise. They are reluctant, fail, or are too stubborn to recognize obsolete materials and goods. The result is that the problem builds to a point where a major hit to earnings becomes mandatory, usually with operational repercussions, including but not limited to changes in executive personnel and production. Hence, not only do reported earnings drop, but an aura of uncertainty cloaks the company as well.

Wall Street hates negative surprises and uncertainty. They cause analysts to become extremely conservative and defensive. Analysts will unmercifully trim their earnings forecasts and question management's ability to manage in the future. Of course, the stock, like the obsolete inventory, will go begging, and the price will fall sharply.

How can individual investors alert themselves to such problems before the fact, rather than suffer after the fact? It's not really difficult to ferret out companies whose inventories are moving toward the danger level. You may once again look to an established service. The best here is the prestigious Value Line subscription service, located in New York City. You can subscribe to this service, or it is more than likely available at your broker's office. It will provide inventory-to-sales ratios. When perusing the data relative to your holdings, look for a ratio that has been rising (it may be a trend) and/or ratios that are comparatively high for their respective industries.

The popular Wall Street adage about the first earnings decline can be modified to include write-offs—that is, "The first write-off is rarely the last." So be among the first to move out in anticipation of the obvious, rather than the last to react to the inevitable.

MONETARY TECHNIQUES

Among the most powerful tools that act upon stock prices are *monetary techniques*. Changes in the supply of money directly affect the general economy through interest rates. Historically, changes in the money supply have led to changes in stock prices.

There are three tools that may signal a change: (1) the Federal Reserve's buying or selling securities; (2) changes in the discount rate; and (3) changes in the reserve requirement. To determine what the environment is, the best approach is to read the daily analysis of the credit markets or special reports as covered in the *Wall Street Journal* or other financial media.

Generally, sales of securities by the Federal Reserve to influence the money supply send a bearish signal. This is because, as the Federal Reserve sells securities for cash, it causes the money supply to shrink. Less money is available for businesses to grow. Thus, this policy is consistent with a restrictive monetary policy and indicates slower general economic growth.

The discount rate and reserve requirements are easier to track. Briefly, when commercial banks borrow reserves from the Federal Reserve system, the interest the banks pay is called the discount rate. The prime rate, the rate charged to a bank's best customer, is heavily influenced by the discount rate. Hence, when the Federal Reserve increases the discount rate, creating a higher interest charge to the borrowing banks, this action pressures banks to increase the prime rate. As the prime rate increases, fewer projects and business expansions become feasible, and fewer loans are made. It is a restrictive monetary policy, and it is bearish for the stock market.

Reserve requirements are the most effective tool of the Federal Reserve. This is because the reserve requirement controls the extent to which new loans are possible. An increase in the reserve requirement means that banks must keep more of their funds on hand to protect against losses. Thus, less money is available for new loans. This in turn slows economic growth.

The most bearish sell signals occur when the Federal Reserve increases both the discount rate and the reserve requirement. In the past, these changes led to or coincided with the top of a bull market.

BREADTH OF THE MARKET

The mood of the market environment at a given time is measured by the breadth of the market. For much of the time, prices of the majority of stocks will move together during a market cycle. But there are times when the first-tier stocks (blue chips, for want of a better label) and lower-tier stocks (AMEX and over-the-counter stocks) do not move in unison. The theory is that, as a market peaks, investors may become wary and withdraw from second- and lower-tier stocks. Thus, it is wise to be cautious when the DJIA continues to rise while the over-the-counter and American Stock Exchange markets decline (or at least don't advance).

However useful it may be, the comparative market concept cannot be used alone. The lead times are quite variable, and institutional domination has distorted the measurement.

To be useful, breadth of the market must be analyzed from the viewpoint of cumulative advances-declines and new highs–new lows. The former measures the number of stocks that advance in price, subtracted from the number of stocks that decline in price. It is popularly measured daily and weekly and reported in all the responsible financial media. The direction of change is more meaningful than the magnitude of change. Obviously, a bearish signal is given when the advance-decline line is headed downward, regardless of whether the market indexes continue higher.

The other aspect of this dual market analysis is the measurement of new highs and new lows. It is formulated by subtracting the number of new low prices from those reaching new highs, then dividing the remainder by the total number of issues traded. This figure too is reported religiously by the financial media and is easy to trace. Again, the interpretation is simple. When the new highs–new lows indicator is declining, particularly if the DJIA is rising, it is an early sign of impending weaknesses.

DEMAND EXPECTATION FACTORS

Another group of market signals consists of demand expectation factors. These are margin requirements, cash position of mutual funds, short sales, and free credit balances.

Margin Requirements

Recalling the previous discussion of margin buying, there is only a little to add here. The Federal Reserve Board has jurisdiction over margins for the entire market and designates securities acceptable for margin purchase. The current margin allowed is 50 percent. This figure bears watching.

If the Fed increases the margin requirement, it is a signal that the Fed believes stocks are trading too high and that speculation has become excessive. It may be the harbinger of more restrictive moves by the government. In any event, it is a red flag that should be heeded.

Cash Position of Mutual Funds

With institutions dominating the stock market today, it is important to closely observe the posture of those institutions, even though the performance of the majority has been less than distinguished. Thus, when mutual fund managers are optimistic, the funds will be close to fully invested in the market.

I take a contrary view. When the funds have a low cash position (are close to being fully invested), it is time to consider withdrawing from the market. Take profits before the market drops, since there is little additional institutional demand to support the high prices. Remember, when the institutional investment community is fully invested, it has no buying power unless it sells something!

Short Sales

Aggressive investors provide a few additional clues to watch as well. The short sale is a useful indicator. As described in Chapter 10, the short sale is a technique used by investors who believe a stock or the market will decline, so they sell stock at the current price, hoping to buy it back and replace the borrowed stock at a lower price. The profit, if any, is the difference between the higher selling price and lower buying price—in that order. It is a gutsy game, since every short sale must be covered (bought back).

When the amount of stock sold short of a company is at a high level (10 percent or more), you are assured of some support should the stock run up; the short-sellers would be squeezed into buying back the borrowed stock. Conversely, should the stock decline, there is also pent up support for the stock when the short-sellers move to nail down their profits by buying in. When there are few short sales and prices have risen, the potential demand through

covering is diminished. These circumstances are a signal to review your portfolio for exposure and sale candidates. Short positions are published monthly in the *Wall Street Journal*. Numerous
subscription advisory services also are available to the investor.

Free Credit Balances

A cynical contrarian indicator is the free credit balances. These
funds are from stock sales where cash is left with brokerage
houses. It is the smaller, less knowledgeable investor who leaves
money with his or her broker, so you should follow the contrary
view. When the small investors have small free credit balances, it
indicates that they are optimistic and buying into the market. The
contrary view is that the individual investor is less knowledgeable
and is buying at the wrong time. So when the free credit balance
is low and prices have risen substantially, consider selling.

Bond Prices

Finally, there is a signal that comes from a study of the long-
standing relationships between the stock and bond markets. A
familiar pattern is that bond prices are a leading indicator for
stock prices. Since after World War II, there have been eight
notable economic expansions and subsequent slumps. In six of
these instances, bond prices reached a peak and declined before
the stock market followed. Though leads and lags varied greatly,
the pattern is clear. In the two instances that bond prices did not
lead a stock market decline, the two markets began to fall together.

The relationship may be best understood within the framework
of a business cycle. As an economy begins its recovery from a
preceding recession, stock and bond prices rise in tandem. As the
business cycle peaks, there is a divergence of the bond and stock
markets. Sensitive to interest rates and credit, the bond market
weakens, and bond prices edge downward. Eventually stocks move
lower, and a recession arrives.

In the 1987 expansion, bond prices reached a recovery peak in
February and began to fall with little interruption to the autumn
of 1987. Stock prices rose through the spring, summer, and fall—
until, of course, the crash of October 19, 1987. While the past is
never a sure predictor of the future, this particular signal is
worthy of attention when determining the market's present status.

ANTICIPATION OF PERIL

It is wise to review your portfolio of stocks frequently. Don't just price the stocks, but study the shareholder and financial reports. It is there you will often be able to anticipate future peril.

First, whenever you review your portfolio, it is important to weed out the poor performers—the "tired stocks." They should go because they aren't pulling their weight, they may deteriorate further in value, and the funds they tie up may be better employed in more promising issues and thus upgrade the portfolio. Clinging to a deteriorating situation usually results in further erosion of value. One of the most respected adages about the process of making investment decisions is "If you wouldn't buy it with new money, don't hold it with old money." This is a rather demanding instruction, but if you think it over, it has much merit and logic.

How do you identify when a stock is tired? There are many hints visible along the way that should be noted. The first clue is obvious: slovenly market action. The stock doesn't rise in value when the market and others do, and it sells off more actively in down markets. If you look to fundamentals, chances are that early sell signals will be present. These include lost earnings momentum, higher liabilities, salary reductions, layoffs, a lowered bond rating.

The point is, these signs can be recognized quite early from the press releases or quarterly statements. The signals are loud and clear. Don't take the optimistic view that the events are an aberration or that the company may turn around. *Get the message promptly—and sell!*

CORPORATE ERRORS

Stocks sell off drastically on the occasion of notable corporate errors. A write-off, a lawsuit, fraud, plant closings, declining corporate solvency, and other problems can all trigger a sharp decline in share prices. Many of these announced or impending disasters can be anticipated.

Corporate blunder, as a depressant of stock prices, is beautifully illustrated in the present-day case of Bolar Pharmaceutical Co. (AMEX symbol BLR). By mid-1989, there were unsettling rumors that certain members of the generic drug industry were involved in unethical and illegal transactions. Evidence surfaced that spe-

cific firms were under investigation for a host of serious impropri-
eties.

All these events were dutifully reported in the press and vehe-
mently denied by managements. As the list of infractions grew in
number and seriousness, the denials became louder and more
frantic. Soon, guilty pleas were made, plea bargaining began, and
there was some public writhing before House subcommittees.
Eventually more heads rolled as greater and more serious allega-
tions unfolded, with evidence mounting in what, at this writing,
may be one of the nation's most odious corporate betrayals of the
public trust.

In the middle of this fray is Bolar Pharmaceuticals. Early warnings of that company's involvement were virtually countless and
included announcements of investigations by a House subcommit-
tee, the SEC, the American Stock Exchange, and the Food and
Drug Administration, as well as criminal investigations. The list
of Bolar's suspected offenses is long, ranging from criminal corporate actions to dumping of stock by management. Yet the stock
pretty much hung in there until late January 1990, when the
weight of these developments caused the SEC, in an uncharacter-
istic action, to suspend trading for 10 days.

When trading resumed on February 5, 1990, the stock, a former
highflier, plunged 6 points to 10¾, as shown in Figure 11-2. Again
the investor had an opportunity to sell. True, the stock had collapsed from its former midyear 1989 high of 32¼, but at least it
was trading and in fact actually recovered a bit to 13⅛. The
investors received one last chance!

Then, only three days later, it was the American Stock Exchange's turn to suspend trading on the announcement that Bolar
had agreed to suspend all drug shipments pending an audit by the
FDA. During the period that the American Stock Exchange
halted trading, there came even another development. Bolar's president and executive vice president resigned on February 12 under
the shadow of the company being the subject of a federal grand
jury investigation and a probe into alleged insider trading by
Bolar management.

On February 19, 1990, the stock resumed trading, closing the day at 8⅛—down 5 on a volume of 1,028,000 shares. A burst of new and expanded charges have been issued.

FIGURE 11-2

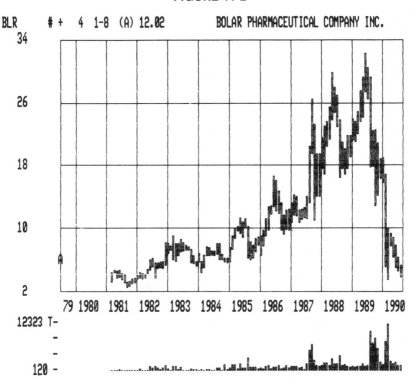

In all my years in the business, I have never known one company to have so many problems. The products withdrawn from the market are estimated to account for 94 percent of Bolar's revenues. I can think of only three reasons for the stock still existing at this writing:

1. Short-seller covering.
2. Support of the American Stock Exchange specialist, so that he can dispose of his long position.
3. The misguided hope that another pharmaceutical firm will purchase Bolar.

I expect the very worst for the Bolar shareholders who are so blind as to not heed the screaming sell signals that preceded this disaster. So much so, that I'm not going to update this portion of the book before publication. I'm that confident of the inevitable total collapse of the stock.

This illustration is significant because of its importance in history and the lessons it teaches about the need to act promptly based upon logic, not emotions. Each year the market provides examples of corporate mistakes and misfortunes. You must not persist stubbornly with your investments. If fundamental data indicate a sale—sell!

MERGERS

Other classic corporate errors that prompt hasty liquidation are mergers. The first rule is that the acquiring company's stock seldom rises following a merger. Rather, it is the target stocks that go up. As for the holder of the shares in the "quarry" company, the more venturesome shareholder may not tender immediately but wait and see whether the acquiring company will bid a higher price to secure the deal or whether some new suitors will enter the picture, adding a new force to the bidding. However, it is important to remember that many of these offers fall through. Taking advantage of the market price increase that results from the merger announcement is a good way to pin down profits.

RETENTION SHARES

Are there certain stocks that should never be sold? We have all heard of the poor soul who sold Computing Tabulating and Recording stock at $5 in 1922. That company turned into IBM, gaining roughly over 20,000 percent. But most stocks are not that vibrant, and few investors are patient enough to hold for 45 years.

Certainly, there will always be dynamic growth issues that stand out from the crowd, featuring pioneering products, services, and inventions. These will not be easy to identify in their early stages of development. You may wish to single out a few situations for special retention in the hopes that they will become the future fortune builders. But remember that the upward curve of even the greatest performance stocks does come to an end when their growth rate flattens.

But the truth is that most investors' holdings will be in stocks of companies that will exhibit cycles when sell decisions toward market and stock tops will pay off handsomely. So know when to hold 'em and when to sell 'em.

CONCLUSION: PEARLS OF WISDOM

Following are some general expressions and observations gathered from experienced investors, all of whom have been confronted with the common goal of making winning exit decisions. They are not absolute truths but are offered as a guide in forming judgments about selling. Remember, success in this business is in being 90 percent right 70 percent of the time.

"Sell when the clamor of the bulls is loudest."

"Don't make waves, ride crests."

"Sell on confirmation of rumor."

"Throw away the charts on major bad news."

"I'll buy the stock and sell it to a bigger fool than I at a higher price."—Don't be the bigger fool!

"The first earnings disappointment won't be the last."

"Sell when you see things you don't believe."

"What goes up (or down) very fast, reverses and comes down (or up) just as fast."

"Selling begets selling."

"Big up markets typically follow exhausted markets and are not necessarily significant."

"Price gaps are a symptom of excess."

"A breakout (major upswing in stock prices) is almost always followed by a pullback."

"How the market reacts to bad news is much more important than the news."

"Always sell too soon."

"In the stock market, nothing recedes like excess."

"Don't hold out for the last eighth of a point."

"Bulls and bears make money; pigs lose money."

"Bull markets require a base."

"Faith, hope, and charity have nothing to do with financial success."

"The first downgrade in a security analyst's rating is only the first of more to come—sell."

"The light at the end of the tunnel may be a freight train coming at you."

"No bull market in history began with institutional buying. Rather, bull markets begin with dumping."

"The market seldom accommodates you."

"The market will frequently do what people least expect."

"An investor can't afford to be stubborn."

"A true breakout doesn't start from the bottom."

"When major damage has been done to the market's structure, the first rally is not likely to be a good one."

"Bear market rallies are usually the most volatile."

"Once the indicators have spoken, don't wait to act."

"Heavy insider selling is an immediate sell signal."

"Sell the acquisitor in any large merger."

"Reduced or omitted cash dividends are foreboding."

"Don't answer a margin call. The first call is not the last."

"Market volume increase accompanied by price decline signals are a bearish trend."

"If several senior management personnel leave voluntarily, you should leave the stock as well."

"Major increase in margin buying is bearish."

"Cash takeover offers at a third or more above prior trading range are a definite profit taker."

"New issues promptly trading at a third or more premium over the subscription price should be sold."

"Don't hold with old money that which you wouldn't buy with new money."

"The market punishes sentimental investment decisions."

"The market doesn't accommodate personal tax deferment. Sell for investment reasons; don't hold to escape taxes."

"Don't be goaded on by the illusion of riches."

Good luck, and don't overstay your market.

12

WALL STREET FOLKLORE

—————————————— Peter J. DeAngelis, CFA

FUNDAMENTAL ANALYSIS, MARKET TIMING, AND TECHNICAL techniques are not the only indicators. Other observations and studies have been made with varying degrees of success. This chapter will discuss the most popular of these. I call them "Wall Street folklore" because on the surface, these indicators defy logic and rational thinking. However, although it is difficult to discern, they may well have a hidden logic.

CALENDAR EVENTS

The calendar offers an interesting sequence of market action. Various types of activity seem to follow a pattern through the year.

JANUARY

The tone of the market is typically set in January, during the first trading week. The general rule is that if the first week of the new year and the month of January as a whole are negative, then there is a strong downward bias for the year. This phenomenon appears to be documented by studies showing that the large majority of down years have been preceded by an off market in January.

Keep in mind that this is only a seasonal barometer. To predict the value of a negative January, you should exercise caution, paying close attention to market conditions that follow. Not every down January is necessarily followed by a down year.

APRIL

The next notable event in the calendar is the April tax-selling period. Historically, the first half of April outperforms the second half. This is contrary to the popular belief that tax selling causes the stock market to decline during the first few weeks of April, then to rebound.

JULY

July's folklore is that the market averages will gain following the Fourth of July. In fact, the month on the whole has declined almost as many times as it has advanced. In 1989 the DJIA gained each day of the holiday-shortened four-session week. For the week through Friday, July 10, the DJIA closed 47.80 points higher, or up nearly 2 percent. By July 31 the DJIA rose to 2635.24, or 7.9% from the July 3 level of 2440.06.

SEPTEMBER

Labor Day has its own characteristics. It is believed to be a reverse barometer. That is, if the market is down during Labor Day week, chances are better for an up market.

The Labor Day holiday of 1989 saw the DJIA fall 42.55 points, or 1.55 percent, through the four-day week. The post–Labor Day decline was the first down week on the DJIA since a string of nine consecutive up weeks began at the end of June. The folklore just barely worked in 1989. Although the market closed the year some 43 points higher on the DJIA, there was that sobering October 13 free-fall and near crash.

FIRST TWO-THIRDS AND LAST ONE-THIRD

Statisticians have also tracked market activity during the first two-thirds and last one-third of the year, beginning in 1945. This folklore is rooted in the fact that in the 45 years since World War II, the market has tended to rise in the first eight months of the year. Statisticians will note that in 31 of those 45 years, or 68 percent of the time, the DJIA increased from January 1 to August

31. Those 31 years with a rising first eight months ended eight times with a declining last four months and 23 times with a rising four months.

Hence, the market statisticians reason, the odds are three to one that stock prices are more likely to rise than fall in the final third of the year if they are preceded by a rising DJIA in the first two-thirds of the year. This proved to be true in 1989, despite the plunge on October 13.

YEAR-END

At year-end during bear markets, declining stocks sell at very low prices as investors liquidate their holdings to offset gains with losses to reduce their tax obligations. As a general rule, when the S&P Composite Index six-day average for the last four days of December and the first two days of January fails to rise, watch out! It may be a bear, not a bull, coming out of the woods.

The stocks that have declined during the year have a habit of getting hammered further in December. This gives way to the market's celebrated "January effect" or "dead-cat bounce." As discussed in Chapter 3, this is the folklore that deals with the anticipated bounce back. Stocks issued by small companies are usually most affected.

It isn't a sure thing, but it happens frequently enough to be a recurrent part of Wall Street folklore and investment strategy. Prices following 1989 didn't fit the pattern. January 1990 was uncharacteristically cruel to the lower-tier stocks. The NASDAQ Composite Index (over-the-counter stocks) plunged 8.6 percent in January to its lowest level in 10 months. This compares with gains of 5.2 percent, 4.3 percent, and 12.4 percent in January 1989, 1988, and 1987, respectively. Nevertheless, each year-end will see the stock pickers, money managers, and the rest lining up their moves in anticipation of the "bounce."

PRESIDENTIAL ELECTION INDICATOR

Election trend years are a well-followed folklore indicator. There is a correlation between presidential elections and stock market performance. Typically, election years for the highest office in the land have generally been good ones for investors. In the eleven such years since World War II, the S&P 500 stock index and the DJIA have risen nine times. Twice—in 1948 and 1960—the indexes fell, but not by much.

Gains were posted in all seven years in which Republicans won. The two election-year market declines occurred in years in which Democrats Truman and Kennedy won.

Further encouraging for investors is that the market has risen in each of the last seven presidential election years (1964–1988), averaging gains over 10 percent. Republicans Nixon, Reagan, and Bush won five of those elections; Democrats Johnson and Carter the other two.

One last note on election year market trends is that the market is likely to rise, more often than not, when the incumbent party wins the election.

THE SUPER BOWL STOCK MARKET PREDICTOR

Sometimes, upon examination, one can find some hidden logic to the stock market's behavior relative to various seemingly unrelated phenomena. But the Super Bowl market predictor, one of the more colorful bits of Wall Street folklore, totally mystifies me by its winning pattern.

Briefly, this predictor puts forth the concept that the stock market will rise in any year when the Super Bowl winner is a team now in the National Football Conference (previously called the National Football League). Any year a team in the American Football Conference wins, the stock market will decline.

Exactly when and how this particular bit of folklore came into play, I don't know. But it has an enviable track record, working out to about a 90 percent success rate. You can get supporting statistics from almost any brokerage firm's market statisticians.

HEMLINE THEORY

There is a long-term relationship between fashion and money. When fashion (the change in mode or style) is mentioned in this context, it refers to the prevailing style in women's dresses—specifically hemlines. The hemline theory, which undoubtedly will be assailed as a male chauvinist concept, contends that there is a relationship between women's fashion and stock prices. Many people claim to have originated this theory, but I believe that the person responsible for the concept is Ira U. Cobleigh, writer of Chapter 7 and a prolific economist and author.

This folklore indicator did not become significant until after World War I. Before then, fashion clothes were custom-made, and dresses were not copied widely or converted into mass production. Before 1914, almost all skirts dragged along the floor, while stock prices were of concern to only a relatively small number of people. In the 1920s an explosion in both stocks and women's fashion developed, as hundreds of thousands more people in the United States could afford both. Volume production of common stocks and dresses emerged.

Interestingly, the centers of popular fashion (Paris aside) and finance are both in New York City. The rationale is that higher income placed many American women in a position to dress more modishly. With the belief that women's fashions reflect the financial mood, it follows that the financial markets will display strength or weakness accordingly. Among financial instruments, stock prices are more publicized, readily measurable, and more responsive to the mood and motion of the economy than any other sector.

Table 12-1 shows the continuing relationship between skirt length and stock prices. The table compares DJIA statistics with historic hemlines in terms of their inches above the floor, so that the varying lengths are directly comparable. A standard five-foot seven-inch tall woman (equivalent to a size 12 dress) was used as the model.

Do skirts and stocks go up together? It appears so. In fact, the table assembled for the 65-year period through 1987 indicates that hemlines were a leading indicator. Hemlines rise before stocks do, and ditto on the downside. For example, hemlines started down ahead of stocks in the 1920–1921 depression. Between 1925 and 1926, skirts rose to knee-high, a daring level by historic standards. The most significant directional guidance to later stock market action was in 1927, when skirts of the flapper era reached new highs (or new thighs). Late in 1927 they started to decline. The downtrend in hemlines preshadowed the market debacle of 1929 by almost two years.

TABLE 12-1

THE HEMLINE INDEX OF STOCK PRICES

Year		Hem to Floor (Inches)	DJIA Median
1922		6.4	91
1927	Hemline peak	18.6	178
1932	Depression	9.8	65
1940–1945	War years	14.5*	140*
1947	Postwar	8.1	175
1955	Rising trend	11.6	438
1967	Miniskirt	25.0	857
1978	Maxiskirt	15.0	825
1982	Miniskirt	24.3	924
1983	Consolidation	21.0	1157
1984	Miniskirt	24.0	1187
1987	Miniskirt	24.0	2361

*Average.

Beginning in late 1932 and pausing to correspond with the slowdown in 1936–1937, hemlines began to rise, reaching eight inches above the ground in 1939 and fifteen inches in 1940, indicating a market top. World War II followed next. Ladies' fashions and the stock market were both on hold for the duration (although, if you are old enough to remember, wartime skirts were fairly short).

Fashion reemerged after World War II, and hemlines were lower in 1947 than on VJ Day. These lower skirt lengths foretold the descending stock market of 1949. The 1950s witnessed a general rise in the DJIA (checked in 1953) and again in 1956. The long dress of 1950–1951 gave way to rising hemlines, especially notable in 1954. By October 1961, skirts were close to knee-high again, which warned that a dip was in the cards. Ten months later, a lull in the market developed. After a pause, skirts continued to rise once more and topped off with the miniskirt. There literally was nowhere else to go. Shortly after, the DJIA peaked at a closing high of 1001 on February 9, 1966. From there, the market suffered a major correction.

Declines in skirt lengths in 1970–1971 predicted the sell-off in 1974. Beginning in 1975, the hemline started a slow rise, foretelling a rising market. Some consolidation in 1983 aside, hemlines continued to rise through the mid-1980s. In the fall of 1987, skirts and stocks were near record highs. Stocks have no theoretical limit, so they continued to soar off the chart, whereas short skirts are definitely limited by modesty. The hemline theory warning was at full red alert. On October 19, 1987, the market crashed! It took a full year for it to recover, but only after severe damage was inflicted. (For a more detailed account of 1987's Black Monday, refer to Chapter 11.)

The fashion watchers therefore rest their case on the general theory that hemlines precede, in their motion and direction, the rise or fall of common stocks. Hence, the slogans "Bull markets and bare knees!" and "Don't sell till you see the heights of their thighs!"

Alas, women's fashion is a mixed bag today. At any given time, a variety of styles is in evidence. Thus, the chronology of hemlines and the relationship between skirts and stocks may have to be modified to a measurement of how much of the wearer there is to look at. Who knows, the sex drive and the money drive may originate from the same emotional sources. Perhaps the fashion trend is a measure of economic health.

CONCLUSION

Wall Street folklore is fun. The wonder is that a goodly amount of the Street's lore seems to work in mysterious ways a majority of the time. The concern to some is that much of this lore has become a legitimate part of professional money management strategy.

In conclusion, while you should be aware of the folklore, it's prudent to recognize that Wall Street folklore, seasonal market trading patterns, and other such phenomena are not foolproof or even necessarily reliable predictors. They are widely observed and can at times, over the short term, be significant. Bearing that in mind, be aware of these peculiarities of the market while paying close attention to the fundamental and technical basics of investment analysis.

GLOSSARY
THE LANGUAGE OF INVESTING

TO INVEST WISELY, YOU HAVE TO SPEAK THE LANGUAGE. Knowing it can make a world of difference in your investment performance. The following definitions can help you boost your investing vocabulary.

All-or-None (AON) Order: An order that must be filled in its entirety or not at all.

American Option: An option that may be exercised at any time before its expiration.

Assignment: The process by which the seller of an option is notified of the buyer's intention to exercise it.

At-the-Money Option: An option whose exercise price is equal to the current market price of the underlying instrument.

Bear: One who anticipates a price decline.

Bear Spread: An option position created by purchasing a call (put) with a higher exercise price and selling a call (put) with a lower exercise price. The strategy is designed to be profitable in a declining market.

326

Bid: A motion to buy a stock, bond, futures or options contract at a specified price.

Bull: One who anticipates a price increase.

Bull Spread: An option position created by purchasing a call (put) with a lower exercise price and selling a call (put) with a higher exercise price. The strategy is designed to be profitable in a rising market.

Calendar Spread: An option position created by purchasing a deferred call (put) and selling a near-term call (put) with the same exercise price. Also known as a horizontal or time spread.

Call Option: A contract between a buyer and a seller giving the buyer the right, but not the obligation, to purchase a specified stock, commodity, futures contract, or cash index at a fixed price on or before a specified date. The seller of the call option assumes the obligation of delivering the stock, commodity, futures contract, or cash index should the buyer wish to exercise the option.

Contingency Order: An order that becomes effective only upon the fulfillment of some condition in the marketplace.

Covered Write: The simultaneous purchase of an underlying instrument and the sale of a call option. For example, the purchase of stock and the sale of a call is a covered write.

Day Order: This is an order that is in effect only until the closing of the business on the day it is placed.

Delta: The sensitivity of an option's theoretical value to a change in the price of the underlying instrument.

European Option: An option which may be exercised only on its expiration date.

Ex-Dividend: Without the right to receive the latest declared dividend. When this right is foregone, the stock is worth less, so its price declines.

Ex-Dividend Date: The date on which investors who own stock will receive a dividend. Those who are short must pay out the dividend to the owner of the stock.

Exercise: The process by which an options buyer notifies the seller of his or her intention to take delivery of the underlying instrument (in the case of a call option) or sell the underlying instrument (in the case of a put option).

Exercise Price: The price at which the underlying instrument will be bought or sold if an option is exercised. Also known as the strike price.

Expiration: The date and time after which an option may no longer be exercised.

Extrinsic Value: The amount by which an option's premium exceeds its intrinsic value. Also known as time value.

Fence: A long (short) underlying position, together with a long (short) out-of-the-money put and a short (long) out-of-the-money call. All options must expire at the same time.

Fill-or-Kill (FOK) Order: An order that must be filled immediately and in its entirety. Otherwise the order will be canceled.

Futures Contract: A standardized contract for the purchase or sale of an underlying commodity, which is traded for future delivery under the provisions of exchange regulations.

Gamma: The sensitivity of an option's delta to a change in the price of the underlying instrument.

Good-Till-Canceled (GTC) Order: An order to be held by a broker until it can be filled or until the investor cancels it. Placing such an order is not a wise move in a volatile stock. If the order is left in too long, events could change dramatically, and the order could be "picked off" to the detriment of the investor. Also called an open order.

Hedger: A trader who enters the market with the specific intent of protecting an existing position in the underlying instrument.

Historical Volatility: The annualized standard deviation of percentage changes in daily prices.

Horizontal Spread: Another name for a calendar or time spread.

Immediate or Cancel (IOC) Order: An order that must be filled immediately, or it will be canceled. IOC orders need not be filled in their entirety.

Implied Volatility: A measurement of the volatility of the underlying market based on the market-traded option premium, as opposed to the calculation of volatility from historical futures prices.

In-the-Money Option: An option that could be exercised and immediately closed out against the underlying instrument for a cash credit. A call is in-the-money if the underlying market is above a call option's exercise price or below a put option's exercise price.

Intrinsic Value: The amount that an options buyer would receive upon exercise of the option. Out-of-the-money options have no intrinsic value.

Leg: One side of a spread position.

Leverage: The use of options to increase the percentage return relative to a move in the underlying instrument.

Limit: The maximum daily price movement allowed for an exchange-traded contract.

Limit Order: An order to be filled at a specified price or better. A buy limit order instructs the broker to purchase the stock at a specified price. In simple terms, the investor wishes to buy stock if it trades at that price. For example, assume that GM is trading at 37¼–37½. An investor wishing to buy at $35 would place a buy limit order at that price. If the stock's market price drops to $35, the trade would go off—assuming that enough shares are traded at that price and the orders placed ahead of the investor are executed.

Or the investor might wish to purchase GM at 37½ maximum. He or she would enter an order to buy at 37½. If enough stock is trading at that level, the order would be executed. In this example, the buy limit order prevents the purchase at a higher price, which could happen with a market order should the stock tick up.

In terms of selling, the opposite is true. In the GM example, an investor wishing to sell above the market would place a sell limit order at 40. An investor wishing to sell at the market price would place a sell limit order at 37½. Typically, sell limit orders are placed above the current market price, and buy limit orders below.

The broker may exceed the order only to the client's benefit. For example, a limit order to sell at a price of 14½ may be executed at a higher price if market conditions provide an opportunity. However, the stock may not be sold at a price below the limit. On the buy side of a limit order, the broker may pay less than the limit, but not more.

If you want to have a limit order executed, you must enter it at a realistic price. Don't place an order to buy or sell at a level too far out of line with the market.

Long: A position resulting from the purchase of a contract. Also, a position that will theoretically increase (decrease) in value should the underlying market rise (fall). For example, a long put position will theoretically increase in value as the value of the underlying instrument decreases. It also refers to a position held in a stock, bond or futures contract.

Margin: Funds or good-faith deposits posted during the trading life of a futures contract to guarantee that the investor will fulfill contract obligations in adverse markets. Margin is also required on short option positions. Stocks may also be purchased on margin.

Margin Call: A demand for additional margin funds when prices move adversely to a trader's position.

Market if Touched (MIT) Order: A contingency order that becomes a market order if a contract or stock trades at a specified price. This order is entered at a price other than the current market price. A buy market-if-touched order is entered at a price below the current market, and a sell at a price above. When the issue trades at the specified price, the broker will complete the order at the best price possible.

Market on Close (MOC) Order: An order to be filled at the current market price as close as possible to the close of that day's trading.

Market Order: An order to be filled immediately at the current market price. This is the most popular and widely used order.

Unsophisticated investors assume that the last sale reported or the current bid or offer is the "market" price they get when placing the order. This isn't necessarily true. Markets change second by second. Chances are that a market order to buy will be filled at a higher price and, conversely, a market order to sell will be sold at a lower price. This is particularly true of over-the-counter and thinly traded issues. So unless you have a compelling reason to buy in at any price or get out at any price, it is foolish to place market orders.

Married Put: The simultaneous purchase of a put option and a position in the market for the underlying instrument.

Naked: A long (short) market position with no offsetting short (long) market position.

Not-Held Order: This is a market order but one that allows the broker flexibility in timing the execution. A broker, at his or her discretion, moves immediately or waits out the market to fill the order.

Offer: A motion to sell a stock futures or option contract at a specified price.

One-Cancels-the-Other Order: This is really two orders in one, generally for the same security. The order instructs the broker to fill whichever order he or she can first, and then to cancel the remaining order. It is not commonly used and then typically only in a fast-moving market. It prevents the investor from making more trades than he or she is willing to, particularly in the same security. For example, this order would be used if an investor wishes to either purchase GM at 35 or sell at 40.

Open Interest: The net total of outstanding open contracts. Any opening transaction increases the open interest, while any closing transaction reduces the open interest.

Option-Pricing Model: A mathematical formula designed to price an option as a function of the underlying price, exercise price, time until expiration, volatility, interest rates, and dividends (in the case of stock options). The Black-Scholes model is one of the most widely used models.

Out-of-the-Money Option: An option that has no intrinsic value. For example, a call is out-of-the-money if its exercise price is above the underlying market price, and a put is out-of-the-money if its exercise price is below the underlying market price.

Over-the-Counter (OTC) Option: An option with no standardization of exercise prices and expiration dates, a direct link between buyer and seller, and no secondary market. Participants are primarily large institutions and banks.

Parity: Another name for intrinsic value.

Premium: The price of an option.

Put Option: A contract in which the seller gives the buyer the right, but not the obligation, to sell a specified stock, commodity, futures contract, or cash index at a fixed price on or before a specified date. Should the buyer wish to exercise this option, the seller of the put assumes the obligation of taking delivery of the stock, commodity, futures contract, or cash index.

Roll-Down: A follow-up action whereby the options trader closes put options at one exercise price and simultaneously opens other options at a lower exercise price.

Rolling: A follow-up action whereby the options trader closes options currently in the position and opens other options with different terms, on the same underlying market.

Roll-Out: A follow-up action whereby the options trader closes out options at a near-term expiration date and opens options at a longer-term expiration date.

Roll-Up: A follow-up action whereby the options trader closes out options at one exercise price and simultaneously opens other options at a higher exercise price.

Short: A position resulting from the sale of a stock or contract. Also, a position that will theoretically increase (decrease) in value should the underlying market fall (rise). For example, a short put position will theoretically increase in value as the value of the underlying instrument increases.

Specific-Time Order: This type of order gives specific timing instructions beyond those of a day order or a good-till-cancelled order. For example, an investor may place an order for execution at around market close or at some other specific time.

Spread: The purchase and sale of two options of the same type, either calls or puts, which vary in terms of exercise prices, expiration dates, or both.

Stop-Limit Order: A contingency order to buy or sell an option at a limit price or better if the option trades at a specified price.

Stop-Loss Order: A contingency order to buy or sell an option at the current market price if the option trades at a specified price.

Stop Order: This type of order instructs a broker to buy or sell an issue once a price threshold is achieved. At that price, the stop order becomes a market order, and the transaction takes place at whatever price the market offers. Stop sell orders must be entered at a price below the current market price. Stop buy orders must be entered at a price above the current market price. Stop orders are sometimes referred to as "stop-loss orders" because they are often used to stop losses or to protect profits.

Straddle: The purchase or sale of both a put and a call having the same exercise price and expiration date. The buyer of a straddle benefits from increased volatility, and the seller benefits from decreased volatility.

Strangle: The purchase or sale of both a put and a call having the same expiration date but different exercise prices. Typically both options are out-of-the-money.

Strike Price: Exercise price.

Theoretical Value: An option value generated by a mathematical model using as inputs the underlying price, exercise price, time until expiration, volatility, interest rates, and dividends (in the case of stock options).

Theta: The first derivative of the Black-Scholes option-pricing model with respect to time. Measures the expected change in an option's theoretical value over a change in time.

Time Spread: Calendar or horizontal spread.

Time Value: Extrinsic or time premium.

Underlying Instrument: The stock, commodity, futures contract, or cash index to be delivered if an option is exercised.

Vega: The first derivative of the model with respect to volatility. Measures the expected change in an option's premium given a 1 percent change in the implied volatility of that option.

Vertical Spread: Bull or bear spread.

Volatility: The degree to which the price of the underlying instrument fluctuates over time.